T0073135

Conjuring
with
Computation

A MANUAL OF
MAGIC AND COMPUTING
FOR BEGINNERS

Conjuring with Computation

A MANUAL OF MAGIC AND COMPUTING FOR BEGINNERS

Paul Curzon

Queen Mary University of London, UK

Peter W. McOwan

Queen Mary University of London, UK

World Scientific

NEW JERSEY · LONDON · SINGAPORE · BEIJING · SHANGHAI · HONG KONG · TAIPEI · CHENNAI · TOKYO

Published by

World Scientific Publishing Co. Pte. Ltd.

5 Toh Tuck Link, Singapore 596224

USA office: 27 Warren Street, Suite 401-402, Hackensack, NJ 07601

UK office: 57 Shelton Street, Covent Garden, London WC2H 9HE

Library of Congress Cataloging-in-Publication Data
Names: Curzon, Paul, author. | McOwan, Peter W., author.
Title: Conjuring with computation : a manual of magic and computing for beginners /
    Paul Curzon, Queen Mary University of London, UK,
    Peter W. McOwan, Queen Mary University of London, UK.
Description: New Jersey : World Scientific, [2023] | Includes index.
Identifiers: LCCN 2022050646 | ISBN 9789811264337 (hardcover) |
    ISBN 9789811264344 (ebook for institutions) | ISBN 9789811264351 (ebook for individuals)
Subjects: LCSH: Computer science--Textbook.
Classification: LCC QA76 .C888 2023 | DDC 004--dc23/eng/20221202
LC record available at https://lccn.loc.gov/2022050646

British Library Cataloguing-in-Publication Data
A catalogue record for this book is available from the British Library.

Copyright © 2023 by World Scientific Publishing Co. Pte. Ltd.

All rights reserved. This book, or parts thereof, may not be reproduced in any form or by any means, electronic or mechanical, including photocopying, recording or any information storage and retrieval system now known or to be invented, without written permission from the publisher.

For photocopying of material in this volume, please pay a copying fee through the Copyright Clearance Center, Inc., 222 Rosewood Drive, Danvers, MA 01923, USA. In this case permission to photocopy is not required from the publisher.

For any available supplementary material, please visit
https://www.worldscientific.com/worldscibooks/10.1142/13085#t=suppl

Desk Editors: Sanjay Varadharajan/Adam Binnie/Shi Ying Koe

Typeset by Stallion Press
Email: enquiries@stallionpress.com

This book is dedicated to my friend and co-author Peter W. McOwan, who was the magical brain behind it. He originally came up with the idea of our doing magic shows to inspire kids about computer science. He also taught me to do magic and gave me the confidence, even as a complete novice, to do live shows. For the book, more or less, he supplied the magic and I fitted the computer science to it. He died before we finished the book. It is not so much fun without him.

Paul Curzon

Contents

Chapter Summaries

Chapter 0. Introduction

This is a book that will teach you some magic, but also explains the many links between computing and magic, with the result that you will learn about both magic and computation.

Interlude: Jean-Eugène Robert-Houdin
PAUSE: Alan Turing

Part 1. Algorithmic Thinking

Algorithmic thinking is about thinking of the solutions to problems as algorithms. We explain what an algorithm is, explain why notation matters, and describe the three control structures that all algorithms can be built from.

Chapter 1. Invisible Palming: What is an Algorithm?

You invisibly move a card from one pile to another.

A self-working magic trick consists of a series of steps that if followed guarantee to achieve a magical effect. An algorithm is also a series of steps that if followed blindly guarantee to achieve a result.

PAUSE: Muhammad ibn Mūsā al-Khwārizmī

Chapter 2. The Möbius Rings: Sequences

You cut a ring in half but magically get two interlocked rings.

Tricks involve following a sequence of instructions. Sequences in algorithms (and so programs) are a fundamental part of computation. Sequencing is the first key control structure and so a building block for describing computation.

Interlude: Felicien Trewey and Harry Blackstone Sr.

Chapter 3. Six Magical Objects: Selection

Given the choice of six magical objects, a volunteer picks the one that you, the magician, predicted.

Branching, or selection, where something different is done depending on the situation, is the second key control structure that algorithms are built from.

PAUSE: George Boole

Chapter 4. Turning the Key: Repetition

A volunteer chooses a card from a pack and then places it back. You, the magician, see neither it being chosen nor replaced, but still can find the card.

Repetition is the final kind of control structure needed. With sequencing, selection and repetition, you have all the building blocks needed to describe the flow of control of any algorithm. All computation (so tricks) can be described with just these three control structures.

Interlude: Penn and Teller

Chapter 5. Calculator Conjuring: Programming Languages

A volunteer types a long number into a calculator based on a shorter number they freely choose. You demonstrate your ability to do lightning calculation by immediately predicting three numbers that divide exactly into it. Even more surprisingly, when the divisions are done, the answer is the original number.

A key step in programming, and a part of computational thinking, is in turning a possibly imprecise version of an algorithm into very precise steps with no room for doubt. That requires a precise language with a very precise mathematically defined meaning. This is a difference to magic where informal descriptions are used.

PAUSE: Grace Hopper

Part 2. Evaluation and Logical Thinking I

We explore the need for evaluation of both programs and tricks, and how thinking logically is at the core of computational thinking.

Chapter 6. Wizardly Book Magic: Testing

Books about witches and wizards are suffused with magic. A volunteer chooses a word apparently freely, and the book then controls them, leading them to the word you predicted in advance with the help of the book.

How can we be sure a program (or trick) always works? We need to evaluate it for correctness. One way is exhaustive testing but with some simple logical thinking, we can reduce the number of tests needed.

PAUSE: Margaret Hamilton

Chapter 7. The 21-Card Trick: Logical Reasoning and Proof

A volunteer freely chooses a card from 21 laid out on the table. No one is told which card was chosen, but you, the magician, read the volunteer's mind to find out which it is.

We can use logical thinking to prove a program (or trick) will always work when the steps are followed correctly.

PAUSE: Edsger W. Dijkstra

Chapter 8. Mental Monte and the Trains of Thought: Reasoning by Cases

You turn your back. A volunteer picks a card from three. They move them around. You turn back, and the three cards are mixed some more. Despite not seeing the card being chosen nor all the mixing, you name the card chosen.

One way mathematicians prove theorems is "by cases". This is really common when proving algorithms correct. Each use of selection turns into another case to check.

Interlude: Bob Hummer

Part 3. Making It Work for People

To develop software that is easy to use, you need to understand people, and in particular the limitations of our brains. Great computer scientists need to understand cognitive psychology.

Chapter 9. The Cyclops' Eye: You Cannot Trust Your Eyes

In this eye-shaped optical illusion, the centre of the eye appears to float off the page.

Optical illusions show that you cannot believe your eyes. Just because you see it does not mean that it is there. When designing interfaces, you cannot assume people see what is there.

Interlude: Hajime Ōuchi and Bridget Louise Riley

Chapter 10. Magically Weighted Boxes: Your Brain Cannot be Trusted at All

Members of the audience take it in turns to pick up a pile of three boxes, but when, after a click of your fingers, they only pick up two of the boxes, the pile is clearly heavier.

You cannot trust your other senses either. This illusion shows you cannot even judge what is heavy and what is light.

Interlude: Lulu Hurst

Chapter 11. The Teleporting Robot: Keep It Simple Stupid

With this magic jigsaw, you make a whole robot appear and disappear just by muddling the jigsaw up and putting it back together again.

Some systems are so complicated we can't take it all in. When designing tricks, we aim to add complexity so the audience do not see what is really happening. When designing usable systems, we need to avoid overloading the senses. Keep it simple stupid!

Interlude: Sam Lloyd and William Hooper

Part 4. Decomposition and Abstraction

When inventing new tricks, we can build them out of a collection of basic parts. Such parts can be reused across other tricks. Likewise we can solve the problem of writing a program by breaking it into parts to write separately, or just reusing bits previously written.

Chapter 12. Pre-booked Picture Magic: Abstraction

An audience member randomly picks a picture from a book of images. You are then able to correctly draw the picture chosen despite not seeing them choose.

This trick relies on the abstraction of images. Abstraction is about simplifying things down to their essence. Variations arise in many disciplines. Computer scientists have many versions including simplified images. Most versions though are both more technical and more precise than that.

PAUSE: Susan Kare

Chapter 13. Trained Rice: Decomposition and Procedural Abstraction

You train a bottle of rice to grip a chopstick so that the bottle can be lifted with the chopstick, whilst the identical bottle of a member of the audience repeatedly falls.

Even simple tricks can be described as a series of parts, making them easier to invent and describe. This is called decomposition. Decomposition of a problem into parts in this way is a fundamental part of computational thinking.

PAUSE: Michael Faraday

Chapter 14. The Teleporting Top Hat: Hiding Detail and Swapping Parts

This is a new version of Invisible Palming, but where a teleporting top hat is used to move a card from one pile to another.

Abstraction and decomposition allow us to think about different parts of a program or trick at different levels of detail at different times. This is a key use of those ideas. It also allows us to swap in and out different parts of a trick/program to give variations, and perhaps even better tricks/programs.

PAUSE: Jeanette Wing

Part 5. Procedures and Procedural Abstraction

There are many different kinds of false shuffles. Just by saying the name of a shuffle, as a step in a trick, a magician would know what was meant and be able to incorporate it into the trick. This is procedural abstraction: a key kind of abstraction used by computer scientists, where named, clear and self-contained pieces of code are created for use elsewhere. Once created, they are incorporated into the program (or "called") by giving their name.

Chapter 15. Overhand Shuffle: Procedures

The overhand shuffle is the standard shuffle used by card players and magicians alike to quickly shuffle a pack of cards. Use it any time you do really want to mix up the cards in a pack.

The core tool for doing decomposition is the procedure. Here we give a sub-trick and specifically a shuffle a name. That allows us to just refer to the name in any trick we wish to use it. Likewise, by naming program code that does a well-defined task, we can then use the name whenever we want to refer to that code. This is called procedure call, and it uses abstraction. We hide the details of how the step is done, just giving the code a name. In this and subsequent chapters, we look at shuffles as sub-tricks.

Interlude: Persi Diaconis

Chapter 16. Swapped Ends Overhand Shuffle: Specifying Procedures

This false shuffle swaps the cards at the top and bottom of the pack while shuffling the cards in the middle of the pack.

By giving a clear description of the effect of a trick (or program), we do not have to worry about how it works (its implementation) when designing other tricks (or programs) that use it.

PAUSE: Nikola Tesla

Chapter 17. Ends Overhand Shuffle: New Procedures from Old and Layers of Abstraction

You shuffle the pack but secretly leave the top and bottom cards of the pack alone while mixing up those in the middle of the pack.

Once we have sub-tricks or procedures, doing well-defined things, we can chain them together to get new ones that do something different overall.

Interlude: Howard Thurston

Chapter 18. False Top Overhand Shuffle: Parameters and Generalisation

This false shuffle leaves the top cards of the pack unchanged.

Often the same sub-trick can be used in different situations but does something slightly different. For example, it might do the same thing but moving a different number of cards depending on what the trick needs. This leads to the idea of parameters: specifying the values needed to fit the procedure to the situation.

PAUSE: Ada Lovelace

Chapter 19. Side Jogging Shuffle: Swapping One Procedure for Another

You shuffle the cards, but unknown to the audience, the top quarter or so of the pack are unshuffled.

If we have decomposed a trick into well-defined parts, then we can swap in equivalent parts to make variations of the same trick, perhaps to improve the presentation of the trick. With programs, having broken them into clear parts that do a well-defined task, we can substitute different implementations (e.g., that are faster) without affecting the rest of the program. That means we do not need to think about the rest of the program when making such a change.

Interlude: John Nevil Maskelyne

Chapter 20. Cyclic False Cut: Libraries of Useful Procedures

You repeatedly cut the cards, but in doing so leave the cyclic order alone.

By making collections of related techniques, like cuts and shuffles, or in programming, procedures about a single topic, we can organise programs so the instructions for the really useful ones are written out once and then just called on whenever needed.

PAUSE: Maurice Wilkes and David Wheeler

Part 6. Building Bigger

We have now seen most of the basic techniques that allow us to build large programs a little at a time. In this part, we go a step further, using results from one subroutine in the next.

Chapter 21. The False Choice: Programming Interfaces

You give a member of the audience a choice of several things, but it is actually no choice at all.

To mix and match sub-tricks, it helps to be clear about what they do. Procedures need to have clear interfaces, i.e., precise descriptions of exactly what they do and when they can be used. Interfaces help avoid mistakes being introduced when using procedures in large programs.

PAUSE: Tommy Flowers

Chapter 22. The Forcing Matrix: Functions

Spectators choose numbers at random from a grid of numbers. They add up to a number predicted by you, the magician.

Sometimes the aim of a particular part of a program is to return a value — a number perhaps. That is what a Forcing Matrix does. Its job is to come up with a number. This could be the aim in its own right, with the magician magically having predicted the number. It can also be used as a component of other tricks.

PAUSE: John McCarthy

Chapter 23. Forced Wizardly Book Magic: Calling Functions — Building Bigger and Better

You first get the audience to pick a random number by choosing numbers from a grid. Then that page in a book is taken, and a volunteer chooses a word from it at random. The book then leads the volunteer onto a new word in the book no one could have known, except that you did predict it.

We can make more new tricks from simpler ones by chaining trick elements together in sequences where they pass information from one to the next. The resulting trick can be much more powerful. The same applies to programs.

Interlude: David Devant

Chapter 24. Invisible Palming (Again): Sequencing Procedures Together

We return to the trick where you magically move a card from one pile to another.

Procedures with parameters allow us to create generalised programs. We can decompose them into parameterised parts and sequence them one after the other, using the same parameters. By matching preconditions and postconditions, we can give an outline argument as to why the whole algorithm works.

PAUSE: Robert W. Floyd and Tony Hoare

Part 7. Abstraction and Data Representation

We've seen abstraction applied to control structures in the form of procedures. Now we explore similar ideas with data: data can have different representations with that representation hidden.

Chapter 25. Drawn to You: Codes Representing Data

Several volunteers each draw a picture of their choice. Just by looking at the drawings, you are able to work out who drew which.

Tricks often rely on representing information in some particular way. Choosing an appropriate data representation is core to computational thinking and programming.

Interlude: Joseph Jastrow

Chapter 26. The Roman Maths Challenge: Roman Numerals

This is a challenge rather than a magic trick: can anyone make a Roman sum add up correctly?

Roman numerals, as used here, are an early example of a number representation different to the one we use. Computers use a different one again. There are many ways to represent the same data.

Interlude: Nevil Maskelyne

Chapter 27. The Lottery Trick: Place–Value Number Representation

You turn the room into a gigantic lottery machine, bouncing lottery balls made of screwed up paper around the room. When a series of balls are chosen, they give a number that does not match anyone's lottery number ... except yours.

We use the Hindu–Arabic numeral system. The really amazing idea is to give digits a position in a number and have their value change depending on the position, so 2 can stand for 2, 20 or 200 depending on its position. This makes large numbers more concise but also makes operations like addition and multiplication easy: they make for simple algorithms.

PAUSE: Charles Babbage

Chapter 28. Cards on Your Mind: How Computers Represent Numbers

Four members of the audience jointly pick a number and concentrate on it helped by a magic set of cards. You can immediately read their collective mind and tell them the number instantly.

This trick uses the same representation of numbers as the one computers actually use: binary.

PAUSE: Gottfried Leibniz

Magicians control your attention, making you miss things that would give the trick away. When designing the interface of an interactive computer system, you need to control their attention too, but making sure the user looks in the right place and so sees everything that is important.

Interlude: Gustav Kuhn

Chapter 32. Supernatural Suggestion: Visual Salience

You show the audience five cards on the screen, asking everyone to focus their attention on just one of their choice. You, however, have controlled them all, and when you remove a card, it turns out everyone was focussing on that same card.

What you see depends on where you focus your attention, and where you focus your attention depends partly on how salient the things in the scene are. If you want important things to be seen on a screen, then you have to make them visually salient.

PAUSE: Peter W. McOwan

Chapter 33. The Numbers Game: Visibility of System State

A member of the audience calls out 10 random numbers that you write on different pieces of paper. A volunteer picks one at random. Amazingly, you tell them the number on the piece of paper they picked.

A key to a good trick is that the audience lose track of actually what is happening. They think the state of the magical system is one thing when actually it is something else. Visibility of the system state is an important interaction design principle in software. Users need sufficient feedback to track the internal state of the system. Planes have crashed when this has been done badly and software has behaved like a trick!

PAUSE: Don Norman and Jakob Nielsen

Chapter 34. The Three-Way False Cut: Conceptual Models and Metaphors

You cut the cards twice and then reform the pack. Unknown to the audience, the pack is completely unchanged from before the cuts.

A good design needs a clear conceptual model that leaves the user in no doubt about what is happening. A good magic trick does the opposite obfuscating what is happening, so the audience think something else is happening.

Interlude: Jay Ose

Chapter 35. The Joker in the Pack: Memory

A volunteer thinks of a number and deals out that number of cards. In doing so, they have brought the only joker in the pack to the top of the deck.

Our working memory is very limited. Give it too much to remember and we start to forget things. Magicians rely on this. Interaction Designers must avoid it.

PAUSE: The Xerox PARC Team

Chapter 36. Are You Psychic? User Experience and Engineering Delight

You test a member of the audience for superpowers. Can they, without seeing any of the values on the cards, end up with a matching pair?

Usability is about whether a system is easy to use. Just as a magician wants more than a trick just working, appearing magical, interaction designers also go further than just ease of use. Magicians show how User Experience can be designed into a system.

Interlude: Fay Presto

Part 9. Evaluation and Logical Thinking II

In this part, we look at more advanced logical thinking including real-world (and magical-world) uses of algebra.

Chapter 37. Are You Psychic? (Continued): Loop Invariants and Inductive Proof

How can we be sure that our volunteer will have the apparent superpowers so that the previous trick definitely will work?

The idea of a loop invariant provides the basis of logical reasoning about repetition.

Interlude: Adelaide Herrmann

Chapter 38. The Red–Black Mind Meld: Abstraction, Algebra and Proof

You are able to meld your mind with that of a volunteer, controlling their choice of cards to make sure a property you predict holds once all the cards are dealt.

Rigorous argument is one way to convince ourselves that an algorithm (or trick) works, but we can go a step further and use algebra. We describe the algorithm with maths, do some algebra on the result, and so prove desirable properties hold. This is a vital way to check safety-critical software is correct.

PAUSE: Shafi Goldwasser

Part 10. More on Computational Thinking

We now look at some more advanced forms and uses of computational thinking: advanced versions of generalisation, decomposition and data representation.

Chapter 39. The Doomsday Clock: Generalisation

The doomsday clock predicts the most important hour in a person's life. A volunteer has a free choice of a starting number, but still the clock stops at the hour predicted for them.

Having worked out a principle (the mathematics underlying a trick), we can use it to make a more general principle that can then be used to design apparently different tricks that underneath rely on the same maths. We can generalise code in a similar way, allowing it to be used in wider situations.

PAUSE: John von Neumann

Chapter 40. Free My Three: Divide and Conquer

Three cards of a kind, chosen by a volunteer, are lost in the pack. You discard cards repeatedly with no sign of them until eventually they turn up ... the very last cards to be revealed.

Decomposition involves breaking a problem into one or more smaller problems that are easier to solve. Divide and conquer is a powerful version of this where these smaller problems are the same problem as the original (just smaller). Those smaller problems are solved in the same way. This gives a way to create very fast algorithms.

Interlude: Alex Elmsley

Chapter 41. The Double-Destination Deception: Data Representation — Graphs and Cycles

A volunteer takes a series of tickets to plan a trip of a lifetime crisscrossing the world. Despite their free choice of route, once done you reveal that you bought in advance precisely the ticket they need to get back from their final destination to their start point.

An important data structure is the graph, and one of the most important problems in computer science involves creating a cycle (i.e., a round trip) through a graph. A famous puzzle about the bridges of Königsberg kick-started the whole idea of graph representations.

Interlude: Dynamo

Part 11. Cyber Security, Privacy and Society

There are overlaps between magic tricks and concepts from cybersecurity. Many magic tricks are about the magician having information the audience think they cannot possibly have obtained. Cybersecurity and privacy are concerned with how to prevent such information leakage.

Chapter 42. Sniff Out that Card: Steganography

A volunteer chooses a card and holds it to their chest. They hide it back in the pack, but you can sniff it out from the faint trace of their scent left on it because they held it close.

Steganography is a way of hiding secret messages in apparently innocuous things. What looks like a normal message or image disguises the real thing being communicated. The same idea can be used as the basis of tricks to allow a magician to know the information he or she could apparently not possibly know.

PAUSE: Sir Francis Bacon

Chapter 43. Classic Mentalism: Codes and Ciphers

Your partner magician leaves the room while a card is chosen. Despite not being there at the time, when they return, they can say exactly which card was chosen.

Classic mentalism tricks involve secret codes between participants. Similar codes based on code books have been the basis of algorithms for sharing secret messages for as long as people have wanted to share secrets.

Interlude: Reginald Scot

Chapter 44. Call the Clairvoyant: Legitimate Channels

A card is chosen from a pack. You phone your friend, the mysterious "Clairvoyant", and when you ask them to do so, they tell the volunteer which card was chosen.

Computer systems are kept secure by having separate areas with different security levels. Nothing from a high-security area should be able to leak to a lower-security area. Hiding information in a legitimate channel (an allowed way to communicate) is one-way information might be leaked. Hackers exploit legitimate channels in computer systems. Magicians build tricks around leaking information via legitimate channels too.

Interlude: Sydney and Lesley Piddington

Chapter 45: Call the Clairvoyant a Second Time: Covert Channels and the Surveillance Society

An object from a table of objects is chosen, and the mysterious "Clairvoyant" is called. They are put straight onto speaker phone, so everything can be heard by all. They can name the object chosen.

Sometimes information is leaked via a legitimate channel. Another way is to set up a covert channel: a way of communicating that is not supposed to be there. Hackers exploit covert channels in computer systems. Magicians also build tricks around them.

PAUSE: Hedy Lamarr

Chapter 46. Reading a Personality with Hot Chocolate: Big Data and Privacy

After stirring it three times, a volunteer drinks a small cup of hot chocolate you make them. You read their personality in the sludge left in the bottom of the cup.

Horoscopes and some personality tests rely on a kind of fakery. Big Tech companies rely on a different kind of fake personality test, gathering as much data as they can about those who use their services. They then make judgements about what kind of person they are and sell the information to advertisers or political parties who exploit this intimate "knowledge" of you to sway opinions.

Interlude: Phineas T. Barnum

Chapter 47. The Chevreul Pendulum: Professional Ethics

A volunteer holds a pendulum made from an old magical key. You ask them questions, and the pendulum, controlled by the spirit world, swings to give the answers.

People mainly use magic for entertainment, but some use it unethically to con people. Likewise, computing skills can be used ethically or unethically. Many magicians debunk frauds by exposing the tricks they are using. Some hackers, called white hat hackers, do a similar thing. They are employed by companies to attack the company's own systems, to protect them against black hat hackers, who can, intentionally or otherwise, cause lots of damage. All professional computer scientists are required to study ethics.

Interlude: James Randi

Part 12. Advanced Technology

Many magic tricks rely on technology to provide the effects. Here are just a few ways such computing-linked technology has formed the basis of tricks.

Chapter 48. The Faerie Cage: Augmented Reality

You reveal to the audience that faeries are not only real but you have trapped one in your special rowan-lined box.

A Victorian invention for theatre, Pepper's Ghost, forms the basis of both illusions and early versions of augmented reality where the real and virtual worlds mix.

Interlude: John Henry Pepper and Henry Dircks

Chapter 49. The Down-Under Deal and Robotic Reveal: Robots

You do the special down-under deal, ending with a card on the table that no one could have predicted. Despite that, as the card is shown to the audience, your helper, a robot, appears from down under the table to reveal that it knew what the card would be.

The final reveal can make a trick extra special. Automata, the precursors of robots, have long been used as props for tricks. Here a robot is revealed to have magically forced the card that was finally selected. Robots are now being used in workplaces and homes, in dangerous environments to make them safe, and as killers.

PAUSE: Ismail al-Jazari

Chapter 50. The One True Sovereign: Curtain Call and Creativity

Who is the one true King or Queen of Britain? You have found a long-lost magical artefact that can reveal the answer.

We finish with a summary of the main links between conjuring and computing and reveal one last trick (about authentication).

Interlude: Richard Garriott

Chapter 0

Introduction

This book is for people who want to learn to do magic tricks for others but who are also interested in learning more about **computation** and how ideas from **computer science** overlap with those of conjuring.

Computer science and magic have a lot in common. Famously, Arthur C. Clarke said that sufficiently advanced technology was like magic. In fact, magicians have always known this and often work at the leading edge of science and engineering to invent new tricks. As it is at the forefront of technology, understanding computer science is important for magicians interested in technology-led magic. The link to computer science is much deeper than just using advanced technology, though.

A popular saying is that Computer Science is no more about computers than astronomy is about telescopes. It is at core about computation, which is what computers do. What is computation? A simple version is that it is just doing calculation by following instructions. A more sophisticated version is that it is about the manipulation of symbols. Conjuring is also closely linked to computation.

Computer scientists also learn to think in a particular way, called **computational thinking**. It is the general skill that underpins programming but is also important in more general situations. Magicians, it turns out, have to think in a very similar way to computer scientists.

Computational thinking is in part about creating precise instructions that always achieve a desired effect. When applied to magic, it is not about the performance of tricks. That is playing the part of the computer following the instructions in a program to get something done. It is more about inventing new tricks, modifying old ones to improve them, and finding ways to be sure they always work. Many more general ideas from computer science have close links to magic too. We can learn a lot about computer science from magic, and vice versa, and that is what this book is about.

All the tricks in this book are simple ones that are fairly easy to perform, and variations of which are widely known and easily found on the Internet or in introductory magic books. Just as computer science is about creating new computer systems, we hope that they will inspire you to start to invent your own tricks. Perhaps at first, you might just make tweaks to these tricks, changing the presentation, or combining effects, but you will ultimately move on to invent your own completely new tricks.

When you do the tricks for others as part of a magic show though, keep the secrets. Never use them for anything other than entertainment (or if you are a teacher, for education).

The best magic, by professional magicians, of course still leaves us as baffled as everyone else.

Interlude: Jean-Eugène Robert-Houdin

Jean-Eugène Robert-Houdin (1805–1871) became a clockmaker after failing in his studies to be a lawyer because he was constantly distracted by mechanical gadgets. Magic started off as a hobby, but he went on to become the greatest magician of his time, pioneering the idea that magic shows should be the height of elegance. He even took over a theatre to perform in. However, in his first show, there was a disaster as he suffered from stage fright and came close to having a breakdown. He was about to abandon the whole idea but then was goaded by a friend telling him it had been a silly idea anyway. That made him determined to prove the friend wrong. His confidence returned, and as a result of carrying on, he completely changed the way magic was both performed and perceived. It went from being seen as a seedy fairground act to high-prestige entertainment. He combined science, engineering and creativity, inventing many gadget-based tricks, and making much use of new scientific discoveries such as electricity and electromagnetism in doing so. He built and used automata in his tricks, some that were magical in their own right such as a mechanical figure that could write. Others were combined with illusions, such as his Marvellous Orange Tree, a machine that apparently grew real oranges, the last one containing an item from the audience that had previously been made to disappear.

PAUSE: Alan Turing

Arguably the most influential computer scientist ever, Alan Turing (1912–1954), set out what it meant to do computation and proved that not everything could be computed, all before any working computer actually existed. His idea of a Turing Machine was a version of a computer simplified to its essence before any computer had been made. He proved that it could do any computation that any computer could possibly do. In the Second World War, he was a key person in the team that cracked the German ciphers, allowing the Allies to read their secret communications. He worked on machines that were the precursors to the first computers and after the war designed a computer himself. He was one of the earliest people to work on the idea of Artificial Intelligence, devising a test, now called the Turing Test, that suggests we should consider a machine intelligent if we cannot tell it apart from a human by questioning both. He sadly died young, committing suicide by eating a poisoned apple because of his persecution for being gay by the British authorities. He had been prosecuted and then "chemically castrated". He was officially pardoned in 2013. Imagine what more he would have achieved, and we lost, had the world been a more tolerant place.

Part 1

Algorithmic Thinking

Computers cannot think for themselves. They just blindly follow instructions. Those instructions must always work when followed. Algorithmic Thinking is the skill of writing such instructions.

Chapter 1

Invisible Palming
What is an Algorithm?

Conjuring

You invisibly move a card from one pile to another. You can do it even as a novice magician who has no idea how it is done.

Computation

An algorithm is a set of instructions that if followed precisely, and in the right order, without thought, leads to a guaranteed result.

The Trick

You need 15 identical cards. One way to get them is to buy several identical packs of playing cards, then take out and use the Jokers so all 15 cards are the same. Have a volunteer put out both hands as though they are playing the piano with fingers and thumbs touching the table (see Figure 1.1). Tell the audience they must chant the magic words: "Two cards make a pair" each time you take a pair of cards.

Take two cards and, as everyone says "Two cards make a pair," place them together between a pair of fingers or finger and thumb of

7

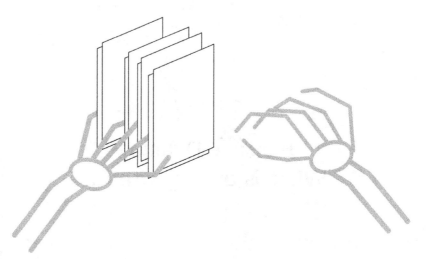

Figure 1.1. In Invisible Palming, the magician places pairs of cards between the fingers/thumb of each hand of the volunteer, with the last place taken by a single card.

the volunteer. Keep doing this until you have one card left. Place it between the final fingers saying there is "one leftover".

Now take the first pair back, again all chanting "Two cards make a pair". Separate them and place them face down on the table to start two piles, one card from the pair in each pile. Take each pair back in turn adding them to the piles: one card from each pair being neatly placed on each pile. As you do, everyone should continue to say the magic words. Eventually, only the final, single card is left. Take this card saying: "We have one extra card." Let the volunteer place it on top of one of the piles of their choice. Square up the piles pointing out: "That pile now has the extra card."

Explain that now the room is full of magic from all the chanting, you are going to do "Invisible Palming". The extra card is on one pile. You are going to invisibly move it to the other. Place your hand over the pile with the extra card. Rub the back of your hand to "make the card go invisible". Lift your palm showing that the card is there but is invisible. Move your hand to the other pile. Tap it, "to make the card drop". Announce that the card has now moved piles.

To show the magic worked, take the pile where the extra card was placed and count off a pair at a time into a new single face-down pile. Everyone still should be saying the magic words as you take each pair: "Two cards make a pair. Two cards make a pair...". Make sure the pile is neat. You find there are only pairs: the extra card has gone! So where is it? Take the other pile and do the same, peeling off pairs and putting them back into a pile. Amazingly the extra card is there. It has moved from one pile to the other!

Before thinking about how the trick works, do it, just following the steps with a friend as the volunteer (you may find the crib sheet of steps below helpful: see The Magical Algorithm below). If you follow the steps precisely, it should just work ... even if you have no idea how you did it. You could even swap with your friend and let them be the magician. It should work for them too.

How can you do a magic trick, magically moving a card from one pile to another without knowing what you did or how it works?

The Magical Algorithm

Here is the trick written out as a series of steps in a structured way similar to the way that computer scientists write out instructions.

TO DO Invisible Palming:
1. Take 15 identical cards.
2. Ask a volunteer to place their hands on the table with fingers arched as though playing the piano.
3. DO THE FOLLOWING 7 TIMES:
   a. Say "Two cards make a pair".
   b. Place 2 cards between two of the volunteer's fingers or finger and thumb.
4. Place the last single card between the remaining fingers or finger and thumb.
5. DO THE FOLLOWING 7 TIMES:
   a. Say "Two cards make a pair".
   b. Take a pair of cards from the fingers and split them placing them one in each of two piles built up on the table.
6. Have the volunteer place the last card on a pile of their choice.

7. Place your hand over that pile, rubbing the back of your hand.
8. Lift your hand, show the palm pointing out that the card is there but invisible, and then place it over the other pile.
9. Tap your hand and remove it, saying the card has moved.
10. Pick up the first pile.
11. DO THE FOLLOWING 4 TIMES:
    a. Add 2 cards from the pile you are holding into a single, neat pile on the table.
    b. Say "Two cards make a pair".
12. Note that the extra card is no longer there.
13. Pick up the second pile.
14. DO THE FOLLOWING 3 TIMES:
    a. Add 2 cards from the pile you are holding to a pile on the table.
    b. Say "Two cards make a pair".
15. Point out that you are holding the extra card: it had moved to the second pile.

How It Works

Magicians call this kind of trick a self-working trick. It always works if you follow the steps precisely. It works whatever the volunteer does given the choices they have (so here wherever the extra card is placed).

There are 15 cards. After dealing out the pairs into the two piles, those two piles are identical: there are 7 cards in each. Of course, you don't give anyone a chance to count the cards. First, think about the pile where you put the last, supposedly "extra", card. That card makes the pile up to 8 cards: 4 pairs. When you count out in pairs, there will only be pairs there, so apparently no "extra"card anymore. It appears to have vanished, but it just finished a pair where it was.

The other pile will be left with 7 cards: 3 pairs with one left over. When you count in pairs, that one left over seems to be the original extra card. It seems to have appeared there, but it was there all the time. You pretend it has magically moved without doing anything. Nothing has to move!

It appears magical only because you have confused everyone. They believe when they add the last card to a pile that they are adding an extra odd card. You are actually completing the last pair, though. It doesn't matter which pile they add the last card to: that card will turn an odd pile into an even pile. You count out the cards in pairs to hide the exact number.

Thinking Computationally

Algorithms, magic and programs

Computer scientists have a similar idea to self-working tricks called **algorithms**. An algorithm is just a set of precise instructions that if followed exactly leads to a guaranteed effect. The instructions have to cover all eventualities, just as a trick does.

Once you have created an algorithm that works, you don't have to think about solving the original problem anymore or what to do to achieve that effect. You just blindly follow the algorithm, and the right thing happens. It is just like following the Invisible Palming instructions: the magical effect of apparently invisibly moving a card just happens. If you followed the steps exactly, it will have worked for you even if you had no idea how it worked. In doing the trick by following the instructions, you were acting like a computer following an algorithm. More specifically you were acting as a **computational agent**. It is something or someone following algorithmic instructions precisely and blindly.

A computer cannot think for itself. It can *only* blindly follow instructions (the instructions are its **program**). They were written for it by a programmer. It does computation as a result. Computers are therefore computational agents. Computer programs are essentially algorithms written in a programming language (like Python, Java or Scratch). They are languages of instructions in a form that a computer can follow.

The detail matters in algorithms. Take our trick. Just saying we should pretend to move a card from one pile to the other isn't good enough. We need to say exactly how to do it in a way that cannot be confused. Similarly, a program needs to tell the computer exactly how to do every little step.

Wizards

A magician who *invents* new self-working tricks is creating algorithms. A programmer writing a program is doing the same. They are both using **algorithmic thinking** skills: working out a series of steps that will always have the effect they are after. Algorithmic thinking also involves writing instructions really clearly and precisely so that there is no confusion about what to do as the instructions have to work when being followed by a Computational Agent.

Expert programmers, male or female, are often called wizards. They really are!

PAUSE: Muhammad ibn Mūsā al-Khwārizmī

The word algorithm derives from the name of Muḥammad ibn Mūsā al-Khwārizmī (c.780–850). This was because of his book, *On the Calculation with Hindu Numerals* which introduced the place-based number system (of 1s, 10s, 100s, 1000s, etc.) to the west that we use today. He described the basic algorithms needed to do arithmetic using decimal numbers on a sand board: a tray of sand that made it easy to write and rub out numbers. Eventually the algorithms from his book removed the need for the abacus to do arithmetic.

Chapter 2

The Möbius Rings Sequences

Conjuring

You cut a ring into two pieces down the middle, only to find you still only have one ring. Try again, and at last, you have two rings, but bizarrely they are linked together.

Computation

There are three fundamental ways to organise instructions. The simplest way is **sequencing**: following instructions one after the other in the given order.

The Trick

Start with a strip of paper about 5 cm wide and at least 30 cm long (ideally longer) and glue it in a loop, but with a twist so the top of one end of the strip is glued to the top of the other end (see Figure 2.1). This is called a Möbius strip. Show it to the audience without mentioning the twist. Explain that you will cut the loop into two thinner rings. Gradually cut it down its centre. When you get back to the start, confidently say you now have two rings. Gently untangle them.

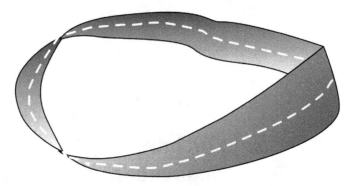

Figure 2.1. A Möbius strip. Cut along the dotted line all the way around the centre to make two interlocked rings.

Look shocked when you see it is still a single ring and wonder out loud how that could possibly happen, saying that you will try again. Take this new longer, thinner ring and carefully cut it down the middle. Say you must have two rings now, and gently untangle them. Look even more shocked as you show that you do have two rings, but somehow they became interlinked as you cut them.

Tell the audience that there is clearly far too much magic in the room if paper rings are going to do that to you.

The Magical Algorithm

TO DO the Möbius Rings:

1. Create a Möbius strip by glueing a strip of paper into a ring with a twist in it so the top of one end is glued to the top of the other end.
2. Say you are going to cut it into two thinner rings.
3. Cut it down the middle.
4. Shocked, show the audience that somehow it is still just a single (longer) ring.
5. Try again, cutting it down the centre.
6. Even more shocked, show the audience that it is now two rings, but somehow they are interlocked.

How It Works

This is another simple self-working trick that relies on an area of maths called topology. Cut a Möbius strip down the middle, and it makes a longer strip. Do it again, and you get two interconnected rings. It is all due to the twist which meant you had created a ring with only one side: draw a pencil line down the middle and it will eventually join back to the start, having covered both sides of the original strip!

Thinking Computationally

The algorithm behind this trick is about as simple as can be as it is only a few steps. There are two aspects of an algorithm that matter: (1) the actual instructions and (2) the order you do them in. The latter is called the **flow of control**. It is the plumbing that connects instructions together.

This algorithm is just a sequence of instructions that must be followed one after the other, in the order given. Follow each step correctly, exactly once and in the right order . . . and the magic will happen. This way of linking instructions is called **sequencing**. It is the simplest kind of **control structure**: constructs that determine the flow of control, the order things are done.

Sequencing of individual commands is the core to other kinds of instructions that people and computers follow including recipes, the way you learnt to add numbers, and programs.

Simple programs are very similar to our magic trick's description. They are a **sequence** of instructions to be followed one after the other in the given order (see Figure 2.2). Here, we have labelled the steps (1) (2) (3) . . . to show the order to do them. Most programming languages just use the order that the instructions are written on the page to indicate the correct sequence, so in most languages the steps tend not to be numbered.

Any computer or computerised gadget that is doing one thing after another is following a sequence of instructions some programmer previously wrote. Take a chip-and-pin card machine. It shows you the amount you owe, asks you to touch your payment device (card, phone, etc.) and

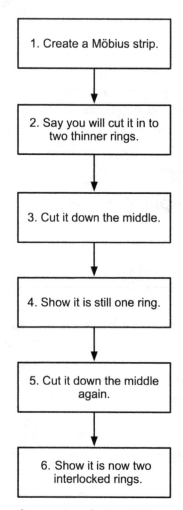

Figure 2.2. The sequence of instructions for the Möbius rings trick as a flowchart. The instructions are followed one after another.

then tells you it's paid: it is following a sequence of instructions in a program to do that.

There are other important forms of flow of control that we use when writing programs (and planning magic tricks). Perhaps, surprisingly though, with only two more kinds of flow of control (described in the next two chapters), it is possible to specify the flow of control of any computation.

Interlude: Felicien Trewey and Harry Blackstone Sr.

The Möbius rings trick was first performed as a magic trick, rather than just a science demonstration, by Felicien Trewey (1848–1920) at the end of the 19th century. Variations of the trick, which are often called the Afghan Bands, have been performed by many magicians since, including Harry Blackstone Sr. (1885–1965). He was one of the great magicians of the 20th century, not only inventing tricks but devising clever variations of existing tricks. He often introduced modern technology twists, such as sawing a woman in half, but in his case with a circular saw. One of his most famous illusions involved a lit electric bulb that, in a darkened theatre, floated away from its lamp, through a hoop, and out over the audience, all while remaining lit. It was designed and built for him by the famous inventor of electronic gadgets, Thomas Edison. It was the first magic trick ever to be considered worth accepting by the Smithsonian museums.

Chapter 3

𝔖ix 𝔐agical 𝔒bjects Selection

Conjuring

A volunteer chooses one from a series of magical objects, only to find that you predicted their choice.

Computation

The second way of determining which instruction to follow next is called **selection**: choosing which of several sets of instructions to follow next based on the truth or otherwise of some test.

The Trick

Before the trick, slide a note into a pack of cards with the message "You WILL choose ME" written on it. Place six different objects, including the pack of cards, in a line on the table. All should have some magical connection. You might, for example, use a magic wand, a cup with a ball underneath, a pack of cards in their box, a silk handkerchief, a coin and a watch. Ideally, all should be solid objects that could not possibly contain a note, except for the cards. The cards should be in the third position from the left. You stand on one side of the objects with a spectator on the other.

Explain that magical objects get infused with magic if they are used in magic shows and all these objects are especially magical because they have all been used in tricks many times.

Ask the volunteer to choose a number from 1 to 6 telling everyone what it is.

The number they choose, when you count to that object, leads to the pack of cards. Explain that as you do lots of card tricks the cards are full of magic and like to be chosen. Ask them to open the pack of cards and see what is inside, then get them to read the note. Note again how magical your cards are.

How It Works

You do something different depending on their choice of number (see Figure 3.1). Whichever number they said gives a different way of counting that forces the choice of the third object: the pack of cards.

If they choose the 1, then you start at your left and count out letters to the third object: O ... N ... E pointing to an object on each step.

If they choose 2, then similarly you count to the third object: T ... W ... O.

If they choose 3, then you just count to the third object: 1 ... 2 ... 3.

If they choose 4, then ask *them* to count out 1 ... 2 ... 3 ... 4 from *their* left (your right) to end on the 3rd object from your left (the 4th from theirs).

If they choose 5, then ask *them* to say the letters of the word FIVE from *their* left (your right) F ... I ... V ... E to end on the 3rd object from your left (4th object from theirs).

If they choose 6, then you count out the letters to the third object: S ... I ... X.

They have been given a false choice: you did not tell them in advance what you would do with the number they picked. As you only do the trick once, you only do one of the alternatives, so they do not get any inkling that it would have happened differently another time.

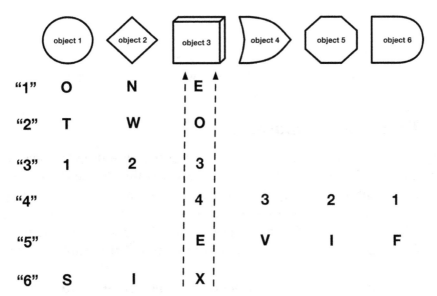

Figure 3.1. Whichever number is chosen, you choose a counting method that counts to the third object.

The Magical Algorithm

TO DO Six Magical Objects:

1. Place a note inside a pack of cards saying "You WILL choose ME".
2. Lay out six objects in a line with the pack of cards at position 3 from *your* left.
3. Ask a volunteer to tell you a number from 1 to 6.
4. IF they say 1 THEN
   a. *You* count to the third object: O...N...E.
   OTHERWISE IF they say 2 THEN
   b. *You* count to the third object: T...W...O.
   OTHERWISE IF they say 3 THEN
   c. *You* count to the third object: 1...2...3.
   OTHERWISE IF they say 4 THEN
   d. *They* count to the third object: 1...2...3...4 from *their* left.
   OTHERWISE IF they say 5 THEN

    e. *They* count to the third object: F . . . I . . . V . . . E from *their* left.
    OTHERWISE IF they say 6 THEN
    f. Y*ou* count to the third object: S . . . I . . . X.
5. Ask them to open the card box and read the message.

Thinking Computationally

The algorithm behind this trick is again a sequence of instructions as steps 1 to 5 are followed in sequence, but now there is something new, a new kind of plumbing. In a sequence, every instruction is followed. Here, there are six possible instructions in step 4 (instructions a–f). However, only one of them is followed each time that you do the trick. These instructions are part of a bigger structure that controls the flow: a **selection**.

Programmers call this kind of structure an **IF statement**. It combines instructions to follow with tests that are either true or false. For example, "they say 1" is a test. Either they did say 1 (it is **true**) or they didn't (it is **false**). Programmers call these kinds of test **boolean expressions** (boolean means true or false). If the test is true, then you do the corresponding instruction and ignore the other tests and instructions in the selection. If the test is false, then you ignore that instruction and move on and check the next test. Whichever instruction you ultimately follow, after doing it you ignore the other tests with their linked instructions and instead move on to the next instruction *after* the whole selection statement (here instruction 5). The selection instruction is just one statement in the sequence of instructions followed in order, but it controls which of several instructions is actually done at that point (see Figure 3.2). In fact, you really only need a simple IF statement that has just a true and a false option. More complicated selection structures like the one here that choose between lots of options can then be built from it.

Every time you used a gadget and it gave you a choice, buried somewhere in the code was a selection statement that a programmer wrote to do that choice. Do you have a choice of avatars? Do you have a choice of buttons to press? Or a choice of links to click? Do you have

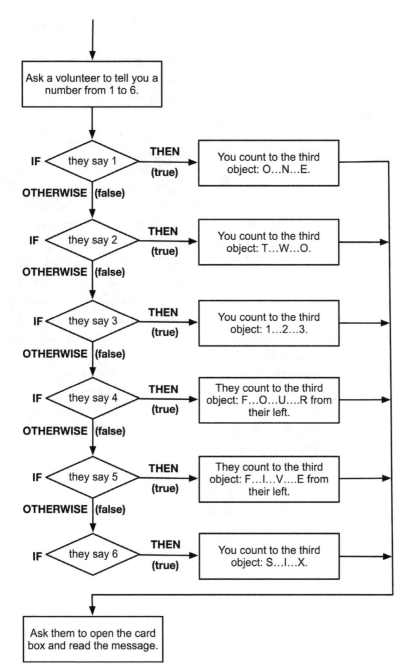

Figure 3.2. The flow of control of the IF statement in the Six Magical Objects trick. It is a sequence of IF statements inside the outer sequence of instructions.

to choose from a menu? What actually makes the machine do something different in each case is some variation on a selection statement.

Selection is our second kind of **control structure**. It gives a new kind of **flow of control**. To be an **algorithmic thinker**, you have to be able to devise and write clear instructions that use both **sequencing** and **selection**.

PAUSE: George Boole

George Boole (1815–1864) was the largely self-taught son of a shoemaker. He became a great mathematician, inventing a new kind of algebra, now called Boolean Algebra or Boolean Logic. It eventually turned out to be ideal for the computer age that was still almost a century away. Instead of working with numbers and arithmetic operations, it works with true and false values and operations like and, or and not. This is exactly what is needed to describe and reason about the logic circuits from which computers are built. It is also the basis of how programs make decisions. True and false values in programs are now called Boolean values as a result. It was a step forward from the Ancient Greek idea of logic as originally developed by Aristotle, and so of the idea of logic as the basis of reasoned argument.

Chapter 4

Turning the Key
Repetition

Conjuring

A volunteer chooses a card. You unerringly find it even though you don't see the card or where it is placed back in the pack.

Computation

The third way of controlling the order instructions are executed is called repetition. It involves following the same instructions repeatedly until a test allows you to move on. If you have sequencing, selection and repetition, you do not need any other control structure. Other control structures just make instructions easier to read and write.

The Trick

Have a volunteer shuffle the deck. When they hand it back, secretly glimpse at the bottom card and remember it. This is your key card. Spread the deck face down and have them pick out a card without you seeing it. Tell them to remember it.

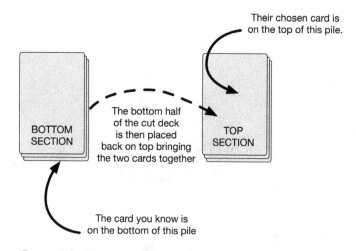

Figure 4.1. The state of the cards in the middle of the cut.

Reassemble the pack face down on the table. Then ask them to place their card on the top of this face-down pile. Turn your back, and ask them to cut the pack wherever they want. Next, have them place the bottom section onto the top section to complete the cut (see Figure 4.1). At this point, turn back around. Point out that their card, which you don't know, is now buried in the pile at a position that you also don't know. This is all true, but unknown to them your key card is now right next to their chosen card.

Start to deal the cards one by one onto the table. Deal until you reach your key card, then turn over one more card. Announce that it was their card.

For a slightly more entertaining variation, you could employ the "magician in trouble" presentation. Deal three cards past their chosen card, then pause. Confidently announce "The next card I turn over will be your card". Of course, they saw you deal past their card, so they think you are going to be wrong. Then, in the final twist, you don't turn over the next card in the pile you are dealing from. Instead, you pull their chosen card out of the face-up pile and turn that over instead.

You have saved yourself, with a nice added comic twist.

The Magical Algorithm

Here is the algorithm for the basic presentation.

TO DO Turning the Key:
1. A spectator shuffles the pack.
2. You glance at and remember the bottom card: this is your key card.
3. You spread the deck face down.
4. The spectator picks out a card and remembers it, but does not let you see it.
5. You reassemble the deck face down.
6. They put their chosen card face down on top of the deck.
7. You turn your back.
8. The spectator cuts the deck into two piles.
9. They put the bottom pile on top to complete the cut.
10. You turn back around and take back the pack.
11. DO THE FOLLOWING UNTIL you see your key card.
    a. Deal the next card face up onto the table.
12. Turn the next card over.
13. Announce that card was their chosen card.

How It Works

Cutting the pack, in the way described, places whatever is at the bottom of the pack directly before the card that is on top of the pack. Therefore, as they put their card on the top, you have guaranteed that it will be the one after the card you remembered.

Thinking Computationally

The third way of connecting instructions to make algorithms is called **repetition**. The line

   DO THE FOLLOWING UNTIL...

indicates we are about to do repetition. We call this kind of instruction a **loop** (there are many variations of loops: this is just one kind).

Immediately following those words is a **test** that is either true or false, just as in our selection instruction in the last chapter. In our repetition instruction, either you see the card (the test is true) or you don't (the test is false). If the test is true at the point when you check it, you move on to the next instruction after the loop (here instruction 12). If, however, the test is false, then you stay in the loop: you do instruction (11a) and deal with the next card. This is called the **body** of the loop, and it is the instruction that is repeated. The body doesn't have to be a single instruction. It could be made up of a sequence of instructions or even contain selection or repetition instructions. The critical thing about a loop is that after following the instructions in the body, you go back and do the test again. It may now have changed. Only when you check it and find that it is true, do you move on to the next instruction. Otherwise, you keep doing the body and then rechecking the test every time you finish the body.

To be an algorithmic thinker, you have to be able to create clear instructions that use all three of **sequencing, selection** and **repetition**. These three kinds of flow of control form the basis of a style of programming called **structured programming**.

One of the most important results in computer science is that if you have a programming language with sequencing, selection and repetition, then it is as powerful as any other language, in the sense that in terms of the flow of control, any computation that can be done in any other language can be done with these instructions. A language that can do any computation that any other language could do is called **Turing complete**. There are many variations of control structures in languages, but they are not to make them more powerful, and they are there just to make programs faster, easier to write, or easier to get right.

Counter-controlled loops

There are other forms of flow of control, but none allow you to write out any algorithm that you can't already do with these three kinds of instruction. They are just variations of these three.

For the more fun version of the trick, you replace steps 12 and 13 with the new steps:

14. DO THE FOLLOWING 4 TIMES:
    a. Deal the next card face up onto the table.
15. Announce that the next card you turn over will be the volunteer's chosen card.
16. Turn over the card four places back in the face-up cards.

Here, we use repetition again but in a slightly different form. The first line tells us we have a loop. Rather than just a test, it says exactly how many times to repeat the instruction in the body. The line labelled (a) is, as before, the body, so the instructions are to be repeated.

This kind of loop is called a **counter-controlled loop**. The difference here is that we know in advance how many times we need to repeat the body and just repeat it that many times. We said we don't need any new kinds of flow of control though and we don't. Having a counter-controlled loop construct like this doesn't allow you to do anything you couldn't do with a general repetition instruction. To do the equivalent with our original general kind of loop, we would just need to add more instructions to keep track of a counter. Our test is just that the counter has counted up to the target number.

Set a counter to 1.

DO THE FOLLOWING UNTIL the counter is 5:

a. Deal the next card face up onto the table.
b. Add 1 to the counter.

All that our new counter-controlled loop structure is doing is packaging together the general loop and instructions to keep count. It is just a shorthand for the above. Either way, we had to keep track of how often we dealt a card. Without the counter-controlled loop, we need to add the appropriate instructions explicitly. The specialist counter-controlled loop structure also makes our instructions more readable to a human. They immediately can see it is a counter-controlled loop from the way it starts, rather than having to work it out by looking at the whole loop. Making instructions easy for a human to understand is really important in programming if mistakes are to be avoided.

Interlude: Penn and Teller

Penn and Teller are an unconventional magical duo, known for combining magic with comedy. They are masters of the "trick gone wrong" ending, though their tricks often go wrong in very violent ways (such as a woman being accidentally sawn in half a second time, apparently for real). Their tricks are often also framed as being about revealing how some specialist trick works, only for there to be a further twist that shows that in their version that could not possibly have been how it worked.

Penn Jillette has a passion for computer technology and the web. He was a regular contributor to a computing magazine in the early 1990s, wrote web articles for a search engine company, and also appeared in the film, Hackers. Based on this interest, Penn and Teller invented (and at the time gave away the secret to) a trick called "The Most Expensive Trick in the World". It was expensive because of the then extremely novel, though now every day, advanced computer science technology it relied upon.

Chapter 5

𝕮𝖆𝖑𝖈𝖚𝖑𝖆𝖙𝖔𝖗 𝕮𝖔𝖓𝖏𝖚𝖗𝖎𝖓𝖌
Programming Languages

𝕮𝖔𝖓𝖏𝖚𝖗𝖎𝖓𝖌

A friend types a six-digit number into a calculator based on a number they thought of at random. Miraculously, when you give them three numbers to divide into it, they all divide exactly. Even though you had no idea what their original number was, they end up back with that original number.

Computation

Computer scientists don't just invent algorithms, they have to be able to formulate them using the specific instructions available in a given **notation** (i.e., a **programming language**). This involves a whole new set of skills of being able to work with a fixed notation.

The Trick

Ask a friend to think of a three-digit number. Give them a calculator, or have them use the calculator on their phone, and ask them to key in the number. Then, say it would be better to have a bigger number, so have

31

them type in the number again to make a six-digit number. Tell them that you haven't seen the number but even so can do some mathematical magic on it. Point out that the chance of a number dividing by 11, so giving a whole number answer, is very slim. Suggest they try it. Amazingly, their number does. Suggest it would be even more surprising if it was also divided by 7. Suggest they try it. Even more staggering, it again gives a whole number. What about 13? Surely they couldn't have randomly chosen a number that would divide by that too! They do so. Point out it would be totally amazing if they were now looking at their original number!

The Magical Algorithm

TO DO Calculator Conjuring:

1. A spectator thinks of a random three-digit number and remembers it.
2. The spectator keys it into a calculator twice and then presses ENTER.
3. The spectator divides it by 11 and checks if they get a whole number.
4. The spectator divides it by 7 and checks if they get a whole number.
5. The spectator divides it by 13 and checks if they get a whole number.
6. You point out that magically they have recovered their original number.

How It Works

The reason this works is all about the number 1,001.

Suppose they thought of the number 123. If you multiply that number by 1,000 then you turn it into 123,000. If you then add the original number to this you get 123,123. This works whatever the number is, as long as it is three digits long. Start with 999: multiply by 1,000 and then add 999, which gives you 999,999. So multiplying a three-digit number by 1,000 and adding the number is the same as making a six-digit number out of a three-digit number written out twice. Now, this is also the same as multiplying by 1,001 as the 1 in 1,001 causes the number to be added to what you get by multiplying it by 1,000. Try it by multiplying any three-digit number by 1,001. So, when your friend puts the number into the calculator twice, they are actually just multiplying by 1,001.

Now, try multiplying 7, 11 and 13 together. The answer is also 1,001. Putting the number end to end and then dividing by 11, then 7 and then 13 is the same as multiplying it by 1,001 and then dividing by 1,001. Dividing is the opposite of multiplying (mathematicians call it the inverse), so that is why we get back to the number we started with.

Written out as an equation, we are using the fact:

$$\text{Secret} \times 1,001 \div 1,001 = \text{Secret}$$

This also explains why it divides by all of 7, 11 and 13. Another way of writing the number in the calculator is

$$\text{Secret} \times 11 \times 7 \times 13$$

since 1,001 is just $11 \times 7 \times 13$. This means that all three numbers we use divide exactly into the total, and when we do each division in turn, we are just cancelling out that number from the total.

Thinking Computationally

We are mainly using similarities between magic tricks and computing concepts to help you understand computing. However, here we focus on a difference that sets them apart.

One thing that distinguishes computer scientists from most magicians is that of precise **notation**. An important part of thinking computationally is to be able to write instructions very precisely and in a precisely defined language: one that can be followed by a computer. You must be able to get the job done using only the commands available.

Magicians put the onus on secrecy rather than sharing their tricks. That means that the need for writing down instructions for anyone but themselves to be able to follow is not a key part of what they do.

Only magicians writing magic books need to worry about the instructions being easy to follow. Magicians (and likewise cooks) tend to fall back on human languages like English to write instructions. That is why sometimes manuals are quite hard to follow as it is quite hard to be really precise in a human language like English. Using human languages is usually fine, but they can be ambiguous or just are not precise enough, with the meaning not always totally clear. If you don't bake cakes, try baking one for the first time following a recipe you've never seen before to get the idea. It probably won't be perfect the first time. The lack of preciseness in languages is the reason why when we try to follow written instructions, whether how to do a trick, fix a puncture or bake a cake, things sometimes go wrong.

Computer scientists, on the other hand, very specifically do want others (both computers and humans) to be able to follow their instructions. This means that ultimately algorithms are written out as a program in a programming language. What that really means is that they are written out using only specific commands with very precise, agreed meanings. Learning to program is in part about deeply understanding what each command does and learning how to convert vaguer plans into the commands available.

Magicians could use precise languages too, and indeed alchemists, those pre-chemists-come-magicians who tried to turn lead into gold, did create notations to write down their "spells".

A magic language for magic tricks might include commands like those given in Figure 5.1.

We can implement the algorithm as a program in our language. It could then be followed by either a human or a robot magician. This involves not only working out what the specific steps are but also the detail. **Attention to detail** really matters in programming. What exactly do you say and when? What numbers do we allow as a "three-digit number". Does 000 count? What about 001? Our program very specifically rules those out.

1. SAY Magician "Think of a three-digit number".
2. STORE secret (SECRET volunteer {100 . . . 999}).
3. SAY Magician "Take this calculator".

STORE x *n*

> This means the number *n* is given the name *x* in the remainder of the description of the trick.

SECRET person {*n*1...*n*2}

> This means the person must choose a number between *n*1 and *n*2, keeping it secret. It delivers a number.

DIVIDE *n*

> This means whoever holds the calculator should divide the current number displayed on the calculator by *n* leaving the result displayed on the calculator and then read out the result. Here *n* is a whole number.

TYPE *n*

> This means whoever is holding the calculator should type the number *n* into the calculator.

PASS person object

> This means give person the object.

SAY person *s*

> This means the given person must say *s* aloud.

In the above, *object* is a magical prop chosen from {wand, hat, silk handkerchief, and calculator} and person is chosen from {Volunteer, Magician} *n*, *n*1 and *n*2 are whole numbers. They could be the name given to a number, an actual number or an operation (like SECRET) that delivers a number.

Figure 5.1. Part of a language for magicians.

4. PASS Volunteer Calculator.

5. SAY Magician "Type in the number you thought of so it is displayed on the screen".

6. TYPE secret.

7. SAY Magician "Let's make it a longer six-digit number. Type in the number you thought of again so it is displayed on the screen twice now. Now I've not seen the number so I've no idea what it is. Despite this, I can do some mathematical magic on it."

8. TYPE secret.

9. SAY Magician "The chance of a number dividing by 11, so giving a whole number answer, is very slim. Try it to see how lucky you are!"

10. DIVIDE 11.

11. SAY Magician "Amazing! It does! It would be even more surprising if it was also divided by 7. Why not try it."

12. DIVIDE 7.
13. SAY Magician "A whole number. That is staggering. What are the chances! Let's try one more. What about 13? Surely you couldn't have randomly chosen a number that would divide by that too!
14. DIVIDE 13.
15. SAY Magician "Wow...it divides exactly too!...And even more magically, you have ended up back at the number you started with! That is mathematical magic!"

To be able to write programs like this requires several extra skills over just thinking up algorithms that computer scientists develop. The first is the ability to formulate instructions using a specific set of precisely defined available instructions. That means a programmer needs to be able to twist what they want to happen to fit what is available. This is a core skill of programming. They also need the ability to think very precisely about detail: had you thought about whether 000 was a three-digit number or not? If you are writing the program, you have to.

Most programming languages are **universal** meaning that a program can be written in the language to do any computation that can possibly be computed. However, the same thing may be done in different ways. Depending on the problem (and so algorithmic solution developed), the algorithm as designed might very directly be converted into the programming language...or not. If it can, then once you have the algorithm, writing the program is relatively easy. In other situations, the constructs used in your algorithm are far from those available in the language. We didn't have a way to say "three-digit number" directly, for example, so had to work out the range we meant instead. That is one reason why there are so many languages. Different languages are designed to make different kinds of problems easier to solve. Choose an appropriate language for the job at hand, and your task as a programmer becomes easier.

A key reason we use programming languages is that the instructions have to be easy to convert into a form that is executable on the machine. However, there is more to writing programs than that. Just as importantly, they are for humans to read too; something many programmers pay too little attention to. Large programs are written by teams, and everyone in the team has to easily understand everyone else's code. Furthermore, once written programs have to be maintained, so changed, both when mistakes are found and when the program is needed to do something new. That means programming is not just about writing code that works, but writing it in a way that is as clear as possible for humans to understand.

In the rest of this book, we will use the slightly more informal **pseudocode** notation we used in the early tricks. It mixes English and notation and aims to be more easily readable. Computer scientists often use pseudocode notations to help them design both individual algorithms and code, an important step towards writing the final code. It is less precise than an executable notation, but easier to work with as you move from initial ideas of how a program will work towards the precise detail.

PAUSE: Grace Hopper

Many people have made contributions to the development of programming languages, but Grace Hopper (1906–1992), ultimately a Vice-Admiral in the US Navy, made one of the biggest. She essentially invented the idea of the high-level language that allows you to write one program that can then be run on lots of different kinds of computers. Before her, programmers had to write code in the specific low-level instructions of the machine it was to run on. Her idea was that programming languages could be based instead on English, and special programs called compilers could translate them into instructions for different machines. She also popularised the word "bug" for programming errors because of a dead moth she found that was the cause of a computer not working: it was stuck in the machine.

Part 2

Evaluation and Logical Thinking I

To create a correct algorithm, whether one behind a magic trick or one behind software, you need to be able to think precisely and logically. It is very easy to get the detail wrong. The flip side to this is that you must also have ways to check that an algorithm is right. Will it always do the right thing?

Chapter 6

𝔚𝔦𝔷𝔞𝔯𝔡𝔩𝔶 𝔅𝔬𝔬𝔨 𝔐𝔞𝔤𝔦𝔠
Testing

Conjuring

You show that books about magic can control people's minds. A volunteer freely chooses a word and then lets the words of the book jump them randomly from place to place until they land on a final word. Amazingly, you had placed that word in a sealed envelope, held by the volunteer throughout.

Computation

It is very easy for programs to contain bugs and subtle mistakes that mean that sometimes they do the wrong thing. A good program will work whatever the situation, and to ensure this, we must actively look for bugs. One way to do this, called testing, is to run the program many, many times and check it works correctly every time. With some logical reasoning, we can do better than that, though.

The Trick

First, you need a copy of the book of Shakespeare's play, *Macbeth*. You can buy a cheap copy from any bookshop. (At the end of this chapter, we will show you how to create your own version of this trick with a book you already own.)

Write the word "HEATH" on a piece of paper, and place it in an envelope clipped onto a clipboard. Place on the clipboard, over it, a piece of paper with the opening lines to Shakespeare's *Macbeth* written out as in Figure 6.1. They are from the famous first scene where the three witches meet. Draw a dotted line after the first sentence. Write the last part of the quotation in bold as shown (or write it in red). Make sure there are no spelling mistakes or missed words.

Now for the trick. Give a volunteer the clipboard and a pen. Give another person an actual copy of the book, *Macbeth*.

Tell the audience how later in the play the witches meet *Macbeth* and predict that he will be King. But words read aloud over and over gain a magic of their own. *Macbeth* has been read so often that the words of the play can control a person's mind and so make other predictions come true.

Ask the person with the book to read the opening lines, while the first volunteer checks that the words on their clipboard are exactly the same words that the witches speak.

> When shall we three meet again
> In thunder, lightning, or in rain?
> -
> When the hurlyburly's done,
> When the battle's lost and won.
> That will be ere the set of sun.
> Where the place?
> -
> **Upon the heath.**
> **There to meet with *Macbeth*.**
> **I come, Graymalkin!**

Figure 6.1. The first lines of *Macbeth* written out as needed for the trick.

Get the volunteer to put their hand on the book and "draw on its magical powers". Have them then pick a word at random from the first sentence of the quotation (before the first dotted line), as spoken by the first witch. It should be one of the words:

When shall we three meet again/In thunder lightning or in rain.

They should circle their chosen word, telling everyone what it is. For example, if they choose the word "three", then that is the word they circle and announce.

Now, explain that they must let the book control them. They will jump from word to word, guided only by the magic of the words themselves. They will stop only when they end a jump on a bolded word (after the second dashed line). That bolded word will be their final chosen word.

To do this, they should count the number of letters in the original chosen word. They then step forward that many *words* to land on a new word. They circle it. For example, if they did choose the word, "three" originally, then it has five letters. They step forward five words and land next on "lightning" which they circle. Have them do this with their word. Double-check that they don't make a mistake.

They do this repeatedly bouncing from word to word, each time counting the number of letters in the *new* word and moving on that far. They should ignore punctuation. They should also ignore the stage direction in the book which is why you've given them a version with only the words spoken.

They keep going until they jump to a bolded word for the first time. Check each step with them and the audience. They should announce what that final bolded word is. Have them agree that it was their own free choice of which word to choose originally and that they had no idea what bolded word they would land on. No one knew.

Finally, explain that using the magic in the book, you made a prediction beforehand. Point out that there is an envelope on their clipboard under the sheet they have been writing on. They should open it and read out what it says. Magically, they find the word written is the bolded word that they finally landed on!

The Magical Algorithm

TO DO Wizardly Book Magic:
  Before the trick starts
  1. Write HEATH on a piece of paper.
  2. Place it in an envelope.
  3. Place the envelope on a clipboard.
  4. Cover it with a piece of paper with the words to *Macbeth* on exactly as shown.

  The trick itself
  5. One volunteer reads the words from the book, while a second who is holding the clipboard checks they are the same.
  6. The volunteer with the clipboard chooses and circles a word from the first sentence.
  7. DO THE FOLLOWING UNTIL the last word circled is a bolded word.
      a. The volunteer counts how many letters are in the last circled word.
      b. The volunteer jumps forward that many words.
      c. The volunteer circles the new word.
  8. The volunteer tells everyone that chosen bolded word.
  9. Tell them about the prediction in the envelope.
  10. The volunteer reveals the predicted word in the envelope.

How It Works

Whatever word they pick from the first sentence, your prediction will be correct (of course). Each word in that first sentence leads to the same bolded word. We will come back to exactly why it works after we have looked at some computational thinking, though.

Deeper magic?

Now you know the trick, you can do it yourself, even if you don't understand how it works (yet). If you start with the words from *Macbeth*, it will always work. In fact, it is even more magical. It will work with just about any book about witches, wizards or magic, though the word to predict will be different for each. Try it with the words from the start of a different book: *The Wonderful Wizard of Oz*. Don't trust me to give you the words. Find a copy. For this book, if you pick a word from the first sentence, you will always end up on the word "FOUR".

Want more evidence? Try another completely different magical book: *The Cat in the Hat* by Dr Seuss. It's about a magical cat. Choose a word from the first sentence. I predict you will land on the word "SAT".

The magic is even deeper than that. It will work with just about any writing, though in some books the sentence to make bold is further on than in others.

A conspiracy?

Is this really some powerful, deep magic? Or has there been a secret conspiracy by authors, all agreeing for centuries to write their books so this trick works? No. It's just a simple, if surprising, property of the words in books. It is another "self-working trick", another algorithm. It always works if you follow the steps, whatever book you choose.

Thinking Computationally

Testing times

I've claimed the trick always works for that passage from *Macbeth*. Do you believe me enough to try the trick for yourself with an audience? How can you be sure it always works? Well, you could try it a few times. Would that convince you? Does that give you enough evidence? What if they pick a word you didn't check? You have no idea whether it works for that one. You will look a bit silly if your prediction turns out to be wrong.

It sounds a bit tedious, but you should check every alternative word that could be chosen does work. You have to be very patient to be a good magician or a good computer scientist! Careful checking and **attention to detail** really, really matter. Miss a step and things can go wrong. Programmers call checking programs like this, **testing**. Programmers spend more time testing programs than writing them. Testing is one kind of **evaluation** of a program: evaluating if it works.

We want to be sure we really have checked all the possibilities. The easiest way to do this for our trick is to start at the first word, check it works, then move to the next, check it, and so on, until we have done all words in the first sentence. That means for *Macbeth* you need to do 12 tests as there are 12 possible starting words. Other books will need more or less tests depending on the length of the first sentence.

We are doing algorithmic thinking again: what I just described is an algorithm for checking our magic trick works. Since we now have an algorithm to do it, we could even write a program based on it to check our trick rather than do it by hand. If you can write programs, you might want to try. If not, check the magic trick really does *always* work for *Macbeth*, *The Wonderful Wizard of Oz* and *The Cat in the Hat*, by hand.

The lazy logical thinker does less

With a little thought, we can actually come up with a slightly better algorithm that involves less work to do the checking. Here is how. Circle each word you come to as you check the paths of each word. Then, if you land on a circled word from an earlier test, stop and move on to a new starting word. You know the path from that point on has already been checked.

Figure 6.2 shows the result of checking every word from the first sentence in *Macbeth* like this. We have added arrows showing where each word jumps to so that we can see the paths taken. Remember, it is only the paths from words in the first sentence you need to check as those words are the only ones that can be chosen.

As part of checking the word "when", for example, we bounce to "meet" and then to "lightning". When it is the turn of those words to be checked, we will have nothing more to do as having checked the trick works for "when" we have already checked those other words too: they follow the same path.

With a bit of logical thinking, we have reduced the number of paths we have to check from 12 to only 7, almost halving the work to do. Some of those paths are shorter, so quicker too. Perhaps you can see a way to reduce the number of paths that we need to check even further?

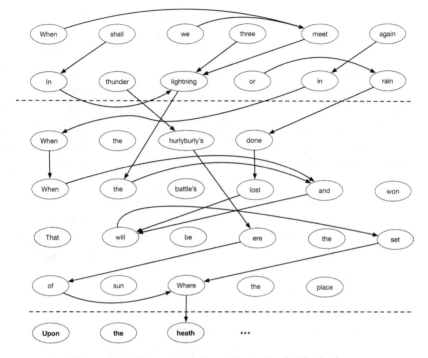

Figure 6.2. The paths followed in the book *Macbeth*.

You have to be very careful when checking. It is easy to make a mistake counting. If you do, then you might find one day your trick doesn't work after all. That means it's best, having done it once, to double-check your work. Drawing the arrows makes that slightly easier. You just need to check every word has an arrow out, and every arrow jumps the right amount.

Why does it work?

Why does it work? Think about what happens in that first sentence as the paths of some words, like "when", "meet" and "lightning", join up. Once paths have joined, they don't split up again. Any short word in that first sentence is just going to join with another word that could have been chosen. They will end up on the same bolded word. Only a few words, mainly ones at the end of the sentence or very long ones, will jump straight to the second sentence. In fact, only four words jump out of that first sentence: "thunder", "lightning", "in" and "rain". What appeared to be 12 possibilities for the volunteer to choose from is actually only four different choices of onward paths: only four paths cross the first dotted line. A similar thing will happen with any book. Long first sentences may look like they are offering lots more choices but actually only a few words will jump the first dotted line and escape as separate paths from that first sentence. Once we are beyond the dotted line, no new paths are created. We don't have to check every word from that point, only those we can land on from one of the existing paths.

So what happens to those four paths for *Macbeth?* Does that still mean there are four possible bolded words we could end up on? Well, no. As their paths bounce around, eventually by chance two paths hit the same word. Then those two paths merge and stay together from then on. Once they do, there is one less possibility for what the final word could be. That is what happens in the diagram for *Macbeth*. The further we go, the more likely it is that the different paths left will eventually meet and so land on the same bolded word. For *Macbeth*, they all meet 31 words from the start. If you go far enough, it is virtually certain all paths will join up whatever the book. You just may have to push the bolded sentence back.

An algorithm to create your own book trick

To create a version of the trick for your favourite book, copy out the start of the book. Draw the start line after the first sentence. Then, check all the paths from words of that first sentence. Find the earliest word they all meet on (if they do). The finish line is the end of that sentence. Make the next sentence the bolded one. Your predicted word is the word where the now single path jumps to first in that bolded sentence. To be extra safe, double-check that every word in the first sentence does take you there!

Bugs

Programmers call the mistakes they make **bugs**, and finding mistakes is called **debugging**. So when double-checking your version of the trick, if you found a word it didn't work for (and so pushed the bolded sentence back to fix it), you are essentially debugging your version of the trick. The word bug had been used before its use in programs as a mistake but caught on in programming supposedly because one of the first times a computer went wrong, it turned out it wasn't because of a programmer's mistake, it was because a real bug (a moth) got trapped in one of the switches! One of the first programmers, Grace Hopper, stuck the moth in her notebook and the name stuck too.

All books?

Does it work for all possible books? How could we check that? We would have to work through every book in turn and see if the paths for each did join together as in *Macbeth*. If ever we found one that didn't work, we would have proof in that book that it does NOT always work. However, each time we check a new book that it does work for, we've proved nothing for certain about all books. We would have to keep testing to be sure it works for the next book, and the next.... To prove that it worked for every book (if it does), we would need to check every single book ever written. That would take forever! Let's hope it doesn't always work! We need some logical thinking.

If it doesn't always work, we should be able to think of a way that a book might be written so that at least two paths don't join up. Well, if two words are the same length, then they will jump to positions the same distance apart. If that keeps happening, their paths will never meet. So if we have a book that is something like the following all the way through, then the trick won't work.

The dog saw the rat,

but the cat ate him.

The dog was sad for the rat...

Here, all the words are three letters long, so we end up with only three paths straight away. However, those paths just bounce along together, never joining up. Check it. If every word in a book is the same length like this, the trick will fail to converge on a single word however far you go. So without checking any real book at all, we have worked out that it is possible for the trick not to work on some books. (Though we still don't know if anyone ever wrote a book like that.)

With similar reasoning, we can also see what will help make it work quickly. The paths will generally join quickly, for example, if the book uses lots of short words but that have different lengths: say lengths 2, 3 and 4 letters.

Avoiding disasters

Just as we originally tested the trick for all possibilities to prove it works, programmers test their programs over and over again to make sure they work, whatever happens.

When a computer program, perhaps a game you are playing, crashes, it means you have just found a situation that the programmers didn't test. It isn't your fault, it's theirs. It is virtually impossible to write complex software, without it containing mistakes somewhere. Why? As real programs can be millions of instructions long, it takes perfect attention to detail and logical thinking to get it right. It is just too easy for the programmer to make a mistake, for a program to contain a bug.

Testers don't find all the problems because there are just too many possibilities to check them all. Testing real software is actually more like checking the trick works for all the books in the world than checking that *Macbeth* or *The Wonderful Wizard of Oz* works. There might be millions, billions or more possibilities to check, and it just can't be done in any sensible time. Instead, programmers often test what they hope is a good enough sample. They then cross their fingers and hope. That is why programs are constantly being updated with "bug fixes". It is only when millions of people start using the software that it starts to get properly tested and the bugs are found. They are using their customers as their testing team.

Testing is an important part of any evaluation, and the testers have to test as completely as possible. But testing alone just isn't good enough to find the problems in really complex programs. There are just too many possibilities to check. There are also problems testing won't find.

Better ways are needed.

Especially, for critical systems, programmers use other **evaluation methods** too. As we did for our trick, they use logical thinking to work out what to test, trying to ensure they cover, if not every situation, a full range of situations.

Both magicians and programmers must check that their algorithms *always* work, whether by testing, logical reasoning or both. This requires a lot of patience, care and attention to detail.

PAUSE: Margaret Hamilton

Testing is a key part of software engineering, which is the idea that programs are not just written but engineered. Margaret Hamilton is a key person involved in the history of how programming was turned from a craft into such an engineering discipline. She was part of, and ultimately led, the team who developed the code for the command module of the Apollo moon landings. Hamilton is responsible for the idea of end-to-end testing where the full system is tested in realistic conditions. One of her other innovations was the priority alarm display, which was included to deal with the problem of the computer becoming overloaded and not being able to do all that was asked of it. When the display showed warnings, Buzz Aldrin was supposedly told to count to 5 before hitting any button to allow it to catch up. Hamilton's foresight actually did help avoid the moon landing being aborted 3 minutes before it was due to touch down.

Chapter 7

The 21-Card Trick
Logical Reasoning and Proof

Conjuring

A volunteer picks a card and thinks about nothing but that card throughout the trick. You show you can read their mind by telling them their card, even though they told no one of their choice.

Computation

Real programs are too complex to test all possibilities in any reasonable amount of time. A complementary method is to use logical reasoning to give a convincing argument or proof as to why a program or specific algorithm always works without doing any testing. By doing both, you increase confidence that the program really is correct.

The Trick

Tell a volunteer that they must think of a card. You are going to read their mind and work out which it is. Explain they must think hard about the same card all the way through the whole trick. First, you need some cards for them to choose from.

Shuffle a pack of cards and then deal 21 cards face up into three piles of seven cards. Deal one card at a time to each row, before moving back to the first pile and so on, making sure all cards are visible.

Ask them to secretly pick any one of the 21 cards and think of it and of nothing else. Explain that if they think of anything else or giggle or laugh, it will make it really hard to read their mind. Go up to them and stare at their forehead, concentrating, warning them not to giggle. If they do giggle or smirk, say that spoiled it. Either way, say they seem to be thinking of other things so it's making it hard. You will need to try again. Ask them to point to the pile their card is in, without telling you which card it was. You collect the cards up and deal them out again for another attempt.

When you collect the cards, collect them in their three piles, placing the pile the volunteer pointed to in the middle. Then deal out the cards again in the same way into three equal piles, across the rows.

Now as you couldn't read their thoughts through the front, the front of the skull is after all pretty solid, try the back this time. Remind them not to move and especially not to giggle but just think of their card. While they do, stand behind them and concentrate on the back of their head.

Again, explain something is going wrong: perhaps they moved or giggled or someone else made a noise. Say you almost had it: you think you got the colour this time. You will need to try again.

Once again, ask them to find their chosen card and only tell you which pile it is in. Collect the cards in the same way as before, casually placing the new pile containing the chosen card in between the other two piles and dealing them out a third time.

As their skull is obviously hard for thoughts to go through this time, you will try through the ear. Again, they think of the same card and you stare at their ear from one side. This time, announce you think you've got it: it is so much easier to read the thoughts coming out of a person's ears, but say you want to triangulate and check from a different angle.

Have them point to the pile their card is in, collect the cards in the same way with their pile going in the middle and deal them out again across the rows for a final time.

Now, go to their other side and stare at their other ear. Announce that yes you've got it and go to the pile of cards. Stare at them saying you've now just got to find it. Turn over all of the first pile saying it is not one of them, checking with the volunteer that you are right so far. Next, turn over the last pile: it is not one of them. That leaves the middle pile. Start to turn most of them over, then pause, go back and turn over the bottom three. Say that it is not any of those, then quickly turn over the top three too, leaving the single middle card face up. Announce that that is their card, asking them to confirm you are right.

The Magical Algorithm

TO DO the 21-Card Trick:

1. Shuffle the pack of cards.
2. Deal the first 21 cards one at a time to make three piles of seven cards with all cards visible.
3. Ask a volunteer to secretly pick a card from the 21 and remember it.
4. DO THE FOLLOWING 3 TIMES:
   a. Ask the volunteer to think of their card and nothing else.
   b. Pretend to read the volunteer's mind but say you haven't quite got it yet.
   c. Ask them to point to the pile their chosen card was in.
   d. Pick the piles up sandwiching the one pointed to between the other two.
   e. Deal out the cards again, dealing the cards one at a time across the piles.
5. Deal out the cards a final time.
6. Ask the volunteer to continue to think of their card and nothing else.
7. Pretend to read the volunteer's mind.
8. Reveal that their chosen card is the one in the centre of the middle pile.

How It Works

There are two important steps to this trick. You must always deal out the cards across the piles. You must also always take the pile they point to and put it in the middle of the other two piles when you pick up the piles. Do that and their card is guaranteed to end up as the middle card of the middle pile after the fourth deal.

Before you read on, have a go at working out why that works. Perhaps try it a few times. Clearly, no one can read your mind. We are just following the steps: the same ones every time. It seems to never fail (as long as the volunteer keeps thinking of the same card all the way through and does not lie about the pile it is in, of course). To trust the magic enough to do it for a live audience, we must be pretty sure it *always* works, though.

Thinking Computationally

One way you could convince yourself is by doing the trick multiple times: by testing. Would that convince you? Try it. What about the next time you do the trick? Will the rules it is following work that time too? How many tests are enough?

You could test every possible way the trick could start and see how it ends. That's what we did first with the Wizardly Book Magic trick. In that trick, it was a bit boring, but it was possible, as there were only 12 different situations to check. What are the possibilities here? There are 52 cards in a pack and any 21 could be used in any order. We would have to test all those different possibilities. There are 9,809,042,663,139,505,407,817,600,204,800,000 permutations to try. That's a lot of times to do a magic trick. For each, we would need to test the case where the volunteer chose each of the 21 cards. So do that 21 times over to be completely exhaustive. That is a *lot* of testing. You would have to stop eventually. Or is there a better way?

Well, as with the book trick, we can do some simple logical reasoning. Here, it is vital. Maybe you worked this part out already. We don't actually have to do all those permutations as it's not what's on the card that actually matters to the trick. It is only where the chosen card is at the start that matters. If, from each starting position, the chosen card always ends in the middle, the trick always works whatever the cards actually are. Thinking that through, it means there are actually only 21 tests we need to do, one for each place the chosen card could start from. It is actually possible to do the trick 21 times to check what happens in each case (if you've an odd hour to spare and are meticulous about keeping track of what positions you check).

Prove it!

However, we can do better than that. In fact, I *know* it always works without any tests. I've proved it (so I can sleep easy at night now before a magic show). With a little logic and proof, I can be sure the rules are right for all 21 possibilities without testing any.

This magic trick works because putting the pile containing the chosen card in the middle of the other two piles and re-dealing the cards in effect limit where their card can go. Let's step through it.

After Deal Number 1: After the first deal of the cards into three piles, the chosen card could be anywhere, but when we pick up the pile pointed to, it goes into the middle seven-card pile. Why? Because we put that pile (whichever it is) in the middle of the other two. There are now only seven positions it could be in within the pack (positions 8–14 in Figure 7.1).

After Deal Number 2: You deal the cards into three new piles dealing across the piles. Where do those seven cards (numbered 8–14) from the selected pile go from the middle pile? They end up in the middle positions of each pile (see Figure 7.2). The chosen card has to now be in one of those seven places. Those places are the fourth or fifth card of the first pile; the third, the fourth or fifth card of the middle pile, or the third or fourth card of the last pile. You ask the volunteer to say which pile, and again put that pile between the other two. Wherever the seven cards were, they are moved to the middle pile. They now must be one of the middle three cards in the middle of the pack (as shown by the arrows of Figure 7.2).

After Deal Number 3: After this deal, the chosen card has to be the middle card of the first, middle or last pile (see Figure 7.3). Why? It was

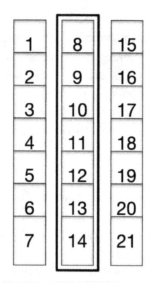

Figure 7.1. The positions of the cards after the correct pile is pointed to and moved to the middle the first time. The cards are numbered by positions 1–21 at this point. Here, we draw the piles as if still laid out. In the trick, they would be in this order in a single pile at this point. The selected card will be ultimately in one of the positions 8–14 in the collected deck.

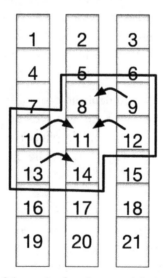

Figure 7.2. The positions of the cards after the second deal. A similar pattern follows if it was in one of the other piles. If the chosen pile is not in the centre, then when the piles are collected up they will have been moved to one of the positions: 8, 11 or 14.

in one of those middle three cards in the middle pile. By dealing across the rows, they all get dealt one after another, one to each pile. Once you are told which of the three piles has the card this time, you already know exactly where their card is. However, when you collect the piles, whichever of the three it is, it is moved to the middle (as shown by the arrows in Figure 7.3).

After Deal Number 4: The fourth deal simply moves the chosen card to the middle card of the middle pile (see Figure 7.4), which really is just for effect.

What we have just done is give a convincing (we hope) argument that the trick, or actually the underlying algorithm, always works. That is all that mathematical proofs are: convincing arguments where there is no room for doubt if you follow the detail. Here, we were just proving that a trick works, but in doing that we have shown we can prove algorithms are correct, more generally. Now, computer programs are based on algorithms. So we can do the same thing for a program and prove it works in a similar way. It is very important that programs always work too.

Testing versus proof

The normal way programmers make sure that a program works is to test it: that is, try it out lots of times. Testing every combination for a program is even more impractical than for our trick. There are many more possibilities to try for any realistic program. Instead, as many as possible are tested. If it works each time, then you assume it also works in the cases you didn't try (and hope!). To improve on this, as we did, testers use logical reasoning to cut down the number of possibilities to test to be more sure it works. Still, for real programs, this leaves more tests than is possible to be totally sure.

The sort of proof we did gives an alternative. If the proof has no flaws, then it proves the trick (or program) works whatever the combination is, and you don't strictly need to test any of them. In practice, it is a good idea to do lots of testing too, as proofs can have mistakes in them just like programs. However, if you want to increase your certainty that your trick (or program) works, try and prove it!

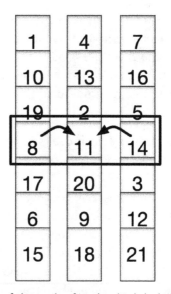

Figure 7.3. The positions of the cards after the third deal. On moving the selected pile to the middle, the selected card will have ended up at position 11.

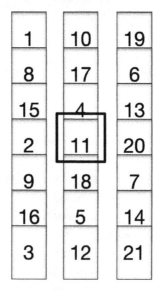

Figure 7.4. The positions of the cards after the fourth deal. The chosen card that was collected into the middle position stays there as the cards are dealt across the rows. It ends in position 11.

Proofs and new versions of tricks

The beauty of doing proofs is they can give you a really deep understanding of why a trick works. Once you understand the mechanics, you can play with changing some of the presentation. As long as you always make sure it doesn't affect the proof, or you can adapt the proof along with the trick, it will still work.

With this trick, we can see from the proof, and so understanding why it works, that the order of the cards in the chosen pile must not be changed. However, the two other piles could each be separately shuffled before being put together. Adding that step doesn't affect the proof. As long as the chosen pile goes undisturbed between the two other piles of seven cards, the order of the other cards doesn't matter. The proof allows us to see what will stop the trick working and what won't. Perhaps you can come up with your own twists now you know how it's done.

Phone crashes, rocket crashes

For games, bugs are just irritating, but there are many situations where they can cause really big problems. For example, when you pick up a phone to dial the emergency services, you don't want to find the phone is dead because of a software bug. On January 15th, 1990, it happened across the USA: 70 million telephone calls failed. Telephone company AT&T's engineers had upgraded the program that makes the connections, so each phone links to the one it is calling. The code in all their 114 switching centres was changed. The new version had a bug, and they all stopped working properly. The mistake was in a few lines of code out of millions, and the programmers who had changed them hadn't tested all eventualities. AT&T lost $1 billion as customers fled to competitors.

NASA's Mariner 1 spacecraft was launched in 1962. It was to fly by Venus. It made it as far as the Atlantic Ocean. A hyphen that should have been there was missed in the program: a simple error, but lethal in a computer language. Testing didn't find the problem. The flight program miscalculated the rocket's trajectory, and the rocket lost control. It had to self-destruct before it caused bigger problems. The mission lasted 290 seconds.

The Ariane 5 rocket had taken 10 years to build and cost $500 million. In 1996, it exploded 40 seconds after liftoff, destroying its satellite cargo. This spectacular software failure was due to squeezing a large number into the computer memory reserved for a small one. As it went faster and the number got larger, there wasn't enough space to hold the rocket's speed. This caused the rocket to veer off course, break up and explode. The testers had missed testing this critical situation, so no one realised the mistake until it was too late, though 40 seconds into a real flight was long enough to find it!

Bug-caused disasters like these show why we need as many ways as possible to avoid bugs being missed in mission-critical software. Arguably, all software should be evaluated more thoroughly. Make sure you do all you can to ensure your tricks always work if you want to avoid onstage disasters.

PAUSE: Edsger W. Dijkstra

Dutch Computer Scientist, Edsger Dijkstra (1930–2002), amongst many amazing contributions to early computer science, revolutionised the way programmers thought about writing programs from the 1960s onwards. He introduced the idea of Structured Programming which led to changes in the design of programming languages. It is a style of programming that helps improve the quality of programs making them easier to write correctly. It involves systematically using specific control structures like selection and repetition, avoiding "spaghetti code" where control is based on jump or goto statements. This makes code both easier to get right and easier to reason about.

Chapter 8

𝔐ental 𝔐onte and the 𝔗rains of 𝔗hought
Reasoning by Cases

Conjuring

A volunteer picks a card from three, then moves cards around, all with your back turned. After more mixing of the three cards, you can still name the card chosen.

Computation

One form of logical reasoning is reasoning by cases. This involves a form of decomposition: splitting your argument into several cases that together prove the whole. It is naturally used at decision points in a program, so with selection instructions. There is one case for each path through the code.

The Trick

Three-card Monte, or Find the Lady, is a popular game which is often used to swindle people. Three cards are used, one a red queen.

The cards are moved around, and the spectator tries to find the queen, normally unsuccessfully. Whilst this game can be rigged by sleight of hand, we present a variation, Mental Monte, that makes it more magic than scam.

Put three cards face up on the table and ask your volunteer to choose one *mentally* and remember its position. You turn your back and ask the volunteer to point at their card, to show the audience which card they chose. Then have them silently switch the two *other* cards, the cards not chosen. They then turn the three cards face down. When you turn round, you ask the spectator to switch pairs of cards in the row of three as many times as they wish, so mixing up the already mixed-up cards. You then turn the cards over. Even after this multiple mixing, you are able to read the volunteer's mind and reveal their chosen card.

Now, you have the basic idea, how about an alternative presentation? You can perform this trick with three train tickets for three different destinations. If you don't have the tickets, just write three places on three bits of identical cards. In this presentation, you can talk about changing the destination, and about long complex train journeys. This gives a natural justification for moving the face-down tickets around. It also gives a strong finish when you reveal the name of the mystery-selected journey.

How It Works

The key to this trick is that you memorise the card in the middle of the three when they are face up at the start. When you turn back around, you need to casually keep an eye on the position of the face-down card in the middle, and track it as it is moved around in the swaps. Once the swapping is finished, you flip over the card you have been tracking.

There are a few possibilities. If the card you flip over is the card you had originally memorised, then you correctly announce it as the chosen card. If it is not that card, then the chosen card is neither this card nor the one you memorised. Flip over the others, and announce that it is the other card (the one neither tracked nor memorised).

To understand why this works, we will need some logical thinking . . .

The Magical Algorithm

TO DO the Mental Monte:

1. Place three different cards face up on the table.
2. Memorise what the middle card is.
3. A volunteer chooses one card and remembers its position.
4. Turn the three cards face down.
5. Turn your back.
6. The volunteer points at their card to show the audience.
7. The volunteer switches the two *unchosen* cards.
8. The volunteer turns all cards face down.
9. Turn back around.
10. The volunteer repeatedly switches pairs of cards while you secretly keep track of where the middle card ends up.
11. Flip the tracked card over.
12. IF the card you tracked (so flipped over) is the memorised card THEN
    a. announce the flipped one is the card they chose.
    OTHERWISE
    b. turn over the other cards and announce the third card (not the one you memorised or the one you turned over first) is the card they chose.

Thinking Computationally

To use logical reasoning to be sure this trick always works, we need to work through the separate cases that can occur. The algorithm has a selection statement, that means you do something different depending on what the card you turn over is. That IF statement gives us two cases to consider. The case when the card flipped over first is the memorised card, and the case when it isn't. We must therefore think through those two cases.

The THEN case

If the card you flip is the one memorised so is still the one tracked, then logic tells us the spectator didn't switch the middle card when your back was turned. If they had moved it, it would no longer be in the middle when you turned around so not be the one you then followed. They must have swapped the two end cards. However, they were told to swap the cards they didn't choose, so the original middle card was their choice.

The OTHERWISE case

If the card you tracked from the middle and so flip is not the one you memorised, then that card must have been swapped from the middle position by the volunteer while your back was turned. If it had not been swapped, it would still have been in the middle and so be the one you tracked. As the non-chosen cards were swapped, the card you flipped over was not the chosen card. The chosen card must be one of the other two cards.

Now the memorised card was originally in the middle. It must have been swapped from the middle as we just saw. Therefore, it also cannot have been the chosen card, or else it would have been left in the middle while your back was turned. It would then have been tracked and be the one you turned over. It wasn't so must therefore have been moved in the original swap.

That means the chosen card, the one that wasn't swapped while your back was turned, must be the other card: neither the memorised nor the tracked one.

Did that just make your head hurt? It may help to understand this second situation better by thinking through an explicit example. Let's suppose the cards at the start are cards 1, 2 and 3, in that order. The middle card is card 2, and you memorised it. Suppose, when your back is turned, the spectator chooses card 3. That means they switch cards 1 and 2 giving the new order 2, 1 and 3. See Figure 8.1.

You turn back around and follow the middle card, card 1. You track its position as the subsequent pairs of cards are swapped. You turn over card 1 wherever it ends up, as it's the card you have been tracking. It is not the card you memorised (2), so they must have been swapped so

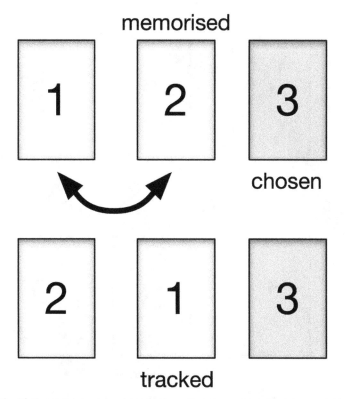

Figure 8.1. If the third card is chosen, the other two are swapped, one being the memorised one, the other the tracked one.

neither is the chosen one. The card they picked was therefore neither the card you memorised (2) nor the one you just turned over (1). It must be card 3.

As the situation is symmetrical, the same reasoning applies if they instead chose card 1. This time they swap 2 and 3 giving the order 1, 3 and 2 and because it is in the middle when you turn back, you track and eventually turn card 3 over. Again the card they picked was neither the memorised card (2) nor the one turned over (3). It must be card 1 (see Figure 8.2).

Our overall logical reasoning is a proof by cases, with one case for each possibility resulting from the IF statement. This idea is the key to logical thinking around algorithms that use selection. You must consider

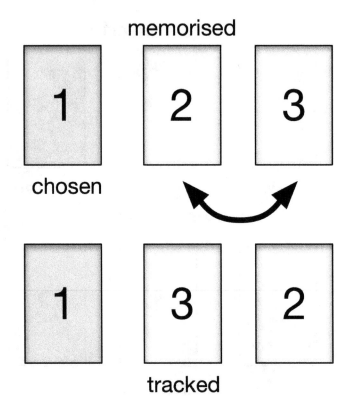

Figure 8.2. If the first card is chosen, the other two are swapped, one being the memorised one, the other the tracked one.

each of the cases. The structure of the algorithm describes the structure of the logical thinking you must do.

Interlude: Bob Hummer

The Mental Monte trick was devised by the great Bob Hummer (1906–1981), a creative magician who performed in and around Chicago. He invented lots of tricks including lots with mathematical angles. Mathematician, Martin Gardner, included some of these in his books on mathematical diversions.

Part 3

Making It Work for People

To develop software that is easy to use, you need to understand people, and in particular the limitations of our brains. Great computer scientists need to understand cognitive psychology.

Chapter 9

The Cyclops' Eye
You Cannot Trust Your Eyes

Conjuring

Stare at the picture of the Cyclops' eye, and it starts to magically move. Don't look for too long or you will be forever trapped by its stare!

Computation

When writing software, you have to understand that our brains have limitations that lead us to make mistakes. You must write the software (and especially its interface) in a way that works with those limitations. If you ignore our limitations, you will produce bad software.

The Trick

This trick is just a few steps: warn everyone that they should not look for too long or they will be trapped forever by the Cyclops' stare, have everyone look at the picture of the Cyclops' eye (Figure 9.1) and move

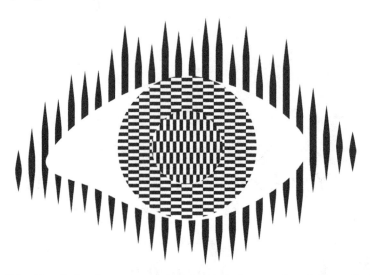

Figure 9.1. The Cyclops' eye was created by Kelly Burrows based on an illusion invented by Japanese artist, Hajime Ōuchi, in his book *Japanese Optical and Geometrical Art.*

their head slowly from side to side. Everyone who looks at it will see the central part of the eye start to hover and float around.

The Magical Algorithm

TO DO the Cyclops' Eye:

1. Warn everyone that they should not look for too long or they will be trapped forever by the Cyclops' stare.
2. The audience look at the image of the eye.
3. The audience move their heads gently from side to side.

How It Works

As with other optical illusions, this is just your brain playing tricks on you. Your brain is fooled because it separately tries to work out what is going on with the horizontal and vertical patterns. As your eyes move, the strong patterns seem to be doing different things, so your brain makes sense of this by assuming they are moving separately.

There is another illusion, here too, although it is one that we perhaps take more for granted. We see the outer shape of the white of the eye even though there is no actual line. Our brains fill in the shape of the eye as though there was a shape outlined there.

Optical illusions like this occur because, in order to process the vast amount of data coming into our eyes, our brains make simplifying assumptions. We have some hard-coded rules that we cannot switch off that illusions are designed to trigger. Essentially, this shows we do not see the world as it really is. It is as though we are living in the Matrix of the film, seeing a made-up version of the world. However, it is not some alien machine that is feeding us a model of the world we see, but our own subconscious brains.

Thinking Computationally

This is our first indication that to be good at developing usable software you need to be much more than a logical, algorithmic thinker. You must understand the way our brains work, and in particular their limitations. As we will see, some of the limitations and simplifications our brains make mean we are highly likely to make mistakes using poorly designed software. When creating software, you must take these limitations into account when you design the **user interfaces** of software (the parts that people see and interact with). Good computational thinkers need to understand people too. Most software now uses some sort of **graphical user interface**: one that tries to make tasks easier to do based on the limitations of our brains. They can be well designed, so easy to use, or poorly designed, so much harder, with mistakes likely.

Interlude: Hajime Ōuchi and Bridget Louise Riley

The central illusion in the Cyclops' Eye was published in 1977 in a book called *Japanese Optical and Geometrical Art* by Japanese artist, Hajime Ōuchi. The book was intended as a sourcebook of ideas for illustrators. The illusion was celebrated and investigated by visual perception researchers, though it was almost 40 years before they tracked down its creator. It follows a tradition of Op Art (optical illusion-based art). The artist best known for pioneering this kind of art was Bridget Riley. She became famous in the 1960s for her black and white geometrical work which gave the illusion of shapes and movement. She had been inspired to experiment with art based on optical illusions by the pointillism paintings of Seurat that used small pixel-like circles of colour.

Chapter 10

𝔐agically 𝔚eighted 𝔅oxes
Your Brain Cannot be Trusted at All

𝔠onjuring

At the snap of your fingers, you make boxes clearly heavier than they were only a moment earlier.

Computation

Our brain's limitations are not just about what we see, but about our other senses too. Multimodal software that makes use of our other senses can make the software easier to use, not least for those with disabilities. However, the software developer must take into account the limitations of the senses being used.

The Trick

Beforehand, take three empty playing card boxes. Stuff the middle one with coins to make it heavy and tissues to make sure the coins don't rattle around.

Place the three boxes in a pile on the table with the heavy one in the middle of the pile (see Figure 10.1). Ask a volunteer to pick up the boxes all at once to feel how heavy the pile is, then put them down.

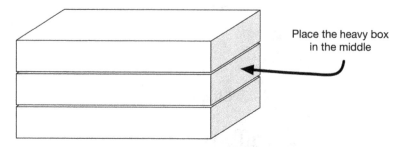

Figure 10.1. First lift all three boxes, then just the top two.

Now explain you can change their weight at the click of your fingers. Click your fingers and ask them to pick only the *top* two boxes up. They will feel immediately heavier than the three did.

How can three boxes be lighter than only two of them?

Repeat this trick, having different people try it in turn.

The Magical Algorithm

TO DO Magically Weighted Boxes:
  Before the trick starts
  1. Fill one box with coins and tissues.
  2. Place the boxes in a pile on the table with the heavy one in the middle.
  The trick itself
  3. A volunteer picks up all three boxes together to see how heavy they are.
  4. The volunteer puts them back on the table.
  5. Click your fingers saying you have changed their weight.
  6. The volunteer picks up only the top two boxes.
  7. Ask them to confirm these boxes feel heavier than all three did.

How It Works

It is all in the mind. It is like an optical illusion, but an illusion of touch rather than of sight. Again, shortcuts made by our brains in making sense of the world are being fooled. This is one example from a whole family of size–weight illusions. Psychologists are still not totally sure exactly why these particular illusions happen.

Thinking Computationally

Illusions can occur with all our senses, not just sight, though for similar reasons. We really do have to accept that our brains have limitations in the way they process information from the world. This matters when designing **multimodal interfaces** that make use of other senses. For example, increasingly computers are being built into physical objects so that manipulating those actual objects in the world acts as an interface to computers behind the scenes. Recognising the limitations of our brains is not just about the way we design graphical user interfaces that are based on sight.

Interlude: Lulu Hurst

Teenage magician, Lulu Hurst (1869–1950) was famous for tricks that involved her showing off her apparently amazing superpower strength. She claimed to have gained it superhero-style during a lightning storm. In one trick, demonstrating how easily she could overcome a massive weight, she had several men sit on a single chair trying to hold it down. She would then show that despite the weight and their efforts, she could easily move it. All her feats were actually based on scientific principles. She retired at age 16.

Chapter 11

The Teleporting Robot
Keep It Simple Stupid

Conjuring

You make a robot appear and disappear from a jigsaw as everyone watches.

Computation

Interaction design principles are rules designers follow to help ensure software is easy to use. One of the simplest rules is to keep the interface simple. The more controls like buttons and drop-down menus you have, the harder a system is to use. One way to keep it simple is to avoid feature bloat. Rather than adding every feature you can imagine, design just so that key tasks are supported and designed to be easy to do.

The Trick

Download a copy of the magic jigsaw (see Figure 11.1) from

https://conjuringwithcomputation.wordpress.com

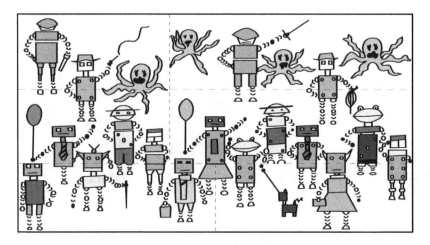

Figure 11.1. The Teleporting Robot magic jigsaw.

Cut out the six pieces of the jigsaw along the dashed lines. Complete the jigsaw by placing the short piece with the grey robot in the top left corner as in the original. With the audience, count the robots out loud, and make sure everyone agrees there are 17. There is also a robot dog and some Hexapus monsters (which are like an octopus but with only six legs).

Now, mix up the pieces and then rebuild the jigsaw, but this time with that first short jigsaw piece with the grey robot in the top right corner. The other pieces still fit together but in different positions. You are building it back with the pieces in the top two layers swapped over. As you mix up the pieces and rebuild it, talk about how you have to keep an eye on robots. As with WALL-E, they have a tendency to disappear on their own little excursions once they start to develop a mind of their own.

Now, with the audience, count the robots again. To everyone's surprise, there are now only 16 robots. The 17th has gone, leaving no trace. Ask which robot has disappeared and where it has gone. Did it wander off? Did a Hexapus eat it, or did it teleport away?

Once everyone is sure that there are 16 robots, shuffle the pieces and put them back the original way. Let everyone see there are 17 robots again. Their challenge is to work out which robot disappeared and how it did it.

If they spot that you rebuilt the jigsaw in a different way, point out that that explains nothing. It is the same pieces with the same heads and bodies. They are just good recycling robots who swap their parts rather than throwing them away. How can one disappear just because they swapped bits?

If someone claims it is a particular robot that disappears, then have them put a finger on the two parts of it, move the pieces around with them pointing at the same two parts and they will see that both parts are still there. That demonstrates their robot cannot be the one that is gone. How could any part of a picture vanish from a physical jigsaw anyway!

The Magical Algorithm

TO DO the Teleporting Robot:
1. Complete the jigsaw with the grey robot in the top left corner.
2. Count the robots out loud with the audience.
3. Note there are 17.
4. Mix up the pieces, then rebuild the jigsaw, this time with a green monster in the top left corner.
5. Count the robots out loud with the audience.
6. Note there are 16.
7. Ask which robot disappeared and how.

How It Works

This works because of a limitation in the way our brains process what we see. Look at the complete jigsaw. There are clearly 17 robots. When you put the jigsaw together the other way, there are definitely only 16. You've fooled yourself!

Error!!! Can't Compute!

This trick is so powerful that you cannot see the robot disappear even when you know what is happening. If you try and work out which specific robot has gone, you have no chance of working it out. It's not one robot. All are involved.

If you have a hard problem to solve, then it is a good idea to simplify it if you can. You may have noticed, for example, that the top four robots are always there, unchanged. They just move position. That means they are not involved. You can discard the top layer of pieces, and the trick still works (just with 12 and 13 robots instead of 16 and 17). Try it. The problem is now a little simpler.

How does it work? The original 13 robots are all that little bit shorter than the 12 robots, something that is easy to miss. Bits of each of the originals have been recycled into others to create a series of new, larger robots. Each loses a small bit (a part of a head say) and gains a bigger new version (a bigger head) from another robot. The first robot involved is the one on the far left. It is completely on the bottom layer of the jigsaw originally, but when the pieces are moved around, it has an extra bit of head on top. That bit of head comes from another robot, which loses that small bit of head but gets a bigger bit in its place. As you move from robot to robot, the place they are cut moves down their body. Eventually, in the final robot in the sequence (the one above the dog), the whole robot starts on the middle piece, and when it is moved, it leaves a gap behind. It also gets taller by joining on to some legs on a bottom piece. All 13 robots along the bottom have squashed together into 12 new taller robots.

We can simplify this even more to help see what is happening by replacing the robots with lines and arranging them so they swap with the adjacent line. Look at the picture of the lines in Figure 11.2.

There are five vertical lines on the left. Now imagine you cut those lines along the black diagonal line and slide the top triangle along by one space. The result is four lines as on the right (draw some parallel lines and try it). Where did the extra line go? It can't just have vanished, can it? No, what's happened is much easier to see here: the final lines are all a little bit longer. The missing line has just combined with part of another line. That other line's remainder combined with part of yet another, and so on.

We've made it more obvious here by only using a few lines and making the differences larger. Why don't we spot it with the robots? Well, people aren't that good at accurately judging small length

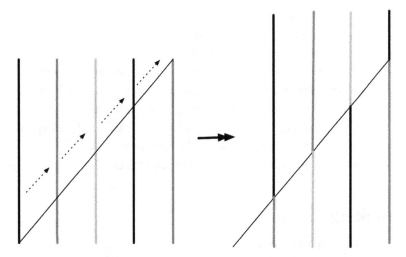

Figure 11.2. A simplified version of the effect used in the magic jigsaw. Slide the top half so each line joins with the bottom of the next along so becomes taller. You are left with one fewer line.

differences by eye. The new robots look "about the same" as before. "About", yes, but "the same", no! That's why we invented rulers!

The robot jigsaw design is more cunning than the lines though. Rather than just having the robots in order, where a simple slide of the top section would make the remaining robots taller, the jigsaw design has lots more confusing detail for our brains to take in but also weaves the vanish across different parts of the picture. That makes it hard to take in everything that you need to see in order to see what is actually happening even when you know.

Presentation matters

Magic is about more than algorithms, about more than the self-working part. You have to get the presentation right too.

Magic = Algorithm + Presentation

Even the most cunning trick can fail to be magical without a good presentation. The two versions of the trick, one with the lines and one with the robots, use the same mechanism. It is the presentation that makes one impossible to see what is happening, whereas in the other it is fairly easy. Here it is done by making the picture more complicated. There is too much going on for anyone's brain to take it all in.

Magicians rely a lot on understanding how our brains work, and particularly how they get things wrong. They rely on an understanding of cognitive psychology: the science of how we think. The key point is that our brain has limited resources. For example, we can only pay close attention to one place at once and only remember a few things at once.

Thinking Computationally

Presentation matters

Computer science, and especially writing software, is about more than algorithms too. You have to get the presentation right, just like a magician.

Software = Algorithm + Presentation

The difference is that a magician makes sure the whole audience makes the same mistake at the same time, whereas when using programs no one should make a mistake as we want programs to be easy to use. Computer scientists need to understand the same cognitive science as magicians, just use it in reverse.

For example, think about the remote control for a TV. It is very complicated with lots and lots of buttons. If someone accidentally presses the mute button switching the sound off, it can be quite hard to find the right button to get it back on again, unless you use it a lot. There is too much information there for our brain to take in.

One thing designers do to help make sure they create usable interfaces is to follow design principles. Our teleporting robot trick and the problems people have with remote controls lead to the "KISS" design principle: **Keep It Simple Stupid!** The best interfaces, that are easiest to use, are often very simple. They aim to support one task at a time and do it well. The things you might want to do at any given time are always really obvious. One thing that helps is to avoid **feature bloat**.

Rather than have your software try to do everything for everyone, focus on designing in a way that makes it easy to do the key tasks one group of people want to use it for. If other people want to do completely different things, then you design a different interface for them.

The reason many people think they are not good at using computers and other gadgets is not because those people are stupid. It is because the people who designed the software or gadget did not think hard enough about people. They made the programs work more like a magic trick than a usable program, so hard to follow and easy to get wrong. If you become a programmer or interface designer, make sure *your* designs are really easy to use, so no one makes mistakes. Make sure they are the opposite of a magic trick.

Interlude: Sam Lloyd and William Hooper

The teleporting robot trick is based on a very old mathematical puzzle. A very simple version of it appears in *The Moscow Puzzles* (1972) by Boris A. Kordemsky where a line is made to disappear. A fairly early and famous version of it was by Sam Lloyd (1841–1911), the great inventor of many mathematical puzzles, though he didn't invent this one. An even earlier version is described by William Hooper in a book published as far back as 1794. It involved cutting up bank notes. It gave a way to cut nine notes up into 18 parts. They were then put back together again to make 10 banknotes. Modern bank notes are now always designed in a way that stops the trick from working!

Part 4

Decomposition and Abstraction

When inventing new tricks, we can build them out of a collection of basic parts. Such parts can be reused across other tricks. Likewise, we can solve the problem of writing a program by breaking it into parts to write separately or just reusing bits previously written.

Chapter 12

𝔓re-booked 𝔓icture 𝔐agic
Abstraction

Conjuring

By reading the mental impression of it in their head, you are able to draw a picture that is selected randomly from a book of images by an audience member.

Computation

An abstraction is a simplification of something. Computer scientists use abstraction a lot, both as a way of making a complex piece of software easier to understand and to help make it possible to write in the first place. Similar ideas can be used in magic.

The Trick

You pass a small notebook around the audience for them to inspect. In it, you have written, on numbered pages, a series of random objects that came to you "in a dream". The spectators check that each page does have a different and unrelated thing written on it. The task is now to choose one.

You use a pack of cards to ensure a random choice. Spread the cards at the start to show the random mix. A volunteer then cuts the cards. They add the values of the bottom two cards of the pack after the cut. Remind them that a Jack is worth 11, a Queen is worth 12 and a King, 13. They secretly note this number. The spectator then takes the notebook to the other side of the room and goes to the page number given by their random card-created secret number. They then close their eyes and visualise the object written on that page.

On the other side of the room, you, the magician, sketch on a pad your mental impression of the thing the spectator is thinking about. The spectator then reveals the identity of the thing on that randomly chosen page. You turn your pad around showing you were able to correctly read the spectators' thoughts from a distance and draw that object.

How It Works

This effect relies on two separate elements: a mathematical technique called the 14/15 stack, used to force page numbers, and the notebook itself.

To create the stack (before doing the trick), you must first remove the Ace of Hearts and the Ace of Spades from a normal pack of cards. The fact that this pack only has 50 cards rather than 52 won't be spotted. You now need to carefully arrange the remaining cards in the following full-deck stack order (where C means Clubs, D means Diamonds, H means Hearts and S means Spades). It should end up with the 7 of Diamonds at the bottom of the deck, with all the cards face down.

7C 8C 6D 9S 5C 10H 4D JS 3C QS 2D KS AC KH 2H QC 3D JH 4S 10C 5D 9C 6S 8S 7S 8D 6H 9H 5H 10D 4C JD 3S QH 2S KD AD KC 2C QD 3H JC 4H 10S 5S 9D 6C 8H 7H 7D

This order is specially created to ensure that every adjacent pair of cards, including the last and the first, add up to either 14 or 15. Cutting the pack does not actually change the cyclic order, it just starts it in a different place. That means when the volunteer cuts the pack, the bottom two cards of the resulting pack will still add up to either page 14 or 15.

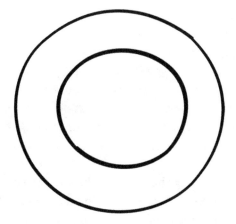

Figure 12.1. The picture you draw.

You now have a way to use a free cut of the pack to force either page 14 or 15. You next need a way of dealing with the problem that there are still two possible outcomes. That's where the way you set up the notebook and make the prediction comes in.

On your prediction pad, you sketch a large circle, with a smaller circle in the middle (see Figure 12.1). This prediction and its simple design allow you to claim it represents either of the two things you write on pages 14 and 15. Use your imagination for the objects you name on pages 14 and 15 of the book. For example, you could write Doughnut, Car Tyre or Porthole. That means you are covered whichever of the two values the spectator uses.

Remember that the spectator will tell you their choice before you show your prediction, so you can be ready with the right convincing argument about how the mental impressions you got made you roughly but correctly draw the answer they gave you. If you really could read minds, it would be difficult, so the fact you didn't get the sugar sprinkles on the particular doughnut they were visualising will be forgiven.

Use a cheap spiral-bound notebook for the book, as it allows for easy flipping of the pages. you need to create the illusion of free choice. Therefore, fill the book with enough random and unrelated things to make it convincing. It should certainly include a lot more than 15 things. Write the names clearly in block capitals so they are easy to read and clearly label the pages in the same place at the bottom, as they need to easily find the page number. Importantly, make sure that you use a separate sheet of paper for each object. Don't write the things on facing pages in case your spectator gets suspicious when they see that the outcomes on both pages 14 and 15 could match your prediction.

There are lots of alternative presentations for this trick. You could, for example, use world landmarks, either writing the names of the landmark or creating a book with pictures of the famous sites. Then your prediction could be an inverted V shape pointing upwards and a line underneath signifying the ground. The landmarks on pages 14 and 15 could then be The Eiffel Tower and Mount Everest. Both are arguably represented by your prediction. Come up with your own version: get creative!

The Magical Algorithm

TO DO Pre-booked Picture Magic:

Before the trick starts

1. Take a spiral-bound notebook and number every second page in the bottom corner, starting from 1 and going up to at least 35.
2. On pages 14 and 15, write the words DOUGHNUT and CAR TYRE, respectively, in block capitals.
3. On each other numbered page, write a noun in large block capitals.
4. Take a pack of cards and discard the Ace of Hearts and the Ace of Spades.
5. Place the remaining cards in the order: 7C 8C 6D 9S 5C 10H 4D JS 3C QS 2D KS AC KH 2H QC 3D JH 4S 10C 5D 9C 6S 8S 7S 8D 6H 9H 5H 10D 4C JD 3S QH 2S KD AD KC 2C QD 3H JC 4H 10S 5S 9D 6C 8H 7H 7D where C, D, S and H mean Clubs, Diamonds, Spades and Hearts, respectively, and A, J, Q and K mean Ace, Jack, Queen and King, respectively.

The trick itself

6. Ask a volunteer to cut the pack, completing the cut by placing the bottom pile back on the top.

7. Have the volunteer take the bottom two cards and add them up, remembering the total.
8. Give them the book.
9. The volunteer goes to the other side of the room, finds the page of their remembered number and silently reads the word on that page.
10. The volunteer closes their eyes and visualises the object given on the chosen page. While they do so, you pretend to focus on their thoughts, telling them you will draw what is coming through to you from their thoughts.
11. Draw two concentric circles on your pad.
12. The volunteer tells you the word they were thinking of.
13. Show them what you have drawn and point out you drew the object they were thinking of.

Thinking Computationally

Sketches are an **abstraction**, a simplification of the real thing. Your prediction is an even simpler version still. Abstraction is all about giving a simplified version of things, but that still captures the essence of the original. The abstraction (like the drawing) discards detail. A good abstraction will only throw away detail that is unnecessary for the task at hand.

Computer scientists use abstraction a lot, though they have very precise versions of it, that we look at in more detail in later chapters. For now, think about it as hiding or discarding detail that is unnecessary for the task at hand (a doughnut is still recognisable as a doughnut even without the sugar sprinkles).

The most important kinds of abstraction we will look at are about program instructions themselves, but computer scientists do use this kind of drawn abstraction in one situation: **icons**. Icons are small pictures used to represent programs. The image is a simplified picture representing what the program is or does. For example, a trash can represents the deletion operation on most **graphical user interfaces**. Drag a file to the trashcan picture and it is deleted. Icons are very simplified versions of the thing they represent, but to work well they must catch the essential detail and be instantly recognisable. The best are really good visual abstractions.

The magic trick, by contrast, relies on a *poor* abstraction in the sense that a pair of circles can represent two different specific nouns in the book (though it is a perfect abstraction for its purpose: to make the trick work). Graphical user interfaces need much clearer ones than this. If you could mistake an icon for meaning two different things, it would be a poor icon. Many modern icons are very confusing in this way. Abstractions generally lose information, but a good abstraction will not lose anything important!

PAUSE: Susan Kare

Susan Kare was part of the team working at Apple on their first graphical user interface. She created the first icons, and her work and ideas were key to the success of Apple both then and since. With no direct experience of Pixel Art to draw on, she instead gained inspiration from pixel-like art of the past: Seurat's pointillism, needlepoint and mosaics. Despite the icons being very small, they were simple and clear, following her design maxims of "meaning, memorability, and clarity". She was responsible for Apple's visual design language designing fonts as well as icons.

Chapter 13

Trained Rice
Decomposition and
Procedural Abstraction

Conjuring

You train rice so that unlike normal rice it can grip onto a chopstick.

Computation

Programs that are millions of lines long cannot be written without ways to simplify the task. The most immediate way is to use decomposition: split the big difficult program into lots of small meaningful parts that can be treated as distinct problems (i.e., mini programs) to solve. These separate parts are called procedures. By giving each a name, we can use them later just by giving their name.

The Trick

For this trick, you need two small plastic drink bottles with narrow necks, chopsticks and uncooked long-grain rice.

Figure 13.1. The bottles are filled with rice and a chopstick is inserted.

You must prepare the bottles by filling them with long-grain rice before you present the trick. Fill the first with rice and leave it as is. Pushing a chopstick into it, the chopstick should go in and then come out easily (Figure 13.1).

With the second bottle, after pouring in the rice, repeatedly tap the bottle on the table so that the rice packs closely together. As you do, you will create more space at the top. Keep adding more rice to fill it up.

When it no longer packs down, try pushing a chopstick into it. It should be harder to do than with the first bottle. If it is ready then, when you pick the chopstick up, the whole bottle should lift and stay in place. If not, keep tapping the bottle packing the rice even closer.

Remove the chopsticks, and you are ready.

Now for the performance. Announce that you have discovered a strain of rice that can be trained to grip things. Show the two bottles and explain that you have normal rice in the first bottle but trained rice in the second.

Place the chopstick in the first bottle and demonstrate that it does not grip the stick. Allow a member of the audience to try. Now place a chopstick in the second bottle and moving your mouth up close, whisper to it over and over "grip the chopstick, grip the chopstick..." Then, slowly lift the chopstick and watch the rice grip and the bottle rise with it.

The Magical Algorithm

Here is the trick written out as a series of steps in a structured way similar to that of the previous tricks. A difference to our previous instructions, though, is that here we have broken (or **decomposed**) the whole trick into two additional smaller *named* steps.

TO DO Trained Rice:
1. DO the preparation of trained rice.
2. DO the performance of trained rice.

TO DO the Preparation of Trained Rice:
{This should be done before the show.}
1. Fill two small plastic drink bottles with rice.
2. Take one of the bottles.
3. DO
   a. Tap the bottle gently on the table to make the rice settle.
   b. If more space appears, refill it with rice.
   c. Push a chopstick into the rice.
   d. Try to pick the bottle up with the chopstick.
   e. Remove the chopstick.
   REPEAT THE ABOVE UNTIL the chopstick stayed in place when picked up.

TO DO the Performance of Trained Rice:
1. Announce that you have discovered a strain of intelligent rice that you have trained.
2. Bring out the first (untapped) bottle, explaining it is normal rice.
3. Place a chopstick in the rice.
4. Try to lift up the bottle just with the chopstick. You can't.
5. Bring out the second (tapped) bottle, explaining it is trained rice.

6. Whisper to the second bottle.
7. Push the chopstick into the second bottle.
8. Lift chopstick and bottle.

How It Works

The secret of this trick is just the laws of physics and, in particular, friction. In the first bottle, the rice is not tightly packed so the grains easily slip past each other. In the second because they are pushed tightly against each other and the edge of the bottle, there is more friction between the rice grains and between the rice grains and the chopstick. This friction is enough to hold the chopstick in place.

Thinking Computationally

Here we have decomposed the algorithm into two subparts: the preparation and the performance. In fact, we did that informally in earlier tricks, though without naming the parts and without giving separate explicit instructions of the order to do them. Decomposition is just the idea of breaking up an algorithm into smaller, easier-to-manage parts like this.

Here, we are using **decomposition** and a programmer's version of **abstraction** (referring to the parts by name) purely as a way to organise the way we write the algorithm. This is to make it easier for a human (a magician or a programmer) to understand the instructions.

This matters a lot when writing large programs. Writing programs is about writing instructions computers can follow. Writing *good* programs is also about making them easy for humans to understand, so follow too! If you don't, then they are likely to have more bugs and, when changes to the program are needed, those changes will be harder to do.

Decomposition into meaningful parts is one of the most important ways of making programs easier for humans to understand. Often programs or even individual algorithms have a setup part, where data is collected or organised, followed by the part that does the actual work, and this is usually a good way to decompose the program. Both parts have very clear tasks to do. What you don't want to do is decompose a program you are writing into arbitrary parts where the separate parts have little real meaning.

There are three important aspects to what we are doing here. The first is **decomposing** the algorithm into parts. The second is to give those parts a unique name that can be used to indicate when those instructions should be followed. The final aspect is to use that name instead of the actual detailed instructions when we do wish it to be followed. These latter points combine to give another key tool in the computational thinking toolkit, that of **abstraction** or hiding of detail. We previously saw abstraction in drawings. Here, we are doing a more technical kind of abstraction. This naming of parts of an algorithm is called **procedural abstraction**. It involves using a name in place of a group of detailed instructions (hiding the detail of the instructions behind the name). These groups of instructions are known as **procedures**. We will explore procedural abstraction more in later chapters.

A Magical Diversion

Magicians can think of the performance of great tricks as being decomposed into three parts[1] in addition to the preparation:

> **The Pledge** is where you set the scene, giving the effect its meaning;
> **The Turn** is where you perform the trick leading them along with the story;
> **The Prestige** is where you reveal the twist at the end, the delight!

For example, we could decompose the Trained Rice performance in this way:

TO DO the Trained Rice Performance:
1. DO the Trained Rice Pledge.
2. DO the Trained Rice Turn.
3. DO the Trained Rice Prestige.

---

[1]Named by author Christopher Priest in his novel, *The Prestige* (1995).

TO DO the Trained Rice Pledge:

Announce that you have discovered a strain of intelligent rice that you have trained.

TO DO the Trained Rice Turn:

1. Bring out the first (untapped) bottle, explaining it is normal rice.
2. Place a chopstick in the rice.
3. Try to lift up the bottle just with the chopstick. You can't.
4. Bring out the second (tapped) bottle, explaining it is trained rice.
5. Whisper to the second bottle.
6. Push the chopstick into the second bottle.

TO DO the Trained Rice Prestige:

Lift chopstick and bottle.

By working with this standard structure, this standard decomposition, you improve the chances your trick will seem magical. For example, missing out the pledge in the above would mean it works less well as a trick even though the mechanics still work. If you are inventing your own tricks, make sure they have pledge, turn and prestige!

PAUSE: Michael Faraday

Michael Faraday (1791–1867) was a self-taught scientist and inventor who also created the inspirational Royal Institution Christmas Science Lectures that still run for children today. He delivered 19 of them personally. He showed that science could be taught to the general public in an entertaining way. He was a critic of spiritualism and seances and ran scientific experiments on how certain seance effects were achieved. As a scientist, his achievements were many across multiple fields including chemistry, physics and environmental science, but he is best known for his work on electromagnetism, with inventions such as the dynamo that ultimately made the widespread use of electricity a reality.

Chapter 14

𝕮𝖍𝖊 𝕮𝖊𝖑𝖊𝖕𝖔𝖗𝖙𝖎𝖓𝖌 𝕮𝖔𝖕 𝕳𝖆𝖙
Hiding Detail and Swapping Parts

Conjuring

We develop a new version of the Invisible Palming trick, replacing the palming part with a top hat teleporter.

Computation

Decomposition, combined with procedural abstraction, allows us to build large programs from small. Once a procedure is written, we can forget about the detail of how it is actually implemented. This also means that we can later completely change the way a step is done without it affecting the rest of the code that uses it.

The Trick

This trick is exactly the same as Invisible Palming (Chapter 1) except that you swap in new steps for those where you pretend to move the card from one pile to the other. Instead, you "move" the card with your magical top hat, into which the card disappears and reappears. At the point where you are to move the card, place your top hat over the pile with the extra card. Tap it with your magic wand and say the

101

magic words. Move the hat to the other pile, tap it once more with your magic wand and say the magic words once again.

The Magical Algorithm

One step of the earlier Invisible Palming trick was to pretend to move a card from one pile to another (no actual movement was needed). The algorithm for it might be split off as follows:

TO DO Pretend to Move a Card Between Piles:
1. Place a hand over the pile with the extra card.
2. Rub the back of that hand.
3. Lift your hand, showing the palm before placing it over the other pile.
4. Tap your hand and remove it, saying the card has moved.

This is then used as one step (step 4) of the whole thing as follows:

TO DO Invisible Palming:
1. Deal out 15 cards in pairs with one left over.
2. Take the pairs back splitting them into two piles.
3. Have a volunteer choose where to put the extra card.
4. DO Pretend to Move a Card Between Piles.
5. Reveal that the extra card has magically moved piles.

Now we can invent our own presentation of the trick (no longer invisible palming), just by changing the instructions of this one procedure. The above instructions do not need to change though.

TO DO Pretend to Move a Card Between Piles:
1. Place your top hat over the first pile.
2. Tap it with your magic wand, saying "Abracadabra".
3. Move the top hat to cover the other pile.
4. Tap it with your magic wand saying "Abracadabra".
5. Say that the card has moved.

The rest of the trick does not change, so the instructions do not need to be changed. This is one way that new tricks are developed: each magician creating a personal version. Don't copy, do your own version, and do better!

How It Works

The mechanics of the trick are exactly the same as they were before. We have actually just changed the presentation of one part. It doesn't change how or why the trick worked. The substituted step does exactly what the original did (nothing to the cards, but a lot to make the audience think something else is going on).

Thinking Computationally

We have used our **procedural abstraction** (giving a group of instructions a name), to make it easy to swap a **new implementation** for one of the steps, i.e., one of the **procedures**. The key point is that the main instructions do not change at all. As long as the new steps have the same effect as the old, nothing else has changed.

The same can be done with programs. If the program is split into procedures, then we can take any of those procedures and change how it works as long as we do not change what it does. The rest of the program is then guaranteed to still work, without any change to anything but the instructions in that one procedure.

The use of procedures makes a program much more **maintainable** because of this. It is easier to improve. It is simple to change the implementation of this part of the program in that when doing so we do not have to worry about any of the rest of the program. We know nothing else has to be changed. We might want to do this, for example, to make a critical part work faster or use less storage space.

Furthermore, if the procedures are used multiple times, improving the procedure improves it everywhere it is used throughout the program with no extra effort: we do not need to track down all the places it is used as no changes there are needed.

PAUSE: Jeannette Wing

A computer scientist who has also become a martial arts expert, Jeannette Wing has worked mainly in the area of using maths-based specification languages to very precisely state what programs should do. However, her biggest contribution has been to promote the idea of computational thinking as a core set of general skills that computer scientists should, and do, learn. The term was first introduced by Seymour Papert many years earlier, but she gave it life. She argued that the skills and way of thinking were generally useful in life, not just for writing programs, and so should be taught to all. As a result, when computer science and programming started to be introduced in school syllabuses around the world, computational thinking was at their core. Her students gave her the nickname "Dragon Lady" because she was a tough teacher. The name then stuck once she started doing martial arts.

Part 5

Procedures and Procedural Abstraction

There are many different kinds of false shuffles and similar well-defined magical manoeuvres that have a specific effect. Just by giving the name of one of these steps, a magician would know what was meant and be able to use it as part of a trick.

This corresponds to procedural abstraction where clear self-contained pieces of code are created for use in lots of programs. Once created, they are incorporated into any running program (or "called") with a command that just gives their name.

We describe a series of shuffles and cuts. In some, you really do mix the pack; in others, you just appear to shuffle it, but actually leave either the whole pack or an important part of it, unchanged.

Chapter 15

Overhand Shuffle
Procedures

Conjuring

This shuffle really does mix up the cards in a random way.

Computation

When we have a meaningful task that we will want our instructions to refer to lots, we package the instructions for that task as a procedure, give it a name and refer to the name, using it as an instruction (call the procedure) at the point we want the task to be done.

How to Do the Shuffle

The overhand shuffle is a commonly used, good way to mix cards. The deck is cupped in one hand (right if you are right-handed, left if left-handed) between the thumb and fingers, and the cards are transferred to the other hand by peeling off a small packet of cards from the original deck with the other hand's thumb. These small piles are deposited at the front of a new deck forming in the second hand. This is repeated until all the cards in the first hand are mixed into a pile cupped in the second hand. The whole thing is then repeated several times until the cards are thoroughly shuffled.

It is a legitimate shuffle and does mix the cards. However, there are various ways it can be performed that keep parts of the pack in the places you want them while still looking like a real shuffle, as we will see.

If you haven't done an overhand shuffle before, practice it for a while, and once you are reasonably good at it, you can start to get sneaky.

The Magical Algorithm

This algorithm can be done repeatedly for more thorough shuffling.

TO DO an Overhand Shuffle:
1. Cup the pack in one hand between thumb and fingers.
2. DO THE FOLLOWING UNTIL all cards are in the other hand.
    a. Pull off a small packet of cards from the front of those in the first hand with the other thumb into the front of the pile forming in the second hand.
3. Transfer the cards back to the first hand.

Thinking Computationally

The overhand shuffle is a generally useful card algorithm. You might use it in a range of tricks where the order of the cards doesn't matter at the start. We don't want to have to explain it in the instructions to tricks every time we need it though. Instead, in the English description, we might just say "Start by shuffling the cards". More precisely and rigorously, the first step of the trick's algorithm might just be:

1. DO an Overhand shuffle.

We rely then on the instructions about how it is done to be somewhere else that is accessible (possibly in the magician's head). When we originally give the instructions, we **define** the procedure: we are writing a **procedure definition**. In this book, the overhand shuffle is defined as this part's "Magical Algorithm". That allows us to refer to it, and you, the reader, now know precisely what we mean, anytime we mention its use!

The definition itself is not telling you to do the trick now (though you may of course want to practice it and check it works now). It is not a trick on its own. Elsewhere you will be told to do it when needed with an instruction like the DO instruction above as part of an actual trick. That is the point when the instructions are followed. Programmers refer to it as the **procedure call**.

This is decomposition and abstraction being used in tandem again. We have split off a part of the instructions and given them their own name. The difference here to our previous use is that we have decomposed our trick in a way that gives us a generally useful procedure that will be used over and over again in lots of tricks, and possibly even several times in the same trick. The benefit is thus much more than organising that one trick. At a stroke, we have set up a decomposition to be used in tricks that we haven't even thought of yet. Whenever we are planning a new trick and need a shuffle, we no longer need to worry about *how* it is done at all. We do not need to think about the *algorithm* of the shuffle, just know *what* it does: i.e., mix up the cards.

This is a really important use of decomposition and procedural abstraction. When deciding how to decompose, one important question to ask is: "can I create a generally useful procedure here." If you can, it is likely to be a good decomposition. In the software world, classic "library" procedures like this are often provided ready written to include in your programs as predefined procedures. Examples include code to search a list of data, sort data into numerical order, print a message to the screen, read some data from the keyboard, write to a file, and so on. The idea is used everywhere in programs. Most languages include lots of libraries of previously written, predefined procedures. Like our shuffle, the instructions can be written down once, made sure they always work, and then referred to by name, in later programs we, or other people, write. When writing instructions that use them, we no longer have to think about how that code actually works, we just need to know what it does so that it is right for our current purposes.

Interlude: Persi Diaconis

Persi Diaconis was a professional magician with a passion for debunking crooked casino games. This drew him back to the advanced maths he vowed as a school dropout that he would one day master. He is now a professor of Mathematics and Statistics at Stanford University where he studies the randomness in events such as coin flipping and shuffling playing cards. He and a fellow mathematician, David Bayer, proved that to randomise a pack of cards, you need only seven riffle shuffles where you cut the pack and then combine them by interleaving cards.

Chapter 16

Swapped Ends Overhand Shuffle
Specifying Procedures

Conjuring

This shuffle leaves the pair of cards that are at the top and bottom of the pack in place, just swapped.

Computation

It's important that it's clear what each procedure does, so we know when to use it. This can be done with English comments or using maths. Important things to be clear about are both what it ultimately does and any assumptions that must hold before the procedure is called if it is to work correctly.

The Trick

Take the deck in your right hand for a standard overhand shuffle. Peel the top card off as a single card, depositing it in the empty hand (Figure 16.1(a)), then proceed normally pulling piles of cards off the pack in a standard overhand shuffle way and dropping them in front of that first peeled card. Continue doing this until you get near the

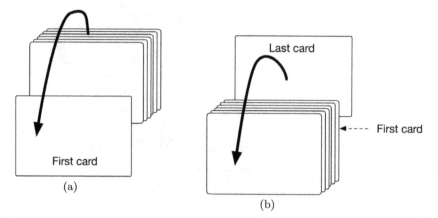

Figure 16.1. To do a Swapped Ends Overhand Shuffle, (a) first peel off the single top card and then drop the rest of the pack as in a normal shuffle in front of it. (b) After doing a normal shuffle for the middle of the pack, leave the last card on its own to be dropped to the front in the last step.

end of the pack. At that stage, pull the last few cards off one by one. In particular, peel off the very last card on its own (Figure 16.1(b)).

The Magical Algorithm

We add a **specification** to this algorithm. In curly brackets, we give any condition that must hold for the algorithm to work at the start. We also state what will have become true after the algorithm has been completed at the end.

TO DO a Swapped Ends Overhand Shuffle:
{*Nothing is assumed.*}
1. Cup the deck of cards in one hand between thumb and fingers.
2. Peel off the top card into your other hand.
3. DO THE FOLLOWING UNTIL you are near but not at the end of the deck.
   a. Pull off a small packet of cards from the front of those in the first hand with the other thumb into the front of the pile forming in the second hand.
4. DO THE FOLLOWING UNTIL all the cards are in your second hand.

   a. Peel off a single card with the second hand's thumb into the front of the pile forming in that hand.

{ The first and last cards have swapped positions.}

How It Works

The first step moved the top card to the bottom. Peeling the last card from the stack alone means that the final card, which was the original bottom card, is now deposited on the top. Cards in the middle have been mixed a little. The top and bottom pair of cards are still at the top and bottom, just swapped over.

Thinking Computationally

An important property of well-written procedures is that they have a clear and clean **specification**. That is you can easily and precisely say what they do (as opposed to how they do it). For example, the algorithm of this shuffle guarantees, whatever the initial order of the pack, to swap the positions of the first and last cards. That is the specification of the algorithm. Nothing is guaranteed about any other cards. That is left unspecified.

Specifications come in two parts. A **precondition** (what must be true before the procedure is followed for it to work) and a **postcondition** (what will then be true afterwards). The precondition here is basically that the cards can be in any order (though it is the case that cards of interest are in the first and last positions). The postcondition is that those two cards have been swapped.

A precondition says what must be true for it to work. We have specified that anything can be true by writing "Nothing is assumed". Computer scientists specify this by just writing "true" (stating that all that matters is "true must be true" which is always the case so not imposing any restrictions!).

Details matter though, and actually here perhaps there could be a precondition. We have referred to the deck of cards in the algorithm, and an implicit assumption is that this is a normal deck. The shuffle works with any cards so if we wanted to take that into account explicitly, then something to note as a precondition is there have to be at least two cards in the deck. The precondition could then be

{ *The deck of cards contains at least two cards.*}

Doing it with two cards wouldn't be very magical though, so actually the number in the precondition ought to be larger for a magical effect.

When writing programs, it is equally important to be clear what the preconditions and postconditions of a procedure are. What the procedure does should also be easily described in English. If it isn't, then it probably wasn't a very well-thought-out procedure. For example, a procedure might find the position of a given number in a list. The precondition might be that the list of numbers is in ascending order. However, English is not really precise enough to write specifications, just as it isn't precise enough to use to write programs.

Well-designed programming languages, used for writing critical code, give a way of writing specifications formally in the program as what are called **assertions**. Rather than being written just in English, as with other aspects of the language, they are written in a precise language with precise meaning.

For the purposes of the magic trick, we could also give a more complex postcondition saying what the aim is in terms of what the audience believe:

{ *The first and last cards have swapped positions AND*
The audience believe the deck is in a random order.}

Of course, we can't be certain of what the audience believe, so such claims are not mathematically checkable results in the same way as the positions of cards. However, if our aim was to make clear the aim of the trick, this would make sense. In fact, specifications about beliefs are used to reason about algorithms called **security protocols**, where the aim is to check that a hacker cannot gain access to a secret (like a password) when the algorithm is followed.

PAUSE: Nikola Tesla

Nikola Tesla (1856–1943) was a prolific inventor of gadgets using electricity and electromagnetism, but also a showman. He held public demonstrations of his ideas and inventions. One such demonstration in the 1890s was of wireless-controlled lighting, where he lit up lights on the other side of a stage. It could just as easily have been presented as a magic show! He predicted similar systems could be used for wireless communications and created the world's first wireless-controlled boat.

He is most famous, though, for his inventions making alternating current (AC as opposed to direct current, DC) a practical reality. It is now used for long-distance power transmission. His AC induction motor used a rotating magnetic field. He created the "Egg of Columbus" demonstration to illustrate this. It used a magnetic field to make a giant egg made of copper stand and spin on its end.

Tesla appeared as a character in Christopher Nolan's film about rival magicians, *The Prestige*. He was played by David Bowie, chosen because the part needed someone who was "extraordinarily charismatic". Rock star Bowie incidentally also invented and co-wrote one of the first programs to help people be creative, helping him write lyrics.

Chapter 17

𝔈𝔫𝔡𝔰 𝔒𝔳𝔢𝔯𝔥𝔞𝔫𝔡 𝔖𝔥𝔲𝔣𝔣𝔩𝔢
New Procedures from Old
and Layers of Abstraction

Conjuring

This shuffle leaves the pair of cards that are at the top and bottom of the pack in their original place.

Computation

Once you have created generally useful procedures and made sure that they work, you can start to build new procedures out of them. You build new reliable code from existing reliable code, rather than creating everything from scratch.

The Trick

In this trick, you just do the Swapped Ends Overhand Shuffle twice.

The Magical Algorithm

TO DO an Ends Overhand Shuffle:
{*You have a normal deck of cards.*}
    1. Do the Swapped Ends Overhand Shuffle.
    2. Do the Swapped Ends Overhand Shuffle.
{*The deck is shuffled, but the first and last cards are unchanged.*}

How It Works

As a single Swapped Ends Overhand Shuffle swaps the places of top and bottom card, doing it twice puts them back to where they started. Cards in between change position.

Thinking Computationally

Once we have created a procedure, we can use it as though it was a core, primitive instruction provided by the language. In particular, we can build new, generally useful procedures out of simpler ones as here.

From the original false shuffle, we create a new false shuffle that does something slightly different (leave the first and last cards alone). We are building **layers of abstraction**. First, we create primitive procedures. We then no longer need to worry about how they work when designing more complex procedures. As long as we know our basic false shuffle swaps the first and last cards, we don't care how. That knowledge is enough to be sure that doing it twice will leave the first and last cards alone. Now, knowing exactly what our new shuffle does, we can use it when designing new tricks, without worrying how the original basic step or the new composite one is actually done while inventing the new trick. The details of lower layers of procedure are hidden in the instructions of later ones (see Figure 17.1). This layering of procedural abstraction is key to creating really large programs that do actually work. Without it, the detail quickly becomes too complex to avoid mistakes.

Really well-designed programs are built out of a set of primitive procedures. A more complex set of primitives are created from those,

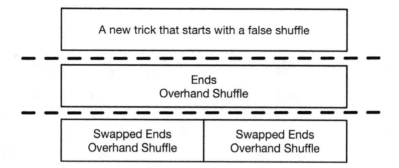

Figure 17.1. Building new components from existing ones in layers of abstraction.

then more complex ones from those, and so on. Groups of such primitives are put into libraries to be incorporated into any program that needs them.

Of course, we are talking here about the process of *designing* new tricks (and programs). You do, of course, need the detail when actually doing a trick using such a shuffle, and those details are there, in the named instructions, when you need them. When practising a trick from a book like this that needs a false shuffle, for example, you just jump to the right page for each step, and when done jump back.

However, this multilayered decomposition probably helps a lot to learn a trick too. You can first learn the basic false shuffle. Only when you have got that down perfectly, and the trick is "loaded" into your brain, do you start to practise the more complex version that uses it twice. Thus this sort of abstraction, this computational thinking trick, is helpful for humans *following instructions*, not just when writing programs or designing instructions.

Interlude: Howard Thurston

Howard Thurston (1869–1936) was one of the greatest magicians of the late 19th and early 20th centuries. He marketed himself as the "King of Cards" based on his skill at card tricks. This included making cards appear and disappear from his fingertips and a trick where cards chosen by members of the audience rise in turn to the top of a pack placed inside a glass. As a boy, he was more street urchin and con artist than his later sophisticated persona might suggest, travelling from city to city by hiding on freight trains. He tried to become a jockey, worked in circuses and nearly became a church minister. He ultimately turned his life around as a result of learning card tricks from a book of magic and spending long hours practising them until he was a master card magician. He also learnt tricks from others but turned those tricks into "masterpieces" through his skill and creativity. Despite his label as being the master of card tricks, ultimately his shows were massive in scale, requiring truckloads of equipment for his elaborate illusions.

Chapter 18

Ƒalse Ⲥop Ⲟverⲏanⲇ Ѕⲏuffle
Parameters and Generalisation

Ⲥonjuring

This shuffle leaves the top cards of the pack in place.

Computation

The procedures we have seen so far give a name to code that does a single task. Parameters allow one procedure to do a whole range of related things by providing the information that makes the difference at the start. They allow a procedure to be generalised: that is work in more general situations rather than just one specific one.

The Trick

Pick up the deck as for a standard overhand shuffle. However, press the bent second finger of the hand holding the cards up against the back of the deck. Peel off a pile of cards from the front into the other hand as in a normal shuffle. Make sure this first pile contains all the cards you want to ultimately leave in place.

Continue with the shuffle, but as you drop the second group into your other hand, pick back up the first cards at the back of the original pack by gripping them between the thumb and other fingers.

You now have two groups of cards in your original hand: the remains of the pack and, behind them, those you split off first with your second finger between them. The new small pile you split off second is in your other hand.

Push the tip of your second finger that is now between the original last card and original first card, up against the original top card. With this finger, you keep the former top cards in place at the back of the pack in your original hand. Continue normally pulling piles of cards from the pack in a standard overhand shuffle way. When you place the cards from the bottom of the original pack into the other hand, you will be left holding the group of cards that came from the top. Slide them down at the front as though they had been at the back of the pack all along.

How It Works

The first cards that you peel off the front of the pack are held at the back through the shuffle. They are put back at the front at the end. It therefore guarantees that those cards are still on the top of the deck at the end. By peeling off more than the number of cards you want preserved in place, you can ensure that definitely that many cards are left alone by the shuffle. You can do this shuffle as many times as you wish, always peeling off a similar number to start.

The Magical Algorithm

This algorithm can be done repeatedly for more thorough shuffling.

TO DO a False Top Overhand Shuffle WITH number of cards to remain in place n:
$\{n < 20\}$

1. Hold the pack of cards in one hand between thumb and fingers.
2. Push the second finger of that hand against the back (i.e., bottom card) of the pack.

3. Peel off a group of more than *n* cards from the front of that hand dropping them into the other hand.
4. Move the rest of the pack in front of these, peeling off a second group of cards from the front into the second hand, while pushing the middle finger against the top card of the original group.
5. Lift off the rest of the pack with the original cards held at the back, leaving only the second group behind.
6. DO UNTIL all cards are in the second hand apart from those being held at the back.
   a. Peel off a small packet of cards from the front of the original deck into the front of the pile forming in the other hand.
7. Drop the remaining cards from the original hand to the front of those in the other hand.
8. Pick up the deck in the original hand.

{ *The deck is shuffled, but the positions of at least the first n cards are unchanged.* }

Thinking Computationally

This procedure can be used in more varied situations than the previous false shuffles. This shuffle doesn't always do exactly the same thing. Some tricks might need only the top card to be left in place. Another might need the first dozen left alone.

We have provided a number *n* to the procedure that is used to guide how many cards to leave at the front. The *n* can stand for different actual numbers depending on what a particular trick needs. This is a **parameterised decomposition**. We have created a description of a general version of the shuffle where, when we use it in a trick, we specify how many cards are to be left alone using the **parameter**, *n*.

In our algorithm, the parameter, *n*, is the number of cards to be left in place. Notice we have a precondition that *n* is less than 20: ($n < 20$). This is essentially saying that you should not rely on this shuffle to leave close to half or more of the pack in place. If you try it, it may work, but it probably won't look so convincing. For it to be convincing, keep the number of cards you preserve to be less than 20.

In an actual trick using this shuffle, we might, in an informal description, say something like

"Do a False Top Overhand Shuffle, leaving 10 cards in place".

The number 10 here is providing a value for parameter *n* on this particular trick's use of the shuffle.

In our slightly more formal notation, to mean the same thing we would write:

(1) DO A False Top Overhand Shuffle WITH number of cards to remain in place 10.

Here the number 10 is called an **actual parameter**, as it gives an actual value to use. In different tricks (so uses of the procedure), this number (so actual parameter) will be different. The variable *n* is called the **formal parameter**. The formal parameter, *n*, is just a name used as a placeholder for each and every value of n we might need. Of course, for the trick to work, you will need to practise judging the right number of cards to take. With a lot of practice, you may be able to do it exactly. For most normal people, it will only be approximate, so best to err on the side of caution and leave more cards alone than needed.

This idea of parameters is key in programming. Real programs are built of lots of procedures each taking parameters in this way. Parameters increase how generally useful a procedure is. For example, if we have a procedure to print out the two-times table, we can change the 2 into a formal parameter, *n*, in the code. Then, the procedure can print out any times table, just by providing a different actual parameter.

This introduces the important computational thinking idea of **generalisation**. Once we have written a program or procedure to solve a specific problem, it is useful to generalise it: make it useful in as wide a set of situations as possible. Adding parameters to procedures is one way to do this.

When I first came across this false shuffle, I just saw it as a way to leave the top card alone. That is useful, but the shuffle generalises to leave a greater number of cards at the top of the deck. By generalising that original shuffle as I understood it, it is now useful in more tricks.

I do not have to invent new false shuffles for tricks that need more cards left in place. Likewise, by generalising procedures, we save coding work later.

PAUSE: Ada Lovelace

A countess, and daughter of poet Lord Byron, Ada Lovelace (1815–1852) is often referred to as the first programmer because of her work on algorithms for Charles Babbage's proposed Victorian computers. His Analytical Engine would have been the first general-purpose computer if completed. She didn't really write programs though, not least because they had not developed a programming language for Babbage's machine. What she did do was work out the sequences of states the machine would go through to follow specific algorithms and, in doing so, found a mistake in an algorithm of Babbage. Programmers today use the same idea to find bugs in programs through logical thinking as part of code walkthroughs. Perhaps Ada's greatest achievement was to suggest that one day computers would take over creative tasks, notably composing music, when Babbage was envisioning the computer as just a souped-up calculator to do arithmetic. She realised that as computers worked with symbols, they could manipulate things other than just numbers.

Chapter 19

$\mathfrak{S}$i$\mathfrak{d}$e $\mathfrak{J}$ogging $\mathfrak{S}$huffle
Swapping One Procedure for Another

Conjuring

This false shuffle leaves the first quarter or so of the pack unchanged.

Computation

If two procedures do the same thing, then you can swap one for the other, and everything else should still work. This allows you to make small changes without needing to change or check the rest of the code.

The Trick

Hold the stacked deck in the overhand shuffle position. You want to ensure the top of the stack (say the top 13 cards) remains intact. On the first part of the overhand shuffle. pull off a large section of cards from the front, more than the number you want to be left in place. Place the next set of cards you pull from the front slightly off to one side. Magicians call this side jogging. Shuffle the remaining cards in small packets by doing a normal convincing overhand shuffle.

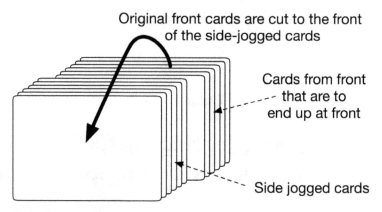

Original front cards are cut to the front
of the side-jogged cards

Cards from front
that are to
end up at front

Side jogged cards

Figure 19.1. Side jogging involves lifting off the front section into the other hand first, then putting the subsequent cards offset slightly. Finally, the original cards are cut back to the front.

All that remains is to cut the cards, which you do by lifting the section containing your protected card stack from the back of the pack. It is easy because it's side jogged from the rest. Move this section to the top of the deck (Figure 19.1).

Practise until it looks like a convincing overhand shuffle and final cut, while you have actually kept your stack in order on the top of the deck.

The Magical Algorithm

TO DO a Side Jogging Shuffle WITH number of cards to remain in place *n*:
$\{n < 20\}$

1. Hold the pack of cards in one hand between thumb and fingers.
2. Pull off a large packet of cards (more than *n*) from the front and drop them into the other hand.
3. Pull off a second small packet of cards from the front of those in the first hand, but drop them slightly to the side in the other hand in front of the first packet of cards.

4. DO THE FOLLOWING UNTIL all cards are in the other hand.
   a. Pull off a small packet of cards from the front of those in the original hand with your thumb. Let them fall into the front of the pile forming in the other hand.
5. Place the cards on the table.
6. Cut the pack of cards at the point where the cards are off to the side.
7. Replace the old bottom part of the pack on to the top of the other pile.

{ *The deck is shuffled, but the positions of at least the first n cards are unchanged.* }

How It Works

The side-jogged cards were the front cards, and they were replaced unchanged back on the top by the final cut.

Thinking Computationally

The specification of this trick is identical to the previous false top overhand shuffle. That means any trick that used that false shuffle could swap in this one instead, and it would work just as well. You might do that because you are doing two tricks in a show that start with the same false shuffle. Therefore, it gives more variety to swap one for the other. Or perhaps you are far better at one false shuffle as you have practiced it more, so in an important show, you switch that shuffle into a trick that is supposed to use the other. Or perhaps one is quicker, and you have limited time to do the trick, or to do the cut, you need a table, but you are doing the trick without one...

This is another important use of **procedural abstraction**. It gives a framework for modifying algorithms, so tricks and programs, in a way that is guaranteed not to affect, algorithmically, whether they work or not.

With programs, we might want to swap in a new version of a procedure that was faster or used less memory, perhaps, or one that was just available in a new standard library that had been developed to make the whole program **easier to maintain** (as we will see in the next chapter).

Interlude: John Nevil Maskelyne

John Nevil Maskelyne (1839–1917) was one of the great Victorian-era magicians. He invented, amongst many other tricks, the original version of the levitation trick where a person appears to float above the ground. His book *Sharps and Flats* (1894) gave a comprehensive overview of the tricks of card sharps and how gamblers cheated at card games. He created the Occult Committee, a group dedicated to exposing frauds claiming to have supernatural powers. In response to his debunking seances, spiritualist Alfred Russel Wallace (famous for working out that evolution worked by natural selection independently of Charles Darwin) just claimed that Maskelyne had supernatural powers. Maskelyne also invented the mechanism behind the pay toilet, where a penny was used to unlock a door, so is ultimately responsible for the phrase "to spend a penny" meaning to go to the toilet.

Chapter 20

Cyclic False Cut
Libraries of Useful Procedures

Conjuring

This cut leaves the cyclic order of the pack unchanged, just starting at a different point in the cycle.

Computation

Programmers collect together similar procedures such as ones needed to manipulate a single data structure into what are called libraries.

The Trick

Fan the cards and allow a spectator to touch the back of a card. Split the pack at that point, moving the top half to the bottom. Repeat this for as long as the spectator wants to, to "mix them thoroughly".

The Magical Algorithm

TO DO a Cyclic False Cut:

{*Nothing is assumed.*}

    1. DO THE FOLLOWING UNTIL the spectator is happy the cards are thoroughly mixed.

      a. Fan the cards.

      b. Ask a spectator to point to a card.

      c. Split the pack at that point, placing the top part underneath.

{*The deck appears shuffled, but the cyclic order of the cards is unchanged, though starting at a different point in the cycle.*}

How It Works

This is actually just a series of normal cuts of the pack. Cutting the pack does not change the cyclic order of the cards. You can do it as many times as you like, and the cycle will be the same, just starting at a different point. To see this, imagine the cards laid out in a circle, before the cut and then again after the cut. The circle is the same before and after the cut, just rotated (see Figure 20.1). The same cards follow each other as before. You can do it as many times as you wish, and the cycle remains. By fanning the deck each time, it is less obvious what is happening than just cutting the deck repeatedly. You can also let lots of people take part, so making it a communal decision as to how the pack is "shuffled".

Thinking Computationally

The techniques from this section are useful components that can form part of a range of tricks. Any good magician will build up a repertoire of them, to call on as needed when inventing new tricks or developing their own versions of old ones. A false shuffle at the start of a trick, that relies on cards being in a known position or order at the start, will throw the audience off the trail of what is actually happening.

In programming, the idea of a **library** is similar to this. Calling it a "library" is actually a **design metaphor** using the idea of a library of

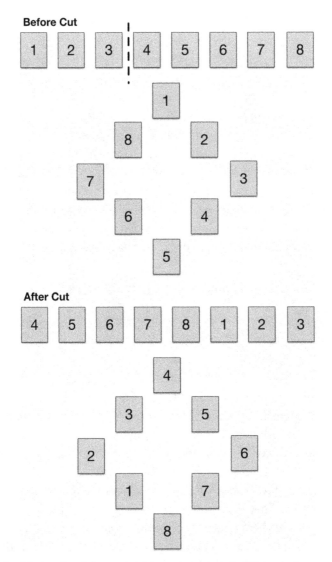

Figure 20.1. The cards of the pack laid out in a circle before and after a cut. The cyclic order is unchanged.

books to make people think of an organised collection. Here we collect together useful similar magical techniques: a magician's repertoire of cuts and shuffles to create a "Cuts and Shuffles" library. In programming, we have libraries of useful operations that can be performed on one data structure, like a list manipulation library, that gives you everything you might need to manipulate lists of things, or a String library of operations for manipulating strings of characters (words, sentences, etc.).

Rather than describing all the procedures in detail whenever they are needed, giving the full algorithm of every trick or program, we can just **include** the library noting they are available. If writing a series of magic manuals to record all our tricks, we might similarly write one book just about cuts and shuffles, and refer to it whenever we mention one. We would then avoid having to explain each, so avoid writing out the instructions, like those for a cyclic false cut, in every book.

This is an organising principle that allows us to make good use of **procedural abstraction** and **decomposition**, reducing the amount of work and actually making our instructions clearer.

PAUSE: Maurice Wilkes and David Wheeler

Maurice Wilkes (1913–2010) and his team developed one of the first digital computers, EDSAC, at Cambridge University. It was immediately used by researchers. Three Nobel Prize-winning teams, in Chemistry, Physics and Medicine, used EDSAC in their research. It hosted the world's first computer game: a noughts and crosses program. With EDSAC team member, David Wheeler (1927–2004), Wilkes created a library of useful procedures that could be included in any program. They were stored on paper tape in a filing cabinet, but descriptions of them (their specification or interface) were stored in a library catalogue. It contained the details of what each procedure was for as well as how to call them. Today we would call this catalogue an Application Programming Interface (or API) specification.

Part 6

Building Bigger

We have now seen most of the basic techniques that allow us to build large programs a little at a time. In this section, we first look at the importance of clear descriptions of what procedures do, then look at how to chain results from one procedure or trick to the next and apply the techniques to a trick we have already seen.

Chapter 21

The False Choice
Programming Interfaces

Conjuring

The false choice is a way of leaving a volunteer thinking they chose one of three things when actually you did.

Computation

Procedures need to have clear interfaces, i.e., specifications or descriptions of exactly what they do and when they can be used if they are to be used in large programs without introducing mistakes.

The Trick

Suppose there are three objects, and you wish to be left with a specific one, say the third. This could be three piles of cards, for example, or three boxes with a reveal hidden in one of them. Ask the volunteer to point to one of the objects. If they point to the one you wish to keep, then say "Ok, we will keep this one". You remove the other two objects.

If, on the other hand, they point to one of the ones that you wish to lose, then say "Ok, we will remove that one". You remove it. You still have, in this second case, another object to lose. You now fill up some time with a story that fits the situation, so everyone loses track of what you did originally. Then you ask them to point to one of the two remaining objects. Whichever they point to, you remove the one you wanted to lose, and keep the other, saying the appropriate thing to justify this, as above (see Figure 21.1).

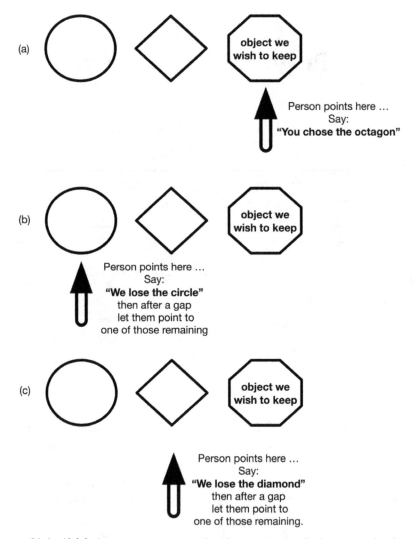

Figure 21.1. If (a) the person points to the object you intend, then you take that as the choice. Otherwise (b, c) you note the pointed-to object is discarded and do a further false choice.

The Magical Algorithm

TO DO a False Choice WITH object *n* chosen:

{*Three objects are laid out. You wish object n of the three to be chosen where n is either 1, 2 or 3.*}

1. Ask a volunteer to *point* to one of the objects.
2. **IF** they point to object *n*

   THEN

   a. Say "OK. You have chosen that one."

   b. Discard the other two.

   OTHERWISE

   a. Say "OK. We get rid of that one."

   b. Discard the object pointed to.

   c. Talk about something related to give time for them to forget exactly what you did.

   d. Ask the volunteer to point to one of the remaining two objects.

   e. **IF** they point to object *n*

      THEN

      i. Say "OK. You have chosen that one."

      ii. Discard the other one.

      OTHERWISE

      i. Say "OK. We get rid of that one."

      ii. Discard the object pointed to.

      iii. Say "We are left with this one, pointing to the remaining object, *n*."

{*Object n is left.*}

How It Works

Make sure you say "point" not "choose" when asking them to pick a pile as that is neutral language that does not imply anything about what you will do once they point to it. Because you did not tell the person what you were going to do with the object they pointed to and used such neutral language they see nothing strange over whether you remove it or keep it. As long as you only do the trick once they have no idea, there was some alternative course of action that could have been taken.

Thinking Computationally

It is not just cuts and shuffles that can be used to enhance different tricks. Here we have given a generally useful false choice. In a similar way, there are many different kinds of procedures that can be written and stored in libraries to be pulled out when needed. Here we have a way of forcing a particular choice while making it look like a free choice. "The Forcing Matrix", described in the next chapter, is another example. We could therefore have a separate collection, or "library", of false choice algorithms too.

Each separate mini trick like this, or library procedure, we create needs a clear **interface** in the sense of it being designed, so there is a clear situation when it can be used having a clear and precise effect. This then makes it easy to give a precise description (i.e., specification) of when it can be used and what the effect is. For example,

> The False Choice can be used when you have three objects (or piles of objects) and wish to be left with just one specific one of the three.
>
> After the false choice, you are left with the one of the three you wanted, but the audience believe that an audience member made the choice.

We have tried to make sure all the cuts, shuffles and false choices described here do have clear interfaces. For example, an interface for the Cyclic False Cut (Chapter 20) is

> The Cyclic False Cut is a false shuffle that can be done any time that the precise order of the cards does not matter, only the cyclic order matters. It will leave the cyclic order alone, just change the starting position.

Specifications like this are often written as **comments** (notes for a human reader) before the actual code in programs.

Using English to do this can sometimes be a problem though, as it is hard to be very precise. This leads to the idea of **logic-based specification languages** where maths is used to give the specification. It would specify precisely, using maths, that a number of cards should be less than 20, for example. We have essentially done that in writing some of the simpler preconditions like $\{n < 20\}$ in our earlier false shuffle algorithms. We could similarly write specifications such as "the cyclic order is unchanged" using logic. Writing mathematical specifications is very like writing programs, as we are using a fixed and precise notation to say what we want to say. The difference is that, rather than saying *how* something is done as we do in a program, we just describe the end result: *what* should be the case, what should have happened. Ideally, a combination of both English and logic would be used, so it is both precise (the logic) and easy to understand in overview (the English). Writing mathematical specifications to describe program interfaces is really important when the code is safety-critical. We won't go into the details here of how to write fully mathematical and logical specifications, as it would take a book on its own.

PAUSE: Tommy Flowers

Tommy Flowers (1905–1998) was an unsung hero of the invention of the computer. He worked for the British General Post Office working on electronic telephone exchanges. He was asked to help Alan Turing and others at Bletchley Park who were trying to make machines to help quickly crack the German ciphers. In particular, he helped build machines to crack messages sent by the German high command using a cipher that was even more complex than the famous Enigma. Flowers came up with the design of the Colossus: the world's first programmable digital computer actually built. It used the kind of valves then used in telephone systems. Others in the team were sceptical, so he worked on the ideas on his own, back at the Post Office, using his own money. His Colossus machines were eventually used at Bletchley Park and cracked one of the most important messages of the war. It showed Hitler didn't believe the Normandy landings would happen, so didn't add reinforcements. Knowing this, General Eisenhower ordered D-day to go ahead the next day, changing the course of the war. Because work at Bletchley Park was kept secret after the war, no one knew of Flowers' contribution for 30 years.

Chapter 22

The forcing Matrix
Functions

Conjuring

The forcing matrix gives a way to always force the selection of the same number, despite a volunteer having a series of free choices, choosing numbers from a grid to add together.

Computation

We have previously used decomposition to create procedures which just get a job done. A variation is the function. The job of a function is to deliver an answer, such as a number or data structure. That answer is used later in the program. We also look at preprocessing data: organising data in advance, with the result used over and over again later in the program.

The Trick

You set out a grid of "random" numbers. There are various ways you can do this such as dealing the top cards from a pack of cards into a 4 × 4 grid, writing out numbers 1–25 in a 5 × 5 grid $(1, 2, 3, 4, 5, \ldots)$, or just having a prepared card containing "random" numbers.

Different members of the audience take it in turns to pick a number on the grid. They circle the number chosen. They then cross out the other numbers in the same row and same column as their chosen number.

You now have a series of randomly picked numbers in the ones circled. You add them up to get a final random number. In doing this as a trick in its own right, you reveal that the final total is the number you previously sealed in an envelope (or reveal as a prediction in some other creative way of your choosing). Alternatively, it can be a forced number used as the basis of some other main trick (such as in the next chapter).

The Magical Algorithm (Part 1)

TO DO Use the Forcing Matrix WITH forcing matrix *f*:
1. DO THE FOLLOWING UNTIL all numbers in the matrix, *f*, are circled or crossed out.
   a. Ask an audience member to pick and circle a number that has not already been circled or crossed out.
   b. Cross out all other numbers in the same row as the circled number.
   c. Cross out all other numbers in the same column as the circled number.
2. Add the circled numbers to get a total, *n*.
3. RETURN the number *n*.

How It Works

To set the trick up, you first need to decide the number you wish to force and the size of grid you wish to use. Let's say the number you want to force is 127 and you want to use a 5 × 5 grid. The grid has 5 rows and 5 columns. You need a "seed" number for each row and each column, so in this case, you need 5 + 5, i.e., 10, seeds. Create any

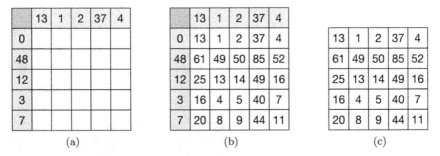

Figure 22.1. Creating a forcing matrix: (a) seed numbers labelling rows and columns that add up to the number you want to force, 127. (b) Fill in the numbers by adding row and column seeds. (c) The final forcing matrix is produced by removing the seed row and column.

10 seed numbers that add up to the forcing number (e.g., $0 + 48 + 12 + 3 + 7 + 13 + 1 + 2 + 37 + 4 = 127$). Write the first 5 seed numbers down the side of a 5×5 grid and the other 5 numbers along the top. Now, for each position in the actual grid, add the seed at the start of that row to the seed at the top of the column, and write the answer in that cell. So with the above seed numbers, you would get the table shown in Figure 22.1.

Removing the seed numbers gives the final forcing matrix to use in the trick to force the number 127.

You now do the trick above using this grid, and the number that results will be 127. If you start with a different initial forcing number, and seeds that add up to it, you can use the trick to force any number you wish.

The forcing number linked to a grid just with numbers 1–25 is 65. Try creating it yourself using seeds: 0, 5, 10, 15, 20, 1, 2, 3, 4, 5. If you did the trick with the resulting forcing matrix, you would always get the number, 65.

Similarly, to force the number 20, you could use a 4×4 grid with seeds: 1, 2, 3, 4, 1, 2, 3, 4. Again try it yourself to see what forcing matrix you end up with. As all these numbers are less than 10, you could create this matrix by dealing out playing cards into a grid (having placed the right cards in the right order at the top of the pack) and even have done a false shuffle such as a false top overhand shuffle (Chapter 18) to appear to have shuffled the pack while leaving those cards in place. Use your imagination to invent more creative ways of making the grid!

Why does it work? Each position is the total of a row and column seed. When you cross out everything else in that row and that column, you cross out all other chances of picking those two seeds. That means each choice gives you two of the seeds that have so far not been used to add in to the total. Eventually, when all numbers are chosen, you have all the seeds represented in the numbers chosen and so part of the addition.

The Magical Algorithm (Part 2)

TO DO Create a Forcing Matrix WITH size *n*, forcing number *f*:

1. Choose 2 × *n* numbers that add up to total, *f*.
2. Write the first *n* of these numbers down the side and the other *n* along the top of an *n* by *n* grid. These are the row and column seed numbers.
3. FOR EACH position in the grid

   a. Add the row seed number to the column seed number.
   b. Write the total in that position in the grid.

4. Write out a neat copy of the grid without the seed numbers. This is your forcing matrix.
5. RETURN the resulting forcing matrix.

Thinking Computationally

We have up to now been decomposing magic tricks (and programs) into procedures whose purpose is to get a job done. Here we are seeing a variation of this. Instead of just getting a job done, we are decomposing into parts whose purpose is to return a result (like a number calculated, or a grid produced). We call these **functions** rather than procedures, as the purpose is often to compute a mathematical function. Both functions and procedures are sometimes more generally called **subroutines** (and all three terms are often interchanged and in some situations also called **methods** just to be even more confusing).

Here we have two functions. We have a function whose job is to create, so **return**, a forcing matrix. We then, as part of an actual magic trick, use the forcing matrix to give us (so **return**) a number. That forced number is used later in the next part of the trick.

Something else important is going on here. It is the idea of **preprocessing data**. Magicians do something like this often. They prepare some prop, like the forcing matrix, beforehand. They only need to do this once, but then can use it over and over again, each time they wish to do the trick.

The equivalent thing programmers do is to write code that prepares a **data structure** that helps do some tasks quickly. Preparing a data structure to make fast searching possible is a good example. We **search** the same data over and over again, so it is worth spending some time preparing the data to make those searches fast. That is what search engine companies do. When you type a search query into a search engine, the search engine is not actually visiting and checking every page out there on the web directly in that fraction of a second. It is checking a pre-prepared data structure that is held by the search engine company; based on them, having preprocessed the web pages, their software bots have found trawling the Internet.

This is exactly the same general idea as an old-fashioned paper telephone directory (or an index in a book like this one). Someone spent time organising (in this case, **sorting**) the data into alphabetical order (to create a **sorted list data structure**) once. That work is done once so that the many later searches for telephone numbers (or pages) can be done quickly later.

PAUSE: John McCarthy

John McCarthy (1927–2011) was one of the founders of Artificial Intelligence and behind the first functional programming language, LISP. It was the language of choice for early programmers working on Artificial Intelligence, trying to write intelligent programs. The idea is that programs are completely built out of mathematical functions. This makes them very mathematically pure and easy to reason about. It turned the ideas of mathematician, Lorenzo Church, who developed a logic based on functions, into a programming language. His logic demonstrated the limits of computation in a similar way to Alan Turing's "Turing Machines": what a computer could and could not do. He was a strong supporter of free speech and argued that computers could have beliefs. He wrote a satirical short story *The Robot and the Baby* about a future society where robots were banned from being human-like or being programmed to have emotions. It predicted the trend for instant social media-based news leading to millions posting their views on news as it happens.

Chapter 23

Forced Wizardly Book Magic
Calling Functions — Building Bigger and Better

Conjuring

A number is randomly chosen. An audience member turns to that page in a book. The selected page then magically directs them to a word. It is both on a random page and a random word on that page: a word no one could have possibly predicted... but you did.

Computation

Once you have decomposed a program into functions and written the functions, those functions provide answers to be passed on to the next procedure or function in a sequence.

The Trick

This trick just combines the forcing matrix trick with Wizardly Book Magic (Chapter 6) to add an extra level of mystery.

Before the trick, find an interesting page (say page 127) in your chosen book (perhaps in *The Wonderful Wizard of Oz*) and work out the predicted word on that page as in Wizardly Book Magic of Chapter 6. Then create the appropriate forcing matrix (say of size 5×5) for that page number, i.e., that forces 127. Write the predicted word from that page in an envelope ready for the reveal at the end.

When doing the trick, use the forcing matrix to pick a page in the book apparently at random, but actually known to you in advance. Then use that page to do the Wizardly Book Magic trick. It finally gives you a word in the book that is your final prediction. Have someone open the envelope to reveal that you predicted the word.

The Magical Algorithm

TO DO Forced Wizardly Book Magic WITH book *b*, forcing matrix size *n*, forcing number *p*1:

1. LET *f* BE THE VALUE RETURNED BY
   DOING Create a Forcing Matrix WITH size *n*, forcing number *p*1.

2. LET *p*2 BE THE VALUE RETURNED BY
   DOING Using the Forcing Matrix WITH forcing matrix *f*.

3. DO Wizardly Book Magic WITH book *b*, page *p*2.

Note as the forcing matrix returns a number we know in advance, we only do the second step for presentation purposes, not really to generate a new number: *p*1 and *p*2 are the same numbers. We have assumed here that we have first written a parameterised version of Wizardly Book Magic set up for a given page in a given book.

How It Works

This is combining two tricks that each is guaranteed to force a result, with one leading to the other. If you understand how each works (see Chapters 6 and 22), then it is clear the combined trick is guaranteed to work.

Thinking Computationally

This involved combining two tricks, by passing the result of one to the next, to give a bigger, better trick. Programmers do the same thing, chaining together existing functions that do separate things. The first provides the input to the next. Programs are often decomposed in this way, using a similar structure to the above algorithm. A first **function returns** a value or data structure that it computes (like the matrix). That value is passed to the next function as a **parameter**. The second function, in its turn, uses the value and calculates from it something new (like the page number). It returns that to be used in the next function, and so on.

In the above, forcing matrix, *f*, is the result of the function that creates the forcing matrix. It is then the actual parameter (i.e., value passed) to the function that gives instructions on how to use a forcing matrix. A similar thing then happens with the page number. It is the result returned by using the forcing matrix, and then that page number value is passed to the actual Wizardly Book Magic trick.

This also shows that to create a better trick, you don't necessarily have to combine just simple trick elements like shuffles. You can sometimes combine whole tricks, that are magical on their own, to get much more powerful tricks.

A similar thing is done with programs, building ever more sophisticated programs, by combining functions that already do something useful and have been used as a self-contained program so that the results of one are passed to another. Procedures are also used when an action is needed on the results calculated so far by the chain of functions. For example, a procedure might be used to display the results of the function on the screen. By building up ever large sequences, more complex programs are created.

Interlude: David Devant

Claimed by some to be the greatest magician of the 20th century, David Devant (1868–1941), was famous for the humour in his magic tricks, ensuring that they were far more entertaining than just the illusion itself. First President of the Magic Circle, he stressed the importance of performance, and once put an arrogant young magician in his place who was boasting about how many tricks he knew, by saying he only knew a few tricks but what mattered was that he could do them very well. He was once accosted in the street by a patient from a psychiatric hospital who demanded he make coins appear out of thin air. Devant kept him entertained by doing so until people from the hospital came to take the patient back. He was passionate about new technology and when cinema was invented became one of the first people to tour the country showing films. Several films were also made of him performing magic including pulling rabbits out of a top hat.

Chapter 24

Invisible Palming (Again)
Sequencing Procedures Together

Conjuring

We return to Invisible Palming and the Teleporting Top Hat and look at them anew.

Computation

Procedures with parameters allow us to create generalised programs. We can decompose them into parameterised parts and sequence them one after the other, using the same parameters. By matching preconditions and postconditions, we can give an outline argument as to why the whole algorithm works without worrying about how the parts work.

The Trick

In this chapter, we are going to just look again at the same Invisible Palming trick from Chapter 1 and its variation from Chapter 14, the Teleporting Top Hat. In doing so, we will put together some of the ideas we have seen so far.

Thinking Computationally

We wrote out the original Invisible Palming trick as a single algorithm that wasn't decomposed at all. We then saw in the Teleporting Top Hat that with a little decomposition we could make it easy to substitute a new part with an identical effect. Here, we are going to see how we could decompose it further into a whole series of procedures, but also use parameters to make it more general. We also use specifications to make clear the intended effect of each part. In doing so, we are seeing the foundations of the way large programs are built.

Generalising the trick

First of all, how can we make the trick more general? The number of cards used in the trick could be a parameter, as it is something that could in theory change. Our main command (a procedure call) to do the trick is then:

DO Invisible Palming WITH 15 cards.

So our definition of the trick now takes a parameter:

TO DO Invisible Palming WITH n cards: . . .

Does it work for any number of cards? See if you can work out what numbers of cards it does work for before reading on.

Fairly obviously, it does not work for all numbers as there must be an extra card to appear to have moved from one pile to another. That means the number of cards, which we are calling n, has to be odd. It would not work with 14 cards or with 16 cards. We can make this clear with an assertion to use as a precondition:

{*There are n cards AND n is odd.*}

That on its own is not enough though. It doesn't actually work for any odd number of cards. When you split the cards into two piles, before the last card is placed, you need two identical piles containing a series of pairs but with one extra in each (so both must contain an odd number of cards at this point). Then, you want to place one extra card in one of the two piles. Fifteen cards work because it splits into 7 cards and

7 cards (both odd) with that last card making 8 cards in one pile. In each final pile, there are 3 pairs, plus one extra in each to make 7 and then that last "extra card" to put on one of the two. As you have two odd piles, that "extra card" disappears into a new pair whichever pile it is placed on.

Thirteen cards doesn't work because it splits into 6 cards and 7 cards: 3 pairs in each pile and one leftover. The 6 pairs form two piles of 6, and now whichever pile you place the "extra card" on cannot complete a pair, so doesn't appear to disappear.

When we take away the extra card (so have $n - 1$ cards), then we need two piles of an odd number of cards. So, that number $(n - 1)$ of cards must divide by 2, and when halved the resulting number of cards should be odd. This gives us a new fact about n that:

$$\{(n - 1) \div 2 \textit{ is odd.}\}$$

Combining this with the fact that n itself also has to be odd, we get the precondition for the trick:

$\{$*There are n cards AND n is odd AND* $(n - 1) \div 2$ *is odd.*$\}$

This says that the trick is only guaranteed to work if these three assertions are true. We could treat it as an instruction to execute that essentially terminates our attempt to do the trick if we find we have the wrong number of cards. If that happens, we need to start again with the right number. I always count the cards to double-check this precondition holds before doing this trick, exactly for that reason.

Our top-level instructions in our new written version now just give an overview of the trick. By the end, a card should have appeared to jump piles.

TO DO Invisible Palming WITH *n* cards:
$\{$*There are n cards AND n is odd AND* $(n - 1) \div 2$ *is odd.*$\}$

1. DO Deal out the cards in pairs with one left over WITH n cards.
2. DO Take the cards back as pairs splitting the pairs into two piles WITH n cards.
3. DO Place the extra card.
4. DO Pretend to move a card between piles.

5. DO Reveal that the extra card has magically moved piles WITH
   n cards.
{*An extra card appears to have moved piles.*}

We can still get the detail of exactly what we need to do when we
want it by looking at the separate instructions for each step. However,
this gives an overview, uncluttered by all the detail.

Chaining assertions

We still need to write out the detailed instructions for each step as its
own procedure. Each can have its own precondition and postcondition,
saying what it does. Actually writing out those procedures' assertions
can help us check overall the trick is going to work BEFORE we worry
about the detail. In the sequence of instructions, each postcondition
should match the precondition of the next step. If it does not, we might
be using an invalid step. The first procedure call has to guarantee the
precondition of the second, and the second has to do the same for the
third. This provides a chain of reasoning as seen in Figure 24.1.

The first step in the algorithm is to deal out the pairs with one left
over. It has the same precondition as the overall algorithm: the same
thing must be true at the start for both. The first step guarantees that
on its completion (its postcondition):

> {*There are an odd number of pairs of cards dealt out with one extra
> card on its own, totalling n cards.*}

That is exactly the precondition of the next procedure to be followed.
Our preconditions and postconditions therefore are giving us an outline
logical argument as to why the trick as a whole works, step by step. The
argument runs something like this:

> *If we start with the right number of cards to make two odd piles with
> one extra card (i.e., n is odd AND $(n-1) \div 2$ is odd . . .*
> *then on dealing them out into pairs . . .*
> *There are an odd number of pairs of cards dealt out with one extra
> card on its own, totalling n cards.*
> *After collecting them back in, there are two piles each holding . . .*
> *and so on.*

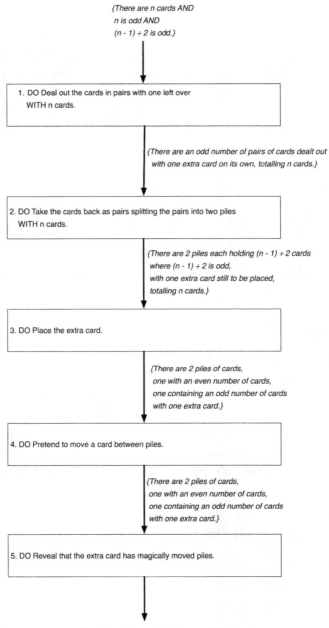

Figure 24.1. Linking the procedures together with matching preconditions and postconditions.

Writing out the instructions for each step as procedures

Now, we have a clear specification for each step. If each step meets its specification, then we know from our logical argument that the whole trick works. Now we write out the detail of each of those major steps, writing the definition of the procedures, separately making sure each does guarantee its postcondition if starting with the precondition being true.

The separate steps are just groups of instructions based on those of our original version of the algorithm, except with parameters, using n instead of the fixed number 15 as in the original. This means the number of times we, for example, place cards is also expressed in terms of n:

DO THE FOLLOWING $(n-1) \div 2$ TIMES...

where $(n-1) \div 2$ is just the number of pairs we have if we have n cards in total.

In summary

Overall, we have written the instructions for a general version of the trick that works with any appropriate number of cards as specified. We have decomposed it into a series of major steps and used preconditions and postconditions for those steps to give an outline argument as to why they work. Finally, we have written the detail of those decomposed instructions. If we can give a convincing argument that each meets its own specification, then our overall argument shows that the whole trick works.

The Magical Algorithm

DO Invisible Palming with 15 cards.

TO DO Invisible Palming WITH n cards:

{ *There are n cards AND n is odd AND $(n-1) \div 2$ is odd.*}
1. DO Deal out the cards in pairs with one left over WITH n cards.
2. DO Take the cards back as pairs splitting the pairs into two piles WITH n cards.

3. DO Place the extra card.
4. DO Pretend to move a card between piles.
5. DO Reveal that the extra card has magically moved piles.

{*An extra card appears to have moved piles.*}

TO DO deal out the cards in pairs with one left over WITH n cards:

{*There are n cards AND n is odd AND $(n - 1) \div 2$ is odd.*}

1. DO THE FOLLOWING $(n - 1) \div 2$ TIMES.
   a. Place 2 cards in a pair.
   b. Say "Two cards make a pair".
2. Place a single card in a pile on its own.

{*There are an odd number of pairs of cards dealt out with one extra card on its own, totalling n cards.*}

TO DO take the cards back as pairs splitting the pairs into two piles WITH n cards:

{*There are an odd number of pairs of cards dealt out with one extra card on its own, totalling n cards.*}

1. DO THE FOLLOWING $(n - 1) \div 2$ TIMES.
   a. Take a pair and split them into the two piles being formed.
   b. Say "Two cards make a pair".

{*There are 2 piles each holding $(n - 1) \div 2$ cards, where $(n - 1) \div 2$ is odd, with one extra card still to be placed, totalling n cards.*}

TO DO place the extra card:

{*There are 2 piles each holding $(n - 1) \div 2$ cards, where $(n - 1) \div 2$ is odd, with one extra card still to be placed, totalling n cards.*}

1. Have a volunteer choose one of the two piles to put the extra card.
2. They place the card on that pile.

{*There are 2 piles of cards, one with an even number of cards, one containing an odd number of cards with one extra card.*}

TO DO pretend to move a card between piles:

{There are 2 piles of cards, one with an even number of cards, one containing an odd number of cards with one extra card.}

1. Place a hand over the pile with the extra card.
2. Rub the back of that hand.
3. Lift your hand, showing the palm before placing it over the other pile.
4. Tap your hand and remove it, saying the card has moved.

{There are 2 piles of cards, one with an even number of cards, one containing an odd number of cards with one extra card.}

TO DO reveal that the extra card has magically moved piles:

{There are 2 piles of cards, one with an even number of cards, one containing an odd number of cards with one extra card.}

1. Pick up the first pile (where the "extra" card was placed).
2. DO THE FOLLOWING UNTIL you are holding no cards.
   a. Add 2 cards from the pile you are holding, to a pile on the table.
   b. Say "Two cards make a pair".
3. Pick up the second pile (where the "extra" card was NOT placed).
4. DO THE FOLLOWING UNTIL you are holding one card.
   a. Add 2 cards from the pile you are holding, to a pile on the table.
   b. Say "Two cards make a pair".
5. Reveal that an extra card is left in your hand. The extra card was in the second pile.

{A card appears to have moved piles.}

PAUSE: Robert W. Floyd and Tony Hoare

Robert W. Floyd (1936–2001) originally studied liberal arts at university, and Tony Hoare studied classics and philosophy. Both went on to become great computer scientists. Floyd's biggest contribution was in the idea of using assertions attached to points in flowchart versions of programs as a way of proving that they did the right thing. These ideas were built on by Tony Hoare, who created a programming logic: a set of rules that could be used to reason about exactly what a program did and so whether it met a mathematical statement of what it should do (its specification). Between them, they kick-started the field of automated program verification, vital for programs that are safety-critical: where bugs can kill. Both made many other contributions to computer science during their lifetimes from inventing really important algorithms to the design of programming languages.

Part 7

Abstraction and Data Representation

We've seen abstraction applied to the way we write out the order of instructions in the form of procedures. Now, we explore similar ideas with data: data abstraction. Data can have different representations which are abstract versions of how the data is really stored. We look at what it means to hide the underlying representation of data.

Chapter 25

Drawn to You
Codes Representing Data

Conjuring

Four people each draw a picture on a piece of paper. The paper is jumbled up, but you are able to read each person's personality and work out who drew each.

Computation

Tricks often rely on representing information in some particular way. Choosing an appropriate data representation is core to computational thinking and programming.

The Trick

You tear the bottom half of a sheet of paper out of an A4 pad. Fold this piece in half, then half again and tear it into quarters along the folds. Hand a piece to each of four friends who you have asked to stand in a line. Next, give each an identical pencil and ask them to secretly draw a simple picture on their piece of paper. You may want to give them a book to lean on while doing this. Each can draw anything they like. Have each crumple their paper into a ball and put it into a small bag where they are well and truly mixed.

You announce that you are able to judge the personalities of people from their drawings. You can also read personalities from their body language (which you have been observing). You will now do a psychological reading of their picture and match each to the person who drew it.

You remove the screwed-up bits of paper one at a time, uncrumple them, and through the psychological reading of the picture you correctly identify which person drew which picture!

How It Works

Though it seems that simply tearing the half sheet into four is an innocent action, it's actually the secret. It encodes information on the bits of paper.

If you look at four bits of paper torn from a pad in this way, you will see that each is similar, but actually subtly different (see Figure 25.1).

- The bottom right quarter has two smooth, clean edges, the original corner of the sheet from the pad you started with. It is the *only* piece that has two such smooth, clean edges.
- The bottom left section has only one smooth edge (from the bottom edge of the original sheet), but that edge is long (about 10 cm if you used A4 paper).
- The top right section also has only one smooth edge (from the side of the original piece of paper), but it is a shorter side (roughly 7 cm if you used an A4 pad).
- The top left quarter has no smooth edges at all. It is torn all around, as it came from the middle of the original piece of paper.

By giving out the paper squares in the above order, each person has been given an identifiable piece of paper. Instead of looking at the drawings, you can just look for the different pieces of paper.

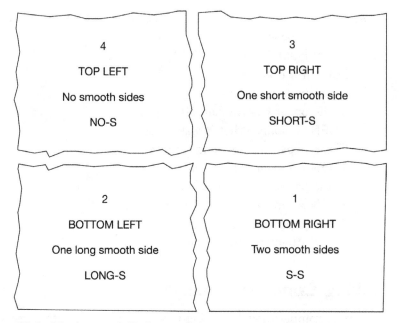

Figure 25.1. The bottom half of a piece of paper torn out of a pad of paper. Each side has different smooth sides.

The Magical Algorithm

TO DO Drawn to you:

1. Ask four people to stand in a line, giving each an identical pencil.
2. Tear the bottom half of a sheet of paper out of an A4 pad.
3. Fold this piece in half, then half again and tear it into quarters along the folds.
4. Hand a piece to each person, in the order they were torn off: Person 1 — bottom right quarter; Person 2 — bottom left quarter; Person 3 — top right quarter; Person 4 — top left quarter.
5. Ask them to secretly draw a simple picture of their choice on their piece of paper.
6. Have them crumple their paper into a ball and put them into a small bag.
7. Mix up the balls of paper in the bag.

8. Announce that you are able to judge the personalities of people from their drawings.
9. DO THE FOLLOWING 4 TIMES.
    a. Pull out a drawing.
    b. Un-crumple it.
    c. IF the paper has two smooth edges
       THEN Announce that it was Person 1.
       IF the paper has one long smooth edge
       THEN Announce that it was Person 2.
       IF the paper has one short smooth edge
       THEN Announce that it was Person 3.
       IF the paper has no smooth edges
       THEN Announce that it was Person 4.

Thinking Computationally

A big part of computational thinking involves working out the best way to **represent information** to make the task at hand easy. Western cultures use characters like A and 1 strung together into words and numbers to represent information, but there are lots of different ways to represent the same information. In many oriental cultures, characters are used that represent words. In South America, knotted strings, called quipu, were once used to represent numbers and possibly words...

Choosing a good representation matters. This trick is based on choosing a representation for four different things (the four people, or equivalently the four numbers representing their positions). The representation is one that you, the magician, can easily see, but they do not notice at all. The audience just see the four bits of paper as the same. However, the performer, in the way they tear them out, is building their own secret representation of the vital information. For them, knowing the representation is just like writing on the corner: Person 1, Person 2, Person 3 and Person 4.

To help remember, you could even go a step further and create a representation in words: a code, where S represents a smooth side: (1) S-S, (2) LONG-S, (3) SHORT-S and (4) NO-S. Remember the code in that order, and it is even easier to remember which is which.

This is made easier still if you organise the people into a line rather than just letting them stand anywhere. By doing that, you physically give the people an order too (their position is now a representation of a number). Their order matches the order you have remembered for the paper. You are organising the information they embody by positioning them in the line. The organisation of information (its structure and representation) makes the task easier to do. Organising information into the most convenient form is what data representation is all about.

Programmers often choose how to organise data before writing code. For example, if you sort names into an alphabetically ordered list first, then it is possible to find a given name much faster. You can use fast search algorithms. That is why dictionaries and the index of a book are in alphabetical order, as were old-fashioned telephone directories. Search engines organise the information from web pages before you do searches, allowing them to search every web page in the world and return a list of those that are relevant in a fraction of a second.

Choose the right way to organise information for the task, and that task can be easy or hard, whether it is a computer or a person doing the computation.

The data representation

Here we represent people as numbers and as properties of pieces of paper, as well as then ultimately remembered code words. There are thus four different representations of the same thing (see Figure 25.2). Actually, there is a fifth too in the drawings, which it is asserted represents the personality of each person, but that is actually ignored.

Person	Position Number	Physical Properties of Paper	Code
First person	1	Two smooth sides	(S-S)
Second person	2	One long smooth side	(LONG-S)
Third person	3	One short smooth side	(SHORT-S)
Fourth person	4	No smooth sides	(NO-S)

Figure 25.2. The way the information about the people is represented in the paper for the "Drawn to You" trick.

Interlude: Joseph Jastrow

The type of mentalism effect where people claim to be able to read personality through objects is called psychometry. Psychometry was hyped by Joseph Buchanan in the mid-1800s as revolutionary science. Experimental psychologist Joseph Jastrow (1863–1944), who made a career of using scientific methods to identify truth from fallacy, denounced it as delusional. There is no scientific evidence behind it at all. The general idea was, however, turned into very many highly popular music hall tricks. In one popular version, the performer identified which name was the name of a dead person from a set of random names offered by the audience. One way to do this is to have the first person write the name of a dead person on their piece of paper, while the other three write the names of living people on theirs, then do the trick as above. While psychometry is nonsense, Jastrow, who denounced it, was a real scientist who discovered and popularised lots of optical illusions as part of his actual scientific work.

Ꮯhe Roman Maths Ꮯhallenge
Roman Numerals

Conjuring

In this challenge, the audience must do some Roman numeral maths, making a Roman numeral sum add up.

Computation

The way you choose to represent numbers affects how hard or easy it is to do different tasks. Addition and subtraction are fairly easy with Roman numerals but multiplication and division are harder. When choosing a representation of data, it is important to think about what you will need to do with the data.

The Trick

Explain that this is more a challenge than a magic trick. Ask a friend if they know Roman numerals. Remind them that Roman numerals are just a different way of writing numbers, though one that makes doing some maths harder than ours. They used I to mean one, V for five, X for 10, counting I, II, III, IV, V, VI, VII and so on. Say "Let's do some Roman maths..." On a pad, slowly write out the start of a sum using

Roman numerals, saying each number after you have written it to check they are the following:

II + II = IV

"Two...plus...two...equals...four"

II + IV =

"Two...plus...four...equals..."

Next, write in the Roman numeral for 9 (IX) saying,

"This is an obviously wrong bit of maths using Roman numerals":

II + IV = IX

Finally, lay the challenge: "The challenge is: can you make it work so that the two sides are equal by adding just a single line?"

Give them a few minutes to try, and if they fail, then show them the answer. (If they manage to do it, praise them for their brilliance!)

How It Works

The solution is to draw in an S before the IX to make the correct sum.

II + IV = SIX

Point out that you didn't say they had to use a straight line! You also didn't say they had to stick to Roman numerals.

The Magical Algorithm

TO DO The Roman Maths Challenge:
1. Explain how Roman numerals represent numbers.
2. Write II + II = IV while saying "Two...plus...two...equals... four".
3. Write II + IV = while saying "Two...plus...four...equals...".
4. Finish the sum by writing IX to give II + IV = IX.
5. Say "This is an obviously wrong bit of maths using Roman numerals".

6. Say "The challenge is: can you make it work so that the two sides are equal by adding just a single line?".
7. Give them a few minutes to work it out.
8. Write an "S" before the IX to make the sum work.
9. Say "I didn't say you had to use a straight line!".

Thinking Computationally

When we think of numbers, we tend to think of the digits we use to write them, but that is just a representation: one particular way of writing them. There are lots of different ways to write numbers. Early civilisations just used tally marks: a very direct representation with one mark for each thing you were counting. If you have 12 goats, then you would write 12 lines.

IIIIIIIIIIII

This representation is called **unary**. It is fine for small numbers, but it gets harder to keep track of what number it is for larger numbers. The first improvement is to make the groups of five more obvious by clustering them, such as making every fifth line into a bar. This representation is called **tallying**.

卌卌II

That makes keeping track of how many you have easier as you can check by counting the tallies in fives. Adding two numbers represented as tallies is fairly easy too for small numbers as you just combine the two lists of tallies, and then arrange any extra ones into clumps of five. It also works well given a limitation of the way our brains work. Scatter some number of coins on the table. If there are less than five or so, you can probably see how many are there at a glance. If there are more though, then you will start having to count to tell. Our brains are good at just seeing small numbers, but can't do it naturally for larger ones. You can probably see how many there are in this sum:

II + III = II III

But, what number is the following? You have to count them all over again! It's just marks you are counting now instead of goats.

IIIIIIIIIIIIIIIIIIIII

Roman numerals are a different way of representing numbers that solves this problem by introducing new symbols to use in ever bigger numbers. It is a different representation that makes quickly seeing what number you have easy, even for really large numbers. The above number is written as

XX

which is much easier to deal with. You can see how many Xs there are at a glance.

However, doing arithmetic in Roman numerals is quite hard. Adding isn't so bad, but multiplication is really hard, by comparison. That's why we no longer use Roman numerals. Now we use a different representation of numbers that in particular is convenient for writing arbitrarily large numbers and also that makes doing all kinds of arithmetic much easier, so is better all around. We use a representation that makes the job easier.

Computers use a different representation again, based on the one we use, but that is a more convenient version for the way computers work. We will look at these other representations in subsequent chapters.

Interlude: Nevil Maskelyne

Nevil Maskelyne (1863–1924) was the son of a famous magician, John Nevil Maskelyne. He became a magician in his own right making use of new communications technology in his mentalism tricks. When Guglielmo Marconi's wireless telegraph (i.e., radio) seemed to be set to pull the plug on the cable telegraph, one of the cable companies hired Maskelyne to spy on Marconi listening in to all his broadcasts. Maskelyne did more than this, debunking Marconi's claims very publicly that radio was private and could not be hacked. He set up his own broadcast station in London and used it to ruin Marconi's prestigious public demonstration of the technology at the Royal Institution by sending his own message picked up by the demonstration receivers before those of Marconi. His fake messages poked fun at Marconi.

Chapter 27

The Lottery Trick
Place-Value Number Representation

Conjuring

Everyone chooses a lucky lottery number. You then turn the room into a lottery machine with everyone bouncing lottery balls around. Three numbers are chosen at random and added, and then we see if anyone has a lucky lottery ticket. The lucky winner is of course you, the magician.

Computation

We use the Hindu–Arabic numeral system. The really amazing idea here is that the value of digits changes depending on their position in the number, so 2 can stand for two, twenty or two hundred depending on its position. This makes large numbers more concise but also makes operations like addition and multiplication easier. It makes for simple algorithms.

The Trick

Before the trick, write the numbers 3, 4 and 8 each on identical pieces of red paper, the numbers 1, 5 and 9 on yellow paper, and the numbers 2, 6 and 7 on blue paper. Secretly, write the number 1,665 on a piece of paper made to look like a lottery ticket and put it in a sealed envelope.

Explain to the audience that you are going to play a lottery game, but where the whole audience will be the lottery machine. Everyone should write down their lucky 4-digit number on a piece of paper and place it in an envelope. It will be their lottery ticket. Hold up your envelope and say you will play too and that the envelope contains your lottery ticket. Tape it to the wall so all can see it, with either masking tape or some other way that will not damage the wall.

First, you need to randomly choose the order of the colours that will determine the order that balls are removed from the lottery machine. Have a volunteer decide the order of the three colours (red, yellow and blue) at random to use. Write the colours in the order they decide on a flip chart.

Explain that you are going to make the lottery balls out of screwed-up coloured paper so they can bounce around the room without hurting anyone. Show the audience the pieces of paper with the numbers. Explain that they will be the lottery balls, noting that just like lottery balls they are coloured and have numbers. You have used three colours and the numbers one to nine.

Next, ask a volunteer to screw each piece of paper up into a ball and toss them into the audience. The audience should then toss the balls of paper around as if they are in a lottery machine.

Next, go to the order of colours chosen, and ask the volunteer to pick out one ball of the first colour. Unscrunch it to find its number. Write this under the colour. Do the same for the next colour, and then the third. Explain you have the first 3-digit random number but that you are going to do this three times and just add the numbers so that all the balls are used. Repeat this process with the same order of colours to get a second 3-digit number and finally a third. You now have three 3-digit numbers (see Figure 27.1).

BLUE	YELLOW	RED
6	9	3
2	5	8
7	1	4

Figure 27.1. This shows what would be written on the flip chart if the colour order chosen was: blue, then yellow, then red; and then balls are drawn randomly as follows: Blue — 6, Yellow — 9, Red — 3, Blue — 2, Yellow — 5, Red — 8, Blue — 7, Yellow — 1 and Red — 4. The numbers 693, 258 and 714 are added on a calculator to give the answer and so the final lottery number, 1,665.

Give the volunteer a calculator and have them add up the three numbers. Then, turning to the next sheet on the flip chart, write the total and circle it. Announce that is the winning number and ask if anyone has won. Finally, have the volunteer open the envelope to reveal your lottery ticket and read out your number. You have indeed picked the winning number, 1,665!

How It Works

The choice of order of colours appears to add randomness to the process, but it actually makes no difference. Let us look at just one colour, red. The three numbers there are 3, 4 and 8. Whichever position red is put in, those three numbers will always be in that same column as that is where the red numbers are written. That means that even though the order they are chosen changes, they will always be added together (and they add up to 15). The three numbers on the other coloured pieces of paper will also always be added together, whatever order the balls are pulled out. The yellow numbers, 1, 5 and 9 will be added also giving 15. Similarly, the blue numbers 2, 6 and 7 will be added together and add up to 15 too.

This means that whatever order the balls are chosen, the three columns of numbers will add up to 15. You will always be adding 15, 150 and 1,500 as each represents a different decimal place so is increased by 10 from the previous one. 1,500, 150 and 15 add up to 1,665, the number you wrote on your lottery ticket.

The Magical Algorithm

TO PREPARE The Lottery Trick:

1. Write the numbers 3, 4 and 8 each on a red piece of A4 paper.
2. Write the numbers 1, 5 and 9 each on a yellow piece of A4 paper.
3. Write the numbers 2, 6 and 7 each on a blue piece of A4 paper.
4. Write the number 1,665 on a white piece of paper drawn to look like a lottery ticket.
5. Seal the white piece of paper in an envelope.

TO DO The Lottery Trick:

1. Have everyone in the audience write down a lucky 4-digit number of their choice and seal it in an envelope.
2. Hold up your envelope noting it contains your lottery number and tape it to the wall.
3. Ask a volunteer to choose the order of colours to pull out balls from the lottery machine from a choice of red, yellow and blue.
4. Write the colours down in the order they choose on a flip chart.
5. Have the volunteer screw up the 9 pieces of coloured paper and throw them into the audience one at a time.
6. The audience toss the balls around as though they are balls in a lottery machine.
7. DO THE FOLLOWING 9 TIMES.
   a. Announce the next colour in turn as written on the board.
   b. Ask the volunteer to choose a ball of paper of that colour from those in the room.
   c. Have the volunteer unscrew the ball and announce the number.
   d. Write the number on the board in a column under the colour.

8. Ask the volunteer to add up the three 3-digit numbers under the colours using a calculator.
9. Turn to the next sheet on the flip chart and have them write the total there and circle it.
10. Announce that that number is the winning number.
11. Ask anyone with a winning ticket to claim the prize.
12. Have the volunteer open your envelope to reveal that you have a winning ticket.

Thinking Computationally

This trick relies on the fact that we use the **Hindu–Arabic number system**. It was invented by Indian mathematicians in the first few centuries BC but brought to the West by Arab scholars and traders. The really amazing idea that matters most about Hindu–Arabic numbers is that digits have a position in a number. Unlike in Roman numerals (where for example X means 10 wherever it appears), their value changes depending on their position. For example, in the Hindu–Arabic system, 2 can stand for 2, 20, or 200, and so on, depending on its position in the number. This is a vital part of the trick that makes it work. The numbers are placed in a position labelled by their colour so that they all come back together to be added.

This representation makes large numbers very concise, so taking up little memory in computer terms. It also makes manipulating numbers by humans relatively easy: it makes for relatively simple algorithms such as the ones we learn in primary school. Counting is easy, for example, as are doing things like addition and multiplication. Multiplication is much easier than with Roman numerals. The choice of representation makes tasks easier or harder.

This is the key idea about choosing a good representation for data, whether numbers or other kinds of data: you want to make it easy to do the key operations. With computers, that usually means you want there to be fast algorithms, though sometimes taking up as little memory as possible matters more, and sometimes you just want it to be easy to get the algorithm right.

PAUSE: Charles Babbage

Charles Babbage (1791–1871) designed the first computer, the Analytical Engine, though never actually managed to build one. It was a mechanical computer with punch cards based on the Jacquard Loom to provide the program. It would have been steam-driven, and the data was stored in a series of cog-like wheels. Unlike modern computers, its data was to be stored as decimal numbers based on the positions of the wheels, so using the Hindu–Arabic number representation. Such wheels were used in his earlier and simpler Difference Engine, a prototype of which was built. He was not a fan of all machines: he hated barrel organs (or at least the people playing them in the street) so much he tried to get an act of parliament to outlaw them. A mechanism based on a barrel organ was included in his design of the Analytical Engine.

Chapter 28

Cards on Your Mind
How Computers Represent Numbers

Conjuring

Four volunteers jointly pick a number and jointly concentrate on it, helped by your set of magic cards. Despite them keeping it secret, you are able to read their collective mind and announce their secret number.

Computation

Digital computers do not use the decimal system that we use but instead use a different place-value system called binary. Binary is also the underlying representation that makes certain tricks work.

The Trick

Ask four volunteers to help in an experiment in mind reading. Give them a list of 15 numbers and ask them to jointly pick one without telling you what it is. Then give each a card which contains a jumble of numbers and letters. They stand in a line facing you, cards hidden from your sight. They each look to see if the jointly chosen number is on their card. If it is, then they must close their eyes and think hard only of that number.

181

Those holding a card without the number choose one of the letters on their card instead and stare at it, thinking only of that letter. That way they won't confuse you, you say. Once they are all concentrating, you close your eyes, think hard, then pick up the thoughts about the secret number and announce what their secret number was!

How It Works

You will need the set of 5 cards shown in Figures 28.1 and 28.2. You can download them from https://conjuringwithcomputation.wordpress.com, print them out, and stick them onto card or write out your own with the same numbers and letters on.

First, you give four volunteers the card with the numbers 1 to 15 to look at (Figure 28.1). They jointly choose one and keep it secret. Next, you give them the 4 special cards with numbers and letters on, one each, in the order as shown in Figure 28.2.

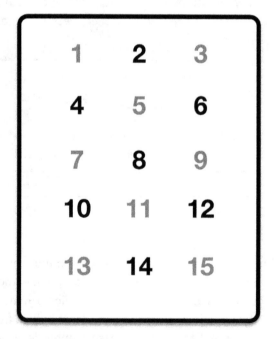

Figure 28.1. The card with the numbers 1 to 15 on, for the "Cards on Your Mind" trick.

Card 4 (Code 8)			Card 3 (Code 4)			Card 2 (Code 2)			Card 1 (Code 1)		
8	**M**	9	4	**S**	5	2	**Y**	3	1	**P**	3
L	10	**H**	**K**	6	**E**	**A**	6	**T**	**B**	5	**Q**
11	**T**	12	7	**U**	12	7	**X**	10	7	**F**	9
13	**D**	14	13	**N**	14	11	**L**	14	11	**G**	13
	15			15			15			15	

Figure 28.2. The 4 cards to give out for the "Cards on Your Mind" trick.

These cards are special in that the numbers on each are carefully selected. Secretly think of them as card 8, card 4, card 2 and card 1. These are the numbers in the top left corner of the card. Stand the volunteers in a line and give out the cards in that order, so the person on the right facing you has card 1 and the person on the left has card 8.

Now, get those with their jointly chosen number on their card to close their eyes. You add up the card numbers of the people closing their eyes, and that is their secret number. For example, if the people holding card 1 and card 8 have closed their eyes and the other two volunteers are staring at their card, eyes open, then add 1 and 8 and announce they are thinking of number 9. If instead the people holding card 2, card 4 and card 8 have their eyes closed, then the secret number is 2 + 4 + 8 so 14. It is that simple. You don't need to be able to read minds, just add up powers of 2.

The Magical Algorithm

TO DO Cards on Your Mind:
  1. Give four volunteers the card containing numbers 1 to 15 (Figure 28.1).
  2. Ask them to jointly pick one number between them without telling you what it is.
  3. Have them stand in a line facing you.

4. Give each a card which contains a jumble of numbers and letters in the order of the cards based on the number in the top left corner, card 1 on the right, card 8 on the left as shown in Figure 28.2.
5. Tell them to keep the cards hidden from your sight and each look to see if the jointly chosen number is on their card.
6. IF the chosen number is on their card
   THEN they should shut their eyes and think only of that number.
   OTHERWISE they should choose a letter on their card and think only of that letter so as not to confuse you.
7. You read off the number by adding the card numbers for the eyes-closed people to give the total.
8. Announce that number as the secret number.

Thinking Computationally

The secret of this mind-reading trick relies on the **binary** representation of numbers. Figure 28.3 gives numbers from 1 to 15 with their binary version. It is a way of writing numbers using sequences of 1s and 0s. It is a positional number system that works just like decimal, but where there are only two symbols: 0 and 1 instead of 10, and the positions increase in powers of 2 (1, 2, 4, 8, ...) instead of powers of 10 (1, 10, 100, 1,000, ...).

To work out the value represented by the number in both decimal and binary, you just multiply the number in a column by the column heading and then add the answers. In decimal, the column headings are powers of 10 (as there are 10 symbols). In binary, the column headings are powers of 2 (as there are 2 symbols).

That means the 1 in the binary number 10 means 2, the 1 in the binary number 100 means 4, and the 1 in the binary number 1,000 means 8. So just as the number 1,204 in decimal represents $1 \times 1,000 + 2 \times 100 + 0 \times 10 + 4 \times 1$, the binary number 1,101 represents $1 \times 8 + 1 \times 4 + 0 \times 2 + 1 \times 1$ (so means 13 as $8 + 4 + 1 = 13$).

You can use any two different things to represent those 1s and 0s as they are just arbitrary symbols. In the trick, eyes open is used for 0 and eyes closed is used for 1. The secret number is then being spelled

```
          8 4 2 1
    1     0 0 0 1  = 0 + 0 + 0 + 1
    2     0 0 1 0  = 0 + 0 + 2 + 0
    3     0 0 1 1  = 0 + 0 + 2 + 1
    4     0 1 0 0  = 0 + 4 + 0 + 0
    5     0 1 0 1  = 0 + 4 + 0 + 1
    6     0 1 1 0  = 0 + 4 + 2 + 0
    7     0 1 1 1  = 0 + 4 + 2 + 1
    8     1 0 0 0  = 8 + 0 + 0 + 0
    9     1 0 0 1  = 8 + 0 + 0 + 1
   10     1 0 1 0  = 8 + 0 + 2 + 0
   11     1 0 1 1  = 8 + 0 + 2 + 1
   12     1 1 0 0  = 8 + 4 + 0 + 0
   13     1 1 0 1  = 8 + 4 + 0 + 1
   14     1 1 1 0  = 8 + 4 + 2 + 0
   15     1 1 1 1  = 8 + 4 + 2 + 1
```

Figure 28.3. The numbers 1 to 15 with their binary representation and as an addition of powers of 2 corresponding to the positions of 1s.

out in binary by the four people's eyes. You can just read the binary to know what the chosen number was.

This works because the numbers on the cards are just those with a 1 in the corresponding position of that number when written as binary. Card 1, for example has all the odd numbers written on it as in binary all odd numbers have a 1 in the first position (the 1s column). See Figure 28.3 and notice how the first column has a 1 for numbers 1, 3, 5, . . .

Similarly, card 8, the leftmost card, has the numbers from 8 to 15 written on it as those numbers have a 1 in the fourth position (the 8s column) in the binary.

By telling people to close their eyes if the number is on the card you are secretly saying close your eyes if there is a 1 in the binary at your position. The volunteers are representing their chosen binary number. Adding up powers of 2, for eyes shut or not, is then just the way you work out what number that binary number actually represents.

You don't actually have to remember the table of Figure 28.3 to work out what decimal number the binary number stands for. You can just do the calculation instead to work out what number your volunteers are thinking of. We put the numbers 8, 4, 2 and 1 above the columns, and you should think of the person in each position corresponding to that number. You then just add up the column numbers to get the secret number. If there is a 1 (eyes shut) in the binary in a column, then that column number is added to the total.

For computers, binary is a better representation of numbers than decimal. In the trick, the 1s and 0s are represented by eyes shut or eyes open. In a computer, they are just differing electrical signals: high and low voltages on wires or transistors that are on or off, for example. These binary signals are easily stored and easily transferred from place to place in the computer, meaning the binary numbers can be moved to where needed to do a calculation. There are also very fast algorithms for doing arithmetic, and it is easy to create specialist hardware for computers to use to do the maths. This all makes binary an ideal representation for numbers in a computer. Therefore, all data are ultimately stored in computers as binary 1s and 0s rather than as decimal numbers.

PAUSE: Gottfried Leibniz

German philosopher and mathematician Gottfried Leibniz (1646–1716) (amongst others) studied the use of binary numbers in the 17th century. In part, he was fascinated by the symbols in a 9th-century Chinese text (a version of the *I Ching*) which shows that binary existed long before its western uses. A form of binary arithmetic was also used even earlier in Ancient Egypt. Leibniz worked out the mathematics behind binary. He was also an important logician setting out the basics of formal logic which is the basis of logical reasoning. He worked on machines to do calculations and even imagined a machine controlled by punch cards with binary numbers represented by marbles long before Charles Babbage envisioned his punch card-controlled machines.

Chapter 29

On the Power of Numbers
Representing Other Things by Numbers

Conjuring

A postcard is chosen from a selection while your guest magician is out of the room, but despite that they can quickly say which card was touched.

Computation

All sorts of things can be represented by numbers and once they are then we can bring them into the digital world, as those numbers in turn can be represented by binary.

The Trick

Explain that your guest magician has extremely heightened powers of observation and can tell when an object such as one of the set of nine postcards on the table has been touched by someone. Have them leave the room, then wearing gloves, take the postcards and shuffle them. Lay them out on the table in a rough three-by-three grid and ask a volunteer to pick one by touching it. They should then remember their card.

Collect the cards back up, shuffle them, and then lay them back down on the table, still wearing gloves. Call in your partner magician. Immediately, just by looking at the cards, they are able to say which card was touched.

How It Works

In advance, you agree a number from 1 to 9 for each card. Both memorise these numbers for the cards. To make this easier, you could choose cards that have different numbers of objects: perhaps the one you label 1 is a picture of a single lighthouse, whereas the one labelled 3 has three seagulls flying in the background, and so on.

As your partner enters the room, facing them, you casually put your hands together, touching that many fingers together as you do so. If you do this as your accomplice enters the room, announcing their arrival, the audience are likely looking at the door not at you to make it even less likely they will see or be suspicious about the movement of your hands.

A variation, rather than labelling the cards (should you find that hard to remember), would be to communicate the position of the chosen card as a pair of numbers giving an x and y coordinate with the fingers you touch together on each hand. So if the card was in the bottom left, you would touch one finger on each hand. If in the top left, touch one finger to three fingers.

The Magical Algorithm

TO DO the Preparation of On the power of numbers:
1. Choose 9 postcards with different pictures.
2. Agree with your partner a number for each picture.

TO DO On the power of numbers:
1. Explain your partner magician has heightened sensory powers and can tell when an object has been touched.
2. Your partner magician leaves the room.
3. Put on gloves and lay the cards out on the table in a rough 3 × 3 grid.

4. Ask a volunteer to choose one by touching it and then everyone remembers their chosen card.
5. Take up the cards and shuffle them.
6. Deal them back into a rough 3 × 3 grid.
7. Call your partner magician back in.
8. Touch together the number of fingers as the number of the chosen card so that your partner can see it.
9. Your partner picks up the card corresponding to that number saying it was the one that had been touched by someone.

Thinking Computationally

We have ways to represent numbers in binary, but numbers themselves can be used to represent other things: cards and the images on them in a simple way as part of this trick. The same can be done for music, images, money . . . just about anything. That idea is the foundation for the digital world.

Images do not have to be represented just by a count of the objects in them. The actual image can be turned into numbers that describe the image in detail. There are several ways to do this. One way, called **vector graphics**, involves describing each line or shape in the image by its size and position. Another, called **raster graphics** or **bitmap graphics**, involves breaking the image into small squares and giving numbers to each square.

To do this, first, we need to represent colours as numbers. One simple way is just to give each colour in the image a single number: red is 1, orange is 2, yellow is 3, and so on. Next divide the image into lots of small squares and note which colour is the main one in that square. Represent that square (or **pixel**) by the number for that colour. Now the list of numbers for all those pixels is a representation of the picture. Each number in turn can be represented by binary so stored on a computer or sent over a network. By sending the list of numbers as binary over the Internet or phone network to someone else, they can reconstruct a copy of the image.

If an image or piece of music or a film or a book can be represented by numbers like this, then it can be converted into a digital object.

Then, it can be copied, shared, streamed...just by copying, sharing, streaming...those numbers.

Interlude: Luca Pacioli

The oldest known book that describes card tricks, *De viribus quantitatis* or *On the Power of Numbers,* included a variation of this trick of the same name. It was a book of mathematical diversions written by Luca Pacioli (c.1447–1517) around 1500. It suggested that a conjurer could train an accomplice to "guess" which card a person had touched, even though they were out of the room at the time, by agreeing in advance numbers linked to the cards. Just like many modern magicians, Pacioli was keen to show that often effects that were classed as magic were really just conjuring tricks. Pacioli was a close friend of the artist and engineer, Leonardo da Vinci, and taught him mathematics as an adult. Leonardo had realised maths would help him gain both a better artistic and scientific understanding of the world. Leonardo's only published illustrations (of three-dimensional shapes) were illustrations for another book by Pacioli.

Chapter 30

The Out-of-Body Experience
Error-Correcting Codes

Conjuring

Someone flips over a card in a grid of cards. Blindfolded, you can leave your body, and hovering from the ceiling watch what happens and so can immediately say which card was changed once you return and the blindfold is removed.

Computation

Computers use special representations to send data over networks. Error-correcting codes are ways to represent, and so store and transmit, data so that if some are corrupted, a computer can not only tell it has been changed but also correct the changes. It can do this without knowing in advance what the original data was.

The Trick

For this trick, you need a partner magician. Explain to the audience that you are able to float out of your body and see things you would otherwise not be able to see. You go to the back of the room where a volunteer blindfolds you. Have them check the blindfold first to ensure there is no trickery. They stay with you throughout the whole trick to both "guard your body" and make sure you remain blindfolded throughout. You explain that your spirit is about to leave your body and as you do so your body slumps.

Once you are blindfolded and spirit departed, your partner magician shuffles a pack of cards. A volunteer then deals them out in a 4 × 4 square. They place some cards face up and some face down at random. Your partner suggests that to make it harder they will make the square even bigger and turn it into a 5 × 5 square which they do by adding more cards at random.

You are blindfolded and lean against the wall at the back of the room with your back to the proceedings through all of this. Your spirit, of course, left your body and flies up to the ceiling so you can watch from above. It has a target to watch in the square of cards. Next a new volunteer chooses any card from the grid and flips it over. No one speaks. You are still blindfolded. You can only know which one was flipped if your spirit really is floating above, watching. You are told by your partner to return to your body, which you do. As you return, you bang against the wall as you re-enter too quickly. As you were upside down on the ceiling, you will be a bit dizzy when you return so you may wobble about a bit. Return to the front and look at the square of cards. You have trouble working out which way up the square was if you were upside down, so struggle to work it out. You turn your head to one side before finally pointing to the one that was flipped over!

How It Works

The secret is in that extra row and column of cards your partner adds apparently at random (see Figure 30.1). It isn't in fact random. It also isn't making things harder, but easier. Your partner counts the number of face-down cards in each row. If that number is odd so that either 1 or 3 of the cards is face down, they put the new card face down. With that added card, there is now an even number of cards (2 or 4) face down in the row. If the number of face-down cards in the row is already even (0, 2 or 4), then instead they put the new card face up. This also leaves the number even.

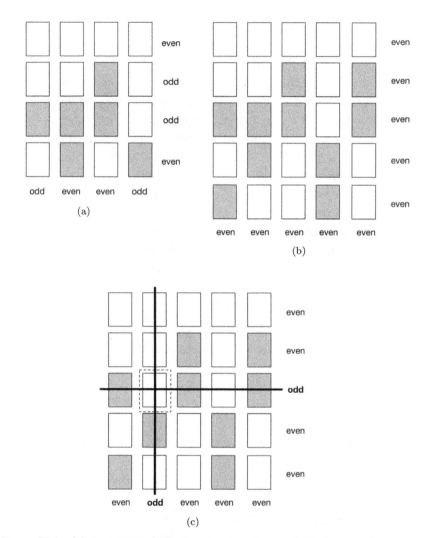

Figure 30.1. (a) An initial layout of cards, some face up (white), some face down (grey). (b) The extra cards added to the rows and columns make each have an even number of face-down cards. (c) When one is turned over, it can be identified by finding the row and column with an odd number of face-down (grey) cards.

Once they have done this for all rows, every row has an even number of face-down cards.

Next they add cards to the bottom of the columns, and do this in exactly the same way, ensuring all columns end up with an even number of face-down cards, including the last card in the corner. That ensures that the extra column of cards added to each row also ends up with an even number of face-down cards.

Working out which card has been turned over is now easy as long as only one card is changed. The row that the turned card is in will now have an *odd* number of face-down cards. Similarly, the column containing the turned-over card will also have an odd number of face-down cards. This is because in each case one has been turned over either turning a face-up card to face-down or vice versa. Turning one card either way means the even pattern is broken but only in one row and one column.

Where the row and column with odd numbers of cards meet is the card that was turned.

The trick works just as well, of course, however big the square of cards is. It does not have to be a 5 × 5 square.

The Magical Algorithm

TO DO The Out-of-Body Experience:

1. Explain to the audience that you are able to float out of your body and your spirit self then sees things.
2. You are blindfolded at the back of the room and "leave your body."
3. Your partner shuffles a pack of cards.
4. A volunteer deals them out in a 4 × 4 grid placing cards face up or face down at random.
5. Your partner says they will make the square bigger so it is harder.
6. FOR each row of cards in the grid

   a. IF there are an odd number of face-down cards in the row, THEN your partner adds a face-down card at the end of the row.
   OTHERWISE your partner adds an extra face-up card at the end of the row.

7. FOR each column of cards in the grid

   a. IF there are an odd number of face-down cards in the column, THEN your partner adds a face-down card at the end of the column.
   OTHERWISE your partner adds an extra face-up card at the end of the column.

8. A second volunteer picks a card and flips it over.
9. Your partner tells you to return to your body and remove your blindfold.
10. You remove the blindfold and come to the front to look at the grid.
11. Point out that you did not see it before the flip, so have no way of knowing what card was changed.
12. Identify the row containing an odd number of face-down cards.
13. Identify the column containing an odd number of face-down cards.
14. Pick up the card that is in both the identified row and identified column and announce that it is the card flipped.

Thinking Computationally

We are using a clever, more advanced kind of data representation here, called an **error-checking code**. They allow us to spot when mistakes have been made, and for some codes like this one, allow the mistakes to be corrected too. If they can correct the error, as here, then they are called **error-correcting codes**.

Everything in a computer is ultimately stored as binary bits: sequences of 1s and 0s. That is also how data is transmitted. If you stream music, the music is represented as a long stream of numbers, but those numbers are each a series of 1s and 0s. Those bits can easily be corrupted in transit: whether zapped by cosmic rays or just corrupted by other electrical interference along the way. If bits are flipped by all this noise, then the music you receive will be corrupted. For some kinds of data, one change could make the message meaningless. We need a way to deal with the problem. Rather than protecting the message as it travels over the network, error-correcting codes allow us to just fix problems when the data arrives.

Instead of thinking about face-up and face-down cards in the trick, now think about binary 1 and 0. The square of cards could just as easily represent 16 **bits** (16 1s or 0s) of computer data. Take 16 bits and organise them in a square and then add the extra bits to make each row and column an even number of 1s. Computer scientists call these extra

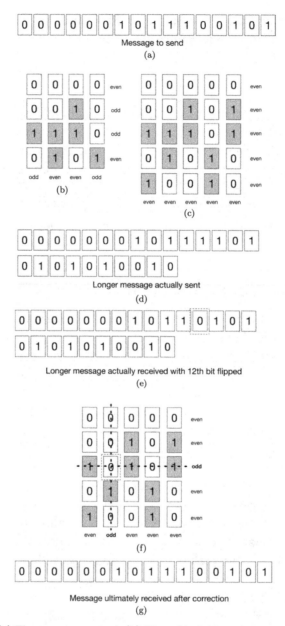

Figure 30.2. (a) The message to send. (b) Those bits laid out in a square. (c) Extra parity bits are added to each row or column. (d) The longer message is sent. (e) A version of that message is received with the 12th bit flipped. (f) The received bits are laid out in a square, and the corrupted bit is identified. (g) The message is ultimately received after the correction.

bits **parity bits**. Now you have a slightly longer message of 25 bits that you can send instead of the original 16.

At the other end, the receiver of those 25 bits can put them into a square and check all the parity bits are correct. If any row or column has odd parity, then a bit was corrupted. If there is one row and one column wrong, then the flipped bit can be determined just as in the trick, and the mistake can just be flipped back (see Figure 30.2).

If more than one bit was flipped, the receiver at least sometimes also knows the data was corrupted and can ask for it to be sent again. If you have more data to send than 16 bits, then you can just split it up into blocks of bits and add the parity bits to each. The receiver checks each in turn. Blocks can also of course be bigger than 16 bits as long as it is a square number. The best size of blocks will depend on how likely it is that bits will be corrupted.

This error-correcting code is a very simple one. There are much more powerful representations that can be used to both detect and correct multiple corrupted bits in data.

Without a variation of the parity trick to help, all digital data transmitted across the Internet, from text messages, websites to emails, or streamed music and films, would be full of errors. Given how integral digital data is now to our lives, it is a pretty important trick.

Interlude: Tim Bell

The "Out-of-Body Experience" trick is a variation of one invented by New Zealand computer scientist, Tim Bell. He pioneered the idea of using conjuring tricks to illustrate complex computer science ideas. He used it, along with other tricks, games and activities, to inspire primary school children about computer science as part of his "CS Unplugged" program. It is the earliest example we are aware of, of a trick being specifically invented to teach computer science, here error-correcting codes.

Part 8

Human–Computer Interaction

We now return to the presentation side of tricks and the importance of understanding people (i.e., cognitive psychology) when developing computer systems. In computing terms, this presentation side is called Human–Computer Interaction or Interaction Design. It is about ensuring programs are usable (usability) and provide a good user experience.

Chapter 31

The four Aces
Usability and Attention

Conjuring

The audience try to keep track of the Aces in a game of cards. The person who clearly held all the Aces turns out to have nothing. Instead, you, the magician, have them all.

Computation

Programmers must make their programs easy to use so that people do not make mistakes using them. Programmers must take our limitations into account. One such limitation is our focus of attention. Programs should actively control our attention to help us both avoid mistakes and recover from mistakes when we do make them.

The Trick

Get a volunteer to the front, and have everyone else gather around the table. Explain that this is a trick about why you should never gamble, and certainly not with magicians or computer scientists. Place the four Aces

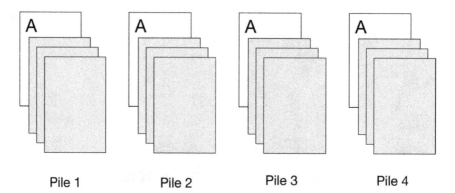

Pile 1   Pile 2   Pile 3   Pile 4

Figure 31.1. The initial position of the four Aces.

from a pack of cards face up onto the table to start four piles. Add three random normal cards face down on top of each Ace showing them to the audience as you do so (see Figure 31.1).

Explain that you have dealt out four hands for the purposes of demonstration. Everyone should imagine that a game had just been played and this was the way the cards fell and that you just happened to notice where the Aces had ended up. In this game, the person with the most Aces wins. That means that anyone who can keep track of where the Aces go will have an advantage and know when to stay in the game and when to drop out, when to gamble big and when not to gamble at all. Everyone should therefore watch where the Aces are at all times.

You turn each Ace face down leaving it at the bottom of its pile and pick up the four piles in order. Point out that if the dealer does not shuffle the cards, then you know exactly where the Aces are and so where they will go on the next deal. They are every fourth card in the pack, so when four new hands are dealt out, all four Aces will land together in the fourth pile. That person will have a winning hand. Start to deal out the cards to illustrate it happening. Count: "1, 2, 3 and an Ace" as you deal the cards face down on the table. On dealing the Ace, stop and, pointing to the Ace with the next card from the deck, ask the volunteer to show the audience it really is an Ace, so all can see that you are definitely right and that person does get the Aces. Have them then leave the Ace face up on the table so everyone can see that that is where the Aces go. Continue to deal the other cards out, counting "1, 2, 3 and an Ace" as you do to emphasise that the Aces end up together in the fourth pile.

Point out that the fourth person (the volunteer) has all the Aces so will win. If this was a gambling game, they would put lots of money on the table. They will keep raising the stakes as long as anyone is willing to match them as they can't lose.

Two hands are then eliminated, perhaps because like us they know where the Aces are, or perhaps they just cannot afford to lose that amount of money. The third hand is yours, so you really ought to drop out too if you had any sense.

In this game, any player still in the game can now swap a card with another player if they wish. The person with all the Aces will pass as it would make their hand worse. You, the magician, do swap a card. Take the face-up Ace from the bottom of the fourth pile and swap it with the bottom card of your pile, turning the other card over to show there is no trickery. Note that you have gained an Ace, but the other hand still wins as it has three Aces left, pointing to the three face-down Aces as you say this. Tell everyone that you really can't win so ought to fold. Instead, you are going to steal those Aces with everyone watching.

Tell them to keep their eyes on the fourth pile. You will make them all look away at just the moment when you steal the Aces. On a count of three, clap your hands in front of the volunteer's face.

Ask if anyone saw you steal the Aces!

Point out that the volunteer definitely had three Aces and a winning hand, but now ... turn the volunteer's pile over ... The Aces are gone. All that money gambled has been lost! So where did the Aces go? Turn over your pile to reveal that you now have all the Aces. You really did steal them without anyone seeing.

That is why you should never gamble, and certainly not with magicians or computer scientists!

How It Works

The secret behind this trick is that you use misdirection, making the whole audience miss something important even though it is there to be seen.

When the volunteer shows the audience the Ace, they are being misdirected. You pointed to that card to take their attention to it, and the volunteer helps keep it there by turning it over and showing that it is an Ace.

So what do you do that they all miss? You use the card that you are holding to point at the Ace. As you stop pointing, you pull that card back to where your other hand with the pack is. You slip that card to the bottom of the pack and slide off the top card in its place. By the time the audience's attention is back to you, unbeknown to them, you are holding a different card. More importantly, as the previous top card is now at the bottom, the next Ace is now only three cards away from the top, not four. That means as you continue to deal the cards, the next Ace will fall on the third pile, not the fourth as everyone expects. The third Ace is still four cards away, so it will also fall on this third pile as will the final Ace. Only the Ace shown to the audience is actually in the fourth pile. The others are placed in the third from the start, but the audience don't know that.

When you later swap the bottom card from the third pile with that of the fourth, you are moving that lone Ace to join the others. Everything from this point on is just performance to disguise what has already happened.

The trick can be made more powerful by combining it with a false choice (Chapter 21). Rather than choosing the two piles to drop out yourself, let the volunteer apparently do so. After making clear the fourth pile with the Aces is theirs, ask them to point to one of the other three. If they point to the third, then you say that that hand will be yours and the other two piles drop out. If they don't, then you say the pile they pointed to drops out. Then, using time misdirection, you talk about other things for a while (like how everyone should drop out if they've tracked the Aces not just the person that has). This is to help people forget exactly what happened. Then, have them point to one of the remaining two piles. Again whichever pile they point to, you ensure the third pile stays and the other pile is removed. This makes it seem far more magical that the Aces end up in that pile, making it seem less likely that the misdirection happened when it did.

The Magical Algorithm

TO PREPARE The Four Aces:

1. Pull out the four Aces and 12 other random cards from a normal pack of cards.

TO DO The Four Aces:

1. Place the 4 Aces face up on the table.
2. Place 3 other random cards face down on top of each.
3. Ask a volunteer to come to the front and stand by the fourth pile.
4. Explain to the audience that the person with the most Aces wins this game.
5. Collect up the four piles of cards, one pile at a time, making a new pack, without shuffling.
6. Note the Aces are every fourth card in this new combined pile.
7. Explain that if you deal the cards now, all the Aces will land together in the fourth pile and that you will now deal out cards to demonstrate this.
8. Deal out the first four cards into four piles saying "1, 2, 3 and an Ace".
9. Pointing to the Ace with the next card, ask the volunteer to turn it over to show everyone it is the Ace.
10. As the volunteer shows the Ace, place the card you were pointing with on the bottom of the pile in your hand.
11. Pull the top card from the pack.
12. Ask the volunteer to leave the Ace face up so everyone can now see that that is where the Aces will land.
13. Carry on dealing out the cards from the first pile while saying "1, 2, 3 and an Ace. 1, 2, 3 and an Ace. 1, 2, 3 and an Ace".
14. Point out that the volunteer has all the Aces so will win.
15. DO the False Choice WITH pile 3 chosen (allowing the volunteer to appear to have a free choice over which of the first three piles stay, but forcing it to be the third).
16. Say the remaining (third) pile is your hand and you should drop out but instead are going to steal the Aces.

17. Introduce the rule that anyone left at this point can swap a card with their opponent. You will, though the volunteer with all the Aces won't as it can only make their hand worse.

18. Turn over the bottom card of the third pile and swap it with the face-up Ace that is in the fourth pile.

19. Note that the volunteer still has more Aces so will still win but should watch those Aces closely as you are now going to make the volunteer blink and steal the cards when they do.

20. Count to three, then clap loudly in front of the volunteer.

21. Ask if anyone saw you steal the Aces.

22. Turn over the fourth pile to show the Aces are gone.

23. Turn over the third pile to show you now have all the Aces.

Thinking Computationally (with Psychology on the Side)

Just like all the other tricks, this one involves a series of steps that must be followed. It has an underlying algorithm. However, it relies on misdirection and some simple sleight of hand too. The audience do not see everything. Presentation matters with all the tricks if they are to feel magical. Here it is key.

The misdirection shows that we have a single focus of attention, and when we focus our attention on an area, we do not see things nearby. Pointing is a very strong social signal, and everyone is curious to check the card is the Ace, so everyone looks at the card. For many in the audience, the magician's hands were not just there to be seen but in their field of view, at least peripherally, at the time. They were looking in the right general direction but still didn't see the card being swapped. Their attention was both moved to the card and also narrowly focussed on it. When our attention is drawn to a point like this, we miss other things even close by.

People make mistakes all the time, and it is not always because they are stupid or negligent. We have limited cognitive resources like one focus of attention. Magic tricks like this show that it is possible to engineer a system so that everyone makes the same attentional mistake at the same time. Magicians engineer the system so we look in the wrong place and miss something important. Good **user interface designers** can use the same understanding of cognitive science to make people look in the right place at the right time. With good design, that takes account of our limitations in the same way that a magician exploits them, designers can help people *avoid* making mistakes or recover when they do.

Programming is not just about writing programs that work. It is also about making them **easy to use**. Computer scientists call designing to make things easier to use, **usability**. Many programmers write programs with themselves in mind rather than the actual users who then find them much harder to use than necessary. After all, the programmer understands deeply how it works. The users do not. Many programs, and features of programs, are so hard to use that they are never used. Making a program easy to use is all about understanding the way our brains work and what their strengths and limitations are.

Good programmers will want to know if people make mistakes with their software and want to fix the problems. When people make mistakes using their software, a good programmer will always ask, "How can I improve it so that no one can possibly make that mistake again. If I can't, then how can I design it so they will always realise they made a mistake and know immediately how to fix the problem."

Some usability problems and the resulting mistakes are just mildly irritating, like closing a program when you meant to minimise it, so having to open it again. Others can lead to a lot of wasted time, like forgetting to save the homework you've spent hours doing. Sometimes the consequences of a mistake are impossible to undo: if you set your alarm clock but didn't realise the volume was muted, so miss an interview, for example. In other situations, the consequences can be about life or death. Hospitals are now full of computer-based gadgets helping cure people or keeping them alive. Someone wrote the program for every gadget. Someone did the **interaction design** (designed the way users use the program), and so made it either easy to use, or conversely, easy to make mistakes with, or most likely they made it somewhere in between. If a nurse accidentally types in a dose that is 10 times too much into an infusion pump, a machine pumping life-saving drugs into a patient, then the mistake could kill them. High doses of otherwise wonderful drugs are often toxic. Avoiding medical error matters.

In all the above cases, different designs can prevent the problems or at least make them far less likely to happen and easier to spot and correct. Word processors can save documents every few keystrokes rather than leaving you to do it. That alarm clock could detect that the volume is muted so know the set alarm will have no effect and ask you to fix the problem before you finish setting it. The infusion pump could know the safe range of doses of each drug and alert the person inputting it that something is wrong.

Thinking about why a nurse might enter the wrong dose without realising leads us back to our trick. There are many possible reasons, but one issue is whether their attention was in the right place. If they are typing in digits on a calculator-style digit keypad, then their attention has to be on their fingers to see what they are doing, not on the screen to see their mistake. When finished, their eye is likely drawn to the start button. Perhaps we can pull the magicians' trick and draw their attention to the screen itself by making it flash so the nurse can check. Even better, we can use a different way of entering numbers that means the nurse's attention stays on the screen as the numbers are entered. One way to do that is to enter numbers using a cursor-based system. For example, you might have two buttons that move a cursor left and right from one digit to the next, and two more to change the value up or down. Once the cursor is in the right place, a person's attention is then no longer on the buttons but on the screen watching the numbers change, where it needs to be.

Controlling people's attention is as important for a programmer as it is for a magician.

Computers solve problems for people. If people are to use the programs developed, then those programs must be designed to be usable. They must be designed to be easy to use, despite the limitations of our brains. Programmers must make sure mistakes are both hard to make and easy to recover from.

Magicians design magic systems so that the whole audience make the same mistake at the same time. Computer scientists must design computer systems so that no one does if their systems are to be usable and safe. They can use the same tricks, the same cognitive psychology, to do so. Rather than directing a person's attention away from things

Figure 31.2. Magic tricks and programs are composed of the same basic components: an underlying algorithm or method and the way it is presented or interaction design.

that matter, designers of software need to use the same understanding of cognitive psychology to direct their attention *to* the things that matter when they matter. Those tricks rely on an understanding of people as well as technology. Both magic tricks and programs have the same two equivalent important parts as shown in Figure 31.2: secret method and presentation ... algorithm and interaction design.

Interlude: Gustav Kuhn

Gustav Kuhn is a psychologist at Goldsmiths, University of London. He investigates the science of magic and has, for example, used eye-tracking technology, which works out where people are looking, to investigate where the audience focus their attention when they watch a magic trick. He found that misdirection is fascinatingly far more complex than just making people look in the wrong place. Our eyes can be looking directly at something, but we can still not be aware of it at all.

Chapter 32

Supernatural Suggestion
Visual Salience

Conjuring

You show five playing cards on the screen and ask everyone to choose the one their eyes settle on. You then show the cards with one removed: the one you think most people will have chosen. When you ask, it turns out EVERYONE chose the removed card.

Computation

What you see depends on where you focus your attention, and where you focus your attention depends partly on how salient the things in the scene are. If you want important things to be seen on a screen, then you have to make them visually salient.

The Trick

You explain that you are going to attempt an experiment in the power of suggestion. Whilst any magician can make one volunteer from the audience choose the card they want, you, by subtle suggestion, will attempt to make as many people in the audience as possible choose the card you want them to. You will try and draw everyone's eyes to the same card. Explain that what you are about to try requires a deep understanding of the way the brain works, of cognitive psychology.

You explain that you will display on the screen a picture containing five playing cards and ask everyone to choose one. They can choose any: perhaps an end one, perhaps the middle, perhaps the ones in between, perhaps to the left and perhaps to the right. They should let their eyes settle on one without too much thought and then stare only at it. It will be their choice. Once they have chosen, they should stand up and remain standing up.

You show the slide with the five cards, reminding them to go with the first one their eyes settle on and stick with it, and then stand up.

When all are standing, you switch to a blank slide and tell everyone they must think about their card and only their card. They must concentrate purely on it. You will then deal out the cards again, but you will have removed one card, the one you were trying to suggest to everyone that they pick. You tell everyone that if they picked the card you have removed, then they should sit down. Note that with five cards you would expect one in five of the audience to sit down if you had no powers of suggestion. Less than that and you would have done the opposite of what you intended. More and your powers of suggestion have worked at least to some extent.

You now show a new slide with the four remaining cards, without the one you were forcing them to choose. Everyone sits down!

How It Works

This is a very simple trick. How it works is that you just replace ALL the cards with a set of four cards that are similar. Everyone's card has gone, so everyone sits down. To make it work, you need to use cards throughout that are very nondescript: so especially no court cards or Aces. Make them all 7s, 8s and 9s of similar red and black suits and swap them for different cards that are also all 7s, 8s and 9s of similar red and black suits. This ensures that the ones not chosen are not very noticeable.

The Magical Algorithm

TO PREPARE Supernatural Suggestion:

1. Create three slides, one with five cards in a line, one with four similar but DIFFERENT cards in a different order. Have a blank slide in between. The cards should be a mixture of 7s, 8s and 9s and a mixture of red and black.

TO DO Supernatural Suggestion:

1. Explain that you are going to use your powers of suggestion to make as many people as possible choose the same card. Talk about the possibilities based on the positions.
2. Show the slide containing pictures of the five cards.
3. Ask everyone to choose a card, the first their eyes settle on, and then concentrate on that card alone, standing up when they have chosen one.
4. When everyone has stood up, replace the slide with a blank one.
5. Explain you are going to remove the card you think most people will have chosen because of your powers of suggestion. If the card you remove is the one they chose, they should sit down.
6. Replace the slide with the one containing the four different cards.
7. Explain, as everyone sits down, that you did more than just control a few people, you controlled everyone and that is the amazing power of suggestion.

Thinking Computationally (with Psychology on the Side)

The story behind this trick is all about how you can make a person's eyes fix on one thing over another. That is what **visual salience** is about, but it just works in a different way than that claimed in the trick. It has nothing to do with suggestions and everything to do with subtle visual cues that draw your eye to some things and not others. Of course, the secret of the trick is a con rather than relying on where your eye is actually drawn to.

The trick does, however, depend in part on a similar thing of people NOT noticing the subtle change from a set of similar cards to different similar cards. It works because some things are more noticeable, more visually salient, than others. That is why we use 7s, 8s and 9s as they are less salient than the court cards and Aces. We want them all not really to be noticed.

Our eyes are drawn to some areas of a scene more than others, and as we have seen, once our attention is focussed, we miss other things completely. So what are our eyes drawn to? Our eyes are, for example, drawn to areas with high-contrast differences. Points in such areas of a scene are visually salient.

This matters when designing interfaces as it can be used by the design team to ensure people's attention is drawn to the right places at the right time. In doing so, the interaction designer can help ensure that users of the interface do not miss important things. Having spent 20 minutes choosing things on a shopping website, the last thing you want is to then not be able to buy them because you can't find a checkout button! That is something your eyes should easily and immediately be drawn to.

PAUSE: Peter W. McOwan

Peter W. McOwan (1962–2019), the co-author of this book before his death, was an amateur magician but a professional computer scientist. His research focussed on biologically inspired computing and specifically understanding the way humans and animals see the world. He and his team, including Milan Verma and Hamit Soyel, created artificial intelligence systems based on our understanding of our vision system. Tools based on his work are now used in a wide range of areas, including marketing, to predict, for example, what our eyes are drawn to in ads. He was also passionate about public engagement in science and a pioneer in using magic to inspire about computer science.

Chapter 33

The Numbers Game
Visibility of System State

Conjuring

A member of the audience calls out 10 random numbers. You write them down, mix them up and spread them out face down, and a volunteer picks one. Somehow, you are able to tell them the number they picked.

Computation

It is really important that the design of a computer system prevents "automation surprises", where a user loses track of the internal state of the system. An important interaction design principle to do this is that of "visibility of system status". This involves ensuring that the important parts of the internal state of a computer system are clearly visible to the user. That means they do not have to mentally track them, reducing the likelihood of such mistakes.

The Trick

Do this as an apparently spontaneous dinner-table trick. Take a piece of blank paper you happen to have in your pocket and tear it up into 16 pieces. Get someone from the table to call out 16 numbers at random that you write on the pieces of paper. Shuffle the pieces of paper so they are thoroughly mixed up. Next, divide them into two piles face down on the table. Ask someone else to point to a pile allowing you to eliminate half of the possibilities leaving only eight pieces of paper. Now spread them out face down on the table and ask a third person to pick one and look at it without telling anyone what it is. Explain that you can tell what it was from the micro-expressions that pass over their face as they look at it. You tell everyone which number you think they have picked. The person shows everyone the one they took. You got it right.

How It Works

What the audience do not realise is that you don't write each number they are calling out, but instead write the first number they said on every piece of paper.

All the numbers on the cards are the same, so of course, you know the number on the card they predict. It is only magical because the audience just assume that you are writing the numbers down as spoken.

For a simpler version, you can skip dividing the paper into two piles. It just gets more people involved and adds an extra layer of confusion over what is happening.

The Magical Algorithm

TO DO The Numbers Game:
1. Tear up a piece of paper into 16 equal pieces.
2. REPEAT 16 TIMES.
   a. Ask the volunteer to call out a number at random.
   b. Write the first number they called out down on one of the pieces of paper.
   c. Place it face down on the table in a pile.

3. Mix up the pieces of paper ensuring they remain face down throughout.
4. Split the pieces of paper into two piles.
5. Ask a second volunteer to choose a pile.
6. Spread out the pieces of paper from that pile, keeping them face down.
7. Ask a third volunteer to choose one piece of paper from the pile and look at it.
8. Announce that, based on their micro-expressions, you can predict which number is written on the piece of paper that they chose.
9. Say the number that you wrote on every piece of paper.
10. Have the volunteer show everyone that you were right.

Thinking Computationally (with Psychology on the Side)

Many card tricks work to some extent because you cannot see exactly what the cards are. This trick is totally about that. If they could see the numbers, it would not be magical at all. Good tricks involve surprises!

All tricks involve the magician engineering a system whereby the audience all make the same mistake at the same time. Part of the mistake normally involves everyone losing track of the hidden things, such as face-down cards or here pieces of paper. In this trick, if the numbers written were all visible so what was on them was clear, then no one would be surprised at all about the result. It is the lack of visibility of the numbers on the pieces of paper that makes it seem magical. When, at the end, the correct number is predicted, you get the sense of delight that you are after.

Interaction designers are after the opposite effect. Rather than wanting users to lose track of the internal state by hiding things, you need to give them enough feedback about the internal state so they do not get confused in a way that matters. Users must be able to track how the system is changing internally so they can make appropriate decisions about what they need to do next.

This leads to a really important interaction design principle concerning the **visibility of the system state**. We do not, in general, want people using our computer systems to be surprised to find the system is in a completely different state to the one they thought. Imagine if this was the case for a pilot flying a plane. As they come into land, they suddenly find they are descending really steeply, so steeply they will hit a hillside, when they thought the plane was set for a shallow angle of descent. When this kind of thing does happen, it is called an **automation surprise**. They are bad because bad things can happen as a result.

The above plane scenario actually happened with tragic results. An A320 passenger plane crashed into a hillside when landing at Strasbourg Airport in 1992. The cause turned out to be that the pilots lost track of what mode the plane's autopilot was in. They entered numbers to control the descent thinking they were entering a shallow angle of descent of 3.3 degrees. In fact, they were telling the plane to descend 3,300 feet every minute. They had no idea until a few seconds before the plane hit the hillside. That is an automation surprise at its worst. 87 people died. Only six survived.

How do you prevent automation surprises? As we use a system, we mentally track what the system is doing and the internal state we think it is in. Automation surprises happen because we lose track so that what we think the state is differs from the actual state. If we make important internal state constantly visible in a clear way, then this mental tracking is less important. Instead, we can just watch the changes as they happen. The Strasbourg plane crash in part happened because the vital information was not visible in a clear way: the mode of the autopilot and the current angle of descent were important but not easily visible. The cockpit design has as a result been changed so that they now are visible. It would have been better for it not to take a crash for it to be improved. Of course, if there is too much information visible, then the information that matters will be lost amongst the rest. A critical part of interaction design is in working out which information is critical for given tasks and finding ways to ensure it is clear at a glance at the time it is needed.

PAUSE: Don Norman and Jakob Nielsen

Much technology is far harder to use than it needs to be. Don Norman and Jakob Nielsen are two of the greatest pioneers of solutions to this problem. Norman introduced the idea of user-centred design with Nielsen introducing the related idea of usability engineering. Both concern making people and their limitations central in the design of computer systems. More than anyone they have promoted the idea that with good design and appropriate engineering methods, software and gadgets can be made far easier to use . . . if only programmers do take people's limitations into account. In Norman's case, his ideas were based on his eclectic background as an electronic engineer and psychologist as well as designer. His book *The Design of Everyday Things* (1988) is probably one of the most influential on the topic and certainly a book all computer scientists should read. Norman and Nielsen have developed practical principles, guidelines, rules, and evaluation methods that help make software more usable if used. They joined together to found a consultancy helping to make technology easier to use.

Chapter 34

The Three-Way False Cut
Conceptual Models and Metaphors

Conjuring

This false cut leaves the whole pack unchanged.

Computation

A way to help make interactive systems easy to use is to give them a clear and simple "conceptual model". The way they work should be obvious. One way to do this is to use a design metaphor: you make the system remind its users of some real-world thing they already know how to use and then have them interact with the computer system in a similar way. On the other hand, if you use a metaphor that does not match the actual design, then the system will be very hard to use.

The Trick

Place the pack on the table (pile 1). Now cut off the top third or so from this pile and place these cards to the right. Call this pile 2. Now cut half of what's left in pile 1 and place this further to the right of pile 2. We'll call this pile 3. All that remains is for you to pause and then reassemble the pack. Place pile 2 onto pile 3 and then take this combined pile and place it on the cards in pile 1 (see Figure 34.1).

To the audience, this looks like a fair series of cuts, but if you try it with a pack, you will discover that the pack is in exactly the same order at the end as it was at the beginning.

The Magical Algorithm

TO DO a Three-Way False Cut:
{ No assumptions}
Let there be three positions on the table, which we will call Position 1, Position 2 and Position 3.

1. Place the pack on the table in Position 1.
2. Cut off approximately the top third to make a second pile in Position 2.
3. Cut half of the remaining first pile in Position 1 to make a third pile in Position 3.
4. Pause.
5. Place the second pile from Position 2 onto the third pile in Position 3.
6. Place the full new third pile from Position 3 onto the first pile in Position 1.

{ The order of the pack is unchanged.}

How It Works

You have just confused the audience. All that takes is to put the piles back together in a different order to the way they were taken apart! They are expecting that a series of cuts is fair. Because we put them back together in a different order to the way the piles were cut, it is easy to lose track of the detail of what is actually being done which is to put each third back on top of the one it started off on top of. The pause in the middle adds a little time misdirection too.

The magician is deliberately projecting an idea of how the world works that is wrong. Everyone who has played cards knows without thinking that if you cut a pack of cards, they end up in a different order.

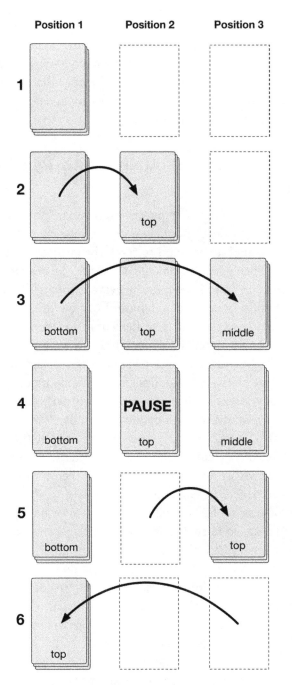

Figure 34.1. The steps of a three-way false cut.

It is a standard way to ensure the cards dealt are unpredictable. Each part of the cut follows the pattern of a real cut. You have removed part of the deck of cards and then put part of the deck on top. By cutting the pack, you set up an expectation, and rather than concentrating on the detail of exactly what is happening, our brain uses this model of the world to predict what will happen.

Thinking Computationally (with Psychology on the Side)

When designing human–computer interaction, we, as in so many situations, need to do the opposite of the magician. Just as with the magic trick, we find it very hard to track the internal state of a program as it changes, even when the change is simple. The design of an interface as presented to us (also known as the **system image**) leads us to create an expectation or a **conceptual model** of how it works. In the trick, the system image presented is of fair cuts. We then do not track the detail, but use this simplified expectation, to work out what we think will happen. If the model we create in our heads (called the **user model**) is not the same as the one the designers actually used, so not how the design actually works (called the **design model**), then we will make mistakes about what the state of the system is.

In this trick, we set up a **system image** so that the viewer creates a **user model** of fair cuts being made. In reality, however, the **design model** is that we are splitting the pack and then putting it back again in the same order, not a different one.

The programmer has a really detailed idea of how the system they are programming works so it is often very hard for them to see how others could be confused. With their detailed knowledge, it is really obvious to them how it works and how tasks are to be done. Their personal user model is the same as the design model and is not created from the system image.

The user interface of the program (projecting the system image) only projects an imperfect version of what is happening. Unlike the programmer, the user only has this to go on. Based on their past experience and what they can see from the interface, a user forms a mental model of how they expect it to work and what they have to do. Those expectations may or may not match the actual system. If it is an accurate version of the system behaviour, then it will help the person use the system with ease. However, if it is not accurate, it leads to misconceptions of what to do when using the system.

For example, if you have seen lots of hand dryers in public toilets that are activated by a large button, then when you see a new hand dryer, you will form a user model that includes the expectation to press a button. If in the place of the button you see something button-like, then this will reinforce that user model. You are likely to press it without thinking. This is likely even if it is actually just a sign in a box saying "DO NOT PRESS: place hands under dryer to activate".

Magicians set up system images of the magical system explicitly so that users form the wrong mental model of what is happening. That is what is happening in this cut. Everyone has seen people cutting packs of cards before, and they know that it is one way to mix up a pack and bring random cards to the top. The first cuts look like that is what is happening, and rebuilding the pack seems to fit what happens with a sequence of fair cuts. The magician's presented system image makes the audience form a user model that the pack is being randomised a little. They do not follow the detail but instead assume they know what is happening.

Programmers and interface designers need to do the opposite. Bad designs work like a trick making the user form a faulty mental model, and good designs help them form a correct one: so hand dryers that are triggered by sensors should have nothing that looks like a button that will reinforce the wrong mental model. Better still they should look completely different and ideally have some very obvious visual clue that you put your hands in the right place. The same considerations apply to interfaces for more complex software.

Design metaphors

One way to help users quickly form the right mental model is to make the controls look like some familiar real-world thing. For example, a paint program might have a set of colours to choose from that look like they are laid out on a painter's pallet. To change colour, the user moves their virtual brush to "dip" it in the paint on the pallet.

This is called a **design metaphor**, and it helps the user understand the way the system works. The actions needed to achieve a task, like choosing a colour, match those in the real world when dipping a paintbrush in paint. The interaction design principle to remember is that if it looks like something familiar, then it should behave like it. If it looks like a painter's pallet, then it should behave like a painter's pallet ... or it will cause confusion.

To take another example, the metaphor of a dustbin is used on many computer desktops so you naturally understand that files you put there are "rubbish" so intended to be deleted. However, they are not deleted immediately. That happens only later when we empty the trash. We have that expectation, and so if that is the way the system works, we naturally understand the right thing to do. There is no actual dustbin in a computer, of course, it is just a metaphor. If instead dropping something in the virtual bin deleted it immediately, then people would likely often make mistakes. That would need a different metaphor to help: a shredder metaphor perhaps. When we shred things, we expect them to be gone for good immediately. It is what we see (the icons), the language used, and the feedback we see that sets up the expectation.

Similarly, in the trick, the magician sets up the metaphor of doing a cut, and so we use that as our conceptual model watching the trick. We use that metaphor to judge what happens. What is done is close enough to our expectations that no alarms are raised. We know what is happening. The design model, what is actually happening, is, however, different. As the magician hopes, our expectations mean that we make a mistake and do not realise the pack is unchanged.

When we design and evaluate computational systems, we don't want people getting confused, so need to ensure we take expectations like this into account. We need to design in a way so that the interface leads to the user's conceptual model matching the design model. We also need to check whether we have succeeded, evaluating the design with real users to ensure that they do understand the metaphor and it sets up the correct expectations.

The magician uses metaphors to confuse us so we miss what is really happening. Good interaction designers use them in the opposite way to help avoid confusion and so make interfaces easy to use.

Interlude: Jay Ose

This false cut is credited to magician Jay Ose (1911–1967). He was amazing at close-up card tricks and was the advisor on various films involving card sharps and con artists, including Steve McQueen's *Cincinnati Kid.* He appeared in a short documentary about the making of the film demonstrating his card-handling skills. He also appeared in other films and TV shows through the 1960s, including an episode of *Mission: Impossible.*

Chapter 35

The Joker in the Pack
Memory

Conjuring

This trick is about finding troublemakers (i.e., jokers) in a classroom and getting them to the front of the class. A volunteer thinks of a number, deals out that many cards, and amazingly they have brought the only joker in the pack to the top.

Computation

No one has a perfect memory. We all forget things, especially short-term things, as our limited working memory can quickly be filled. Forgetting something we know we have to do in the future is a particularly common mistake, especially in stressful situations. Interaction designers need to keep our memory limitations in mind, ensuring the interface only requires us to remember things if they can't be avoided.

The Trick

Tell the audience that teachers must be able to spot troublemakers: the jokers of the class. You will show them a test for prospective teachers to see if they can do the necessary crowd control. The person being tested will use their natural talent at detecting problems before they happen. They will try and find a joker in the pack. A volunteer thinks of a number, say between 2 and 8, and announces what it is. You shuffle the pack and then show them what you want them to do. You count out their chosen number of cards aloud 1, 2, 3, ... from the top of the pack of cards onto the table, face down. When their stated number of cards have been dealt, turn over the last card dealt and point out what it is. Place the cards back on top of the pack and hand the whole pack to them. Take some time to remind them that they are looking for the joker, which stands for a naughty student who is about to cause trouble. They must get them to the front of the class (so the top of the pack), where you can see them before they have a chance to make mischief. While doing this, you shuffle the pack.

They now do as you instructed, counting out the cards, 1, 2, 3, ... up to their number. Before they turn over the top card, take back the rest of the cards that weren't dealt out and spread them face up on the table, pointing out that there are no jokers. Pull out some single cards and say aloud what they are, to emphasise they are not jokers. Remind everyone that you shuffled the pack. Now have them check to see if they found the joker by turning over the top card of the pile they dealt. Amazingly, the card they turn over is the joker!

Despite it being the only one in the pack, they have brought the troublemaker to the front with no trouble at all. They are a natural at crowd control and a natural for the classroom.

How It Works

To make the trick work, before the performance, you simply place a joker on top of a shuffled pack. Each time you shuffle the cards during the trick, you do a fake shuffle that leaves the top cards unchanged while appearing to mix the cards up (e.g., a False Top Overhand Shuffle: see Chapter 18).

When you count the cards onto the table, do it casually so that they think nothing of it: you are just showing them what to do.

The joker starts at the top of the pack. The fake shuffle leaves it there. Suppose the person chooses the number 4, then in your demonstration, you count 4 cards onto the table face down. The joker is now at the bottom of these cards, so in this case, it is the fourth from the top. You place the cards back on the top of the pack so it is now the fourth card in the whole pack. A similar thing happens whatever number is chosen (see Figure 35.1). The fake shuffle again leaves the

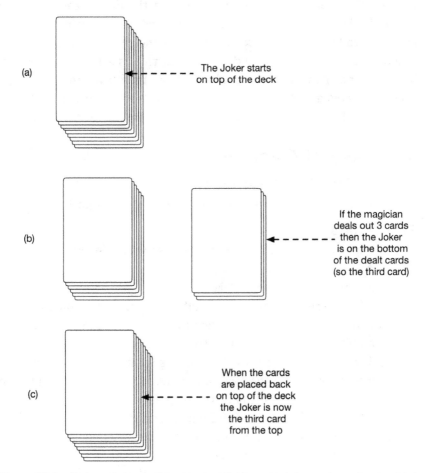

(a)   The Joker starts on top of the deck

(b)   If the magician deals out 3 cards then the Joker is on the bottom of the dealt cards (so the third card)

(c)   When the cards are placed back on top of the deck the Joker is now the third card from the top

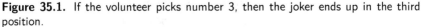

Figure 35.1. If the volunteer picks number 3, then the joker ends up in the third position.

top cards alone, so given they were asked to pick a small number, the shuffle should leave their card in the same position from the top. You hand the pack to them, and they now do exactly as you did. However, now counting four cards out actually brings the fourth card (the joker) back to the top. It is the card they later turn over. Whatever number they choose, they exactly undo what you did.

Your extra patter between you dealing and them dealing and also between them dealing and then finally revealing the joker are important. It takes the audience's attention away from the cards dealt and from the pack. The time delay it causes also helps, as this, combined with all the extra things you are doing, increases the chance that they forget exactly the detail of what you did at the start. This is time misdirection. If you are not confident doing fake shuffles, then leave them out: the trick still works as long as you have time misdirection, it is just slightly less powerful.

The Magical Algorithm

TO PREPARE the Joker in the Pack:

1. Place a joker face down on the top of a shuffled pack.

TO DO the Joker in the Pack:

1. Explain this is a test for whether someone can find troublemakers.
2. Ask a volunteer to pick a small number, between 2 and 8, say and tell everyone what it is.
3. DO a False Top Overhand Shuffle, preserving the top 8 cards.
4. Show the volunteer what they must do by dealing their chosen number of cards onto the table.
5. Turn over the last card dealt saying what it is and noting they are trying to find the joker and bring it to the top then put the dealt cards back on top of the pack face down.
6. DO a False Top Overhand Shuffle, preserving the top 8 cards.
7. Take time talking about keeping troublemakers near you.
8. Give the volunteer the pack.
9. Have them count out their chosen number of cards.
10. Turn over the remaining pack and show that there are no jokers there.

11. Have them turn over the top card of the dealt pack.
12. Point out they brought the joker to the top of a shuffled pack so are a natural at spotting troublemakers.

Thinking Computationally (with Psychology on the Side)

This trick relies on our fallible memory. The audience at the time do not understand the importance of you counting out the cards. Your intention is that by the time they can make sense of what has happened, they have completely forgotten you even did it. This is done by a combination of time misdirection and giving people other things to think about.

As an interface designer, you have to take into account human fallibility, and there are many ways we are fallible and so make mistakes. As we have already seen, we have limited attention. We also have very limited working memory: that is only a small and fixed amount of short-term memory. Many kinds of mistakes that we make are linked to the fallibility of our short-term memory.

Take car lights, for example. It is quite common for drivers to get out of their car having forgotten to turn the lights off. It is easy to end up flattening your car battery as a result of such forgetfulness. Why is this so common? They switched the lights on so knew they were on. They knew they needed to switch them off before leaving the car. Some may even have made the mistake before with bad consequences like a flat battery. Still, they forget. They were relying on their working memory to remember, but in the meantime, there was a long delay while they did all the driving. Driving involves concentrating on lots of other things that fill up working memory. Eventually, they arrived at their destination, so had achieved what they were trying to do, and now had new things to think about: greeting their family or getting on with work, for example. The little step of switching off the lights went out the window!

This kind of human error is called a **prospective memory error**: knowing you have something to do in the future but then forgetting about it when the time comes. In this case, what was forgotten was a tidying up task that could only be done after the person's goal had been achieved. You cannot turn off your headlights until after you have arrived! Ever gone to find something in your bedroom and forgotten to turn the light off when you left? Your goal was to get the thing you were after. Turning off the light is just a tidy-up task. Experiments have shown that that particular kind of prospective memory error happens when a person's working memory is filled. The more short-term things you have to remember the more likely you will make this kind of mistake. No one is immune. Everyone can get it wrong if given too many things to remember, though some people have a bigger capacity than others.

People make this kind of mistake in all sorts of situations, not just with lights, and including using computer systems. Rather than human error, they should be thought of as the fault of the designer of the system. Some simple design changes can make them far less likely, and sometimes impossible. A really simple example is in the design of cashpoints. Cashpoints that give money before returning the card are setting up people to make this kind of mistake. The person's goal is to get money, so retrieving the card becomes a tidy-up task to be done afterwards. If the machine requires the card to be retrieved first, then the person is less likely to forget as it would mean leaving without the money they came for too. Forgetting the money is possible but less likely as it is the reason for using the machine.

In some similar situations, like paying with a card at a supermarket or a garage, the problem can be eliminated if the person only scans the card rather than giving it up. Then there is no longer a possibility at all of forgetting to take it back as it is never handed over in the first place.

There are a range of ways that memory can lead to problems with poor design. Another common source of problems occurs when a person is interrupted in the middle of doing a task. Then, when they try to continue, they are likely to either redo the last step they did (forgetting they did it) or skip a step because they think they did the last step when they only thought about doing it. Interface designers can help avoid such problems by ensuring that in a sequence of steps the interface clearly shows what step the person is actually on.

PAUSE: The Xerox PARC Team

One of the biggest steps forward in making computers easy to use was the Graphical User Interface (GUI). It makes a massive difference for lots of reasons but part of it is because it removes the need for people to remember obscure commands to get things done. Instead of typing commands, they can just click on things they recognise and, e.g., drag them about ("drag and drop"). A big team from Xerox PARC were responsible for creating the first GUI. It included Alan Kay, Larry Tesler (1945–2020), David Smith, Clarence Ellis (1943–2014) and Dan Ingalls. They all made significant contributions and went on to do other amazing things too. For example, Clarence Ellis went on to work on early versions of shared documents that allow lots of people to edit them at once (as is now taken for granted with Google Docs), and David Smith came up with the idea of icons (pictures to click on that run programs) and a way to program robots by demonstrating actions, Larry Tesler had the idea of cut and paste as a way of copying things and later helped improve shopping websites, and Dan Ingalls came up with pop-up menus. Alan Kay, as well as working on the first GUI, also made massive contributions to the design of object-oriented programming languages: where programs are thought of as a collection of objects that send messages to each other, as opposed to being like recipes to be followed.

Chapter 36

Are You Psychic?
User Experience and
Engineering Delight

Conjuring

You test the psychic abilities of a volunteer and show that they have great power. They successfully match pairs of cards that had been mixed up, even though those cards were face down the whole time.

Computation

Ideally, you do not want your software just to be usable, you want the user to have a great experience. To give a good experience, you need to engineer that experience.

The Trick

First, you need two sets of matching cards. You can do it with any cards that can be paired. Zener cards, which you can buy from magic shops, are ideal as they are the cards that scientists have used to test for psychic powers (or at least to prove people aren't psychic). They have different patterns: a circle, a cross, wavy lines, a square and a star. You can, however, do the trick with happy family cards or playing cards if you have two identical packs. We will do the latter here. You also need four "magical tokens". Anything that looks a bit magical will do like gems, toy crystals, tokens or just coins.

Beforehand, take five cards: if using normal cards, an Ace, a King, a Queen, a Jack and a 10, and shuffle them. Then take another set of identical cards and put them in the same order. Place one pile of five cards on top of the other. So, for example, if the first five end up in the order King, 10, Jack, Ace and Queen, then the whole sequence is King, 10, Jack, Ace, Queen, King, 10, Jack, Ace and Queen.

Do a Cyclic False Cut (Chapter 20) by showing a volunteer from the audience the cards face up, fanned out in your hands so they can see there is a mix of different cards. To then mix up the cards, turn the cards face down and allow the volunteer to point to a card. Split the pack at that point, putting the top part to the bottom. Keep doing this until they are happy the cards are mixed. If doing the trick as close-up magic with people gathered around the table, you can have different people touch the cards.

Next deal the top five cards, one at a time, into a pile on the table. Place the remaining undealt cards into a second pile beside them.

Tell the volunteer that, now the cards are mixed up, they must try to end with two cards that match without seeing any of the cards. This will prove whether or not they have psychic or magical powers. Explain that they have four magic tokens to channel their powers. Each will stand for a move. A move involves taking the top card from one of the piles and placing it at the bottom of the same pile. They can put all four tokens on one pile, and none on the other; two on each; or three on one and one on the other. It is their choice, remembering that their aim is to be left with two matching cards. You will do the number of moves on each pile that corresponds to the number of tokens there. The volunteer will therefore be the one deciding what happens by placing the magic tokens on the piles. Once the tokens have been placed, you make that many "moves" on each pile. A "move" just involves moving a card from the top of the pile to the bottom. So if a pile has three tokens placed on it, you move three cards from top to bottom, one at a time (see Figure 36.1).

Next, remove the top card from each pile and place them aside in a pile together. Place one of the magic tokens on top of them to show they are discarded. It does not matter what they are; it is the cards left at the end that must match.

Now there are four cards in each pile. Give the volunteer the three remaining tokens to repeat the process. Once the moves are done, remove the top two cards from the piles again, placing a token on them as before. There are now three cards left in each pile and two tokens. Do it all again, again removing the top card from both piles. This leaves two cards in each pile and a single magic token. This is their final chance to get it right. One move remains, and one card can make all the difference. They choose where to put the token, you make the last move, and the top two cards from each pile are discarded.

Now it's time to reveal the final two single cards left on the table. No one has seen them through the whole process, they were mixed at the start, and the number of cards moved was completely chosen by the volunteer. Ask the volunteer again if they think they have psychic powers. Tell the audience to cheer if the cards do match, but give a loud groan if they don't. Turn one card over, asking if they think the other will be the same, then turn the final card over. They match!

The volunteer chose freely which cards to eliminate, so it was their secret psychic powers that came through to ensure a match at the end.

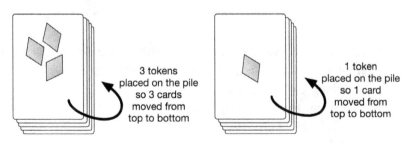

Figure 36.1. Tokens are spread between the two piles. The number of tokens is always one less than the cards in each pile (here five cards, so four tokens). The same number of cards are moved from top to bottom as tokens are placed on a pile.

Give their jaw time to drop, then say that once you have found someone with magical powers, it is worth checking how powerful they are. One pair at a time, dramatically reveal that all the pairs of cards they removed match too!

Point out that they should stop denying their powers, go and buy a superhero costume, and start using their powers for the good of humanity!

The Magical Algorithm

TO PREPARE Are You Psychic?

1. Take the Ace, King, Queen, Jack and 10 of the same suit from two identical packs of cards.
2. Shuffle the five cards from the first pack.
3. Put the five cards from the other pack in the same order.
4. Place one set of five cards on top of the others.
5. Place four "magic tokens" (e.g., gems) on the table.

TO DO Are You Psychic?

1. Spread the cards fanned face up to show that they are a mixture of cards.
2. Ask a volunteer to come to the front.
3. DO THE FOLLOWING UNTIL the volunteer is happy the cards are sufficiently mixed.
   a. DO a Cyclic False Cut.
4. Deal the top five cards onto the table, one at a time.
5. Place the other five cards together in a pile on the table next to them.
6. Explain that the volunteer must, without seeing the cards, use whatever psychic powers they have to try to be left with two matching cards at the end.
7. Give them the four "magic" tokens.
8. DO THE FOLLOWING FOUR TIMES.
   a. Ask the volunteer to place each token on one pile or the other to direct what you do.
   b. Move the number of cards equal to the number of tokens on each pile, one at a time, from top to bottom of that pile.

     c. Remove the top card from each pile and place them aside together with one of the tokens on top.

     d. Give any remaining tokens back to the volunteer.

9. Turn over the two cards that remain to reveal that the volunteer does have psychic powers! Take the applause.

10. Point out that once you have found someone with psychic powers, it is worth seeing how powerful those powers are.

11. DO THE FOLLOWING FOUR TIMES.

     a. Turn over one of the remaining pairs put aside during the trick to show that they match.

12. Suggest the volunteer should stop denying their powers, buy a superhero costume, and start using their powers for the good of humanity!

How It Works

The trick works because of a combination of the starting order, the way the cards are then mixed up, the way they are placed on the table at the start, and then the fact that there is always one less token to place than the number of cards remaining in each pile.

First, the cards start off in a pile with five cards followed by the same five cards. The way the cards are mixed is then via a Cyclic False Cut (see Chapter 20). Each time you cut the pack at the point of their choosing, you are just rotating the order of the cards. At all times, there are still five cards followed by the same five cards as at the start. The sequence just starts with a different card. It is the cyclic order that matters though, and that is unchanged.

Next, you count the first five cards out onto the table. Critically, this reverses their order. The remaining cards are placed straight onto the table. Their order is unchanged. That means the two piles hold the same five cards but in opposite orders.

We finally always have one magic token less than the cards in each pile. It turns out that when the cards are organised as they are (an identical sequence except with the order reversed), how ever you share the tokens between the piles, you will always end up with a pair of matching cards on the top of the piles. That pair of matching cards is the pair that is discarded. We will leave the details of why this happens to the next chapter (see if you can work it out in the meantime). Here, the important point is that on every round, you are actually guaranteed to discard two cards that match. That means the final pair must too, and it allows you to take the audience by surprise with your twist of a final reveal.

Thinking Computationally (with Psychology on the Side)

This trick shows that you can engineer a system in a way that increases the delight that results. It uses a fairly simple principle. Set up an expectation. Meet that expectation. Then go further and do something unexpected (but rewarding).

Here the audience almost certainly expected the final two cards to match. It wouldn't be magic if they didn't. While that is entertaining because it is hard to see how it could have happened, it is not unexpected. However, few will have expected all the cards to match as that seems very unlikely and you did not imply at all that it would happen, so that is a surprise. Given matching two cards by chance seemed unlikely, matching all of them is by comparison astounding and so leads to greater delight.

Just as we can build that idea into the experience of a magic trick, we can build it into the experience of using software. Engineering delight, in this way, is a part of a wider aspect of design and evaluation of software: that of **user experience**. User experience is about provoking the right emotions in your users.

Why does this matter? Well, if, for example, the software is a shopping website, it does if you wish to build customer loyalty. Suppose a disabled person has bought a concert ticket online but finds that they have to change the date. They hope they can do it, though worry they won't, but they assume it won't be easy and expect they will have to pay a charge and will have trouble getting a new disabled access seat. That has been their experience in the past. They go to the website and immediately see a clear way to change tickets. The system has very good usability in that it is easy to use. That is providing a good experience. However, it is also manipulating their emotions. They were worried (an emotion) before in case they couldn't work out how, or that it might be impossible, but now are relieved. Better still, and surprisingly, it tells them it has automatically booked a disabled seat on the new date rather than them having to even mention it. Finally, they find not only is it all easy to do but also are explicitly then told that there is no charge. They are delighted and rave about the ticket site to others, and vow to always use that site in the future.

One of the most powerful ways of delivering delight is to design something that people hadn't realised they needed, but suddenly do so. For the delight to last, it must actually fulfil a need they really did have, though. For example, I bought a soap dispenser on the begging of my then 5-year old who loved the cartoon on the label. After we had bought it, we found out that it wasn't a normal soap dispenser but an interactive one. It giggled every time you pressed the button to get soap. That in itself was delightful the first time. What really delighted me long term though was that we no longer had to nag about handwashing as my 5-year old now actively wanted to wash his hands. It delivered what I expected, but surprisingly, then went much further, and delivered something I needed without realising it.

Finding such needs takes a lot of experience. The important thing, though, is to know the people you are designing for well. You need to understand their **unfulfilled needs**. Rather than having a preconceived idea of what they need, you must understand their lives. For example, if you are tasked to come up with a product for families, then by talking to parents, you might discover that getting kids to wash their hands is a problem. That is the need so becomes the design goal. Design a good solution, and you have a big advantage over competitors, especially if those who buy it are delighted when they realise their tricky problem is solved.

Interlude: Fay Presto

Self-working tricks like this one are often suitable for close-up magic where, rather than the magic taking place on a stage, distant from the audience, it takes place anywhere, including on the street. Spectators gather around and watch from all angles. If spectators are expected to be watching from a distance but instead are allowed close up, it improves their experience of the magic. Involving everyone in a trick is also a way to increase everyone's pleasure in watching it. Fay Presto is credited with starting a revolution in this kind of close-up magic by doing tricks in bars and restaurants, rather than on a theatre stage. She also held a residency in a London brasserie. Her most famous trick, passing a bottle through a table, was voted one of the top 50 tricks of all time.

Part 9

Evaluation and Logical Thinking II

We now look at more advanced logical thinking about tricks and programs including real-world uses of algebra.

Chapter 37

Are You Psychic? (Continued)
Loop Invariants and Inductive Proof

Conjuring

We return to the trick that proves an audience member has superhero powers and prove here it will always work.

Computation

When proving that loops do the correct thing, the idea of a loop invariant provides the basis of logical reasoning: reasoning by induction.

The Trick

Rather than showing you a new trick, we return to the previous one ("Are You Psychic?", Chapter 36) and look at why it always works. The trick is made up of several parts, but the core part is the repeated placing of tokens. Below, we give that key part of the algorithm that we now focus on. The first part of the trick sets up a precondition: on the table are two piles of five cards each, face down, with the same cards in each but in the opposite order. At the end of this part of the algorithm, it guarantees the postcondition that all pairs of cards match.

The Magical Algorithm

{ On the table are two piles of five cards each, face down, with the same cards in each but in the opposite order.}
1. Give the volunteer the four "magic" tokens.
2. DO THE FOLLOWING FOUR TIMES.
   a. Ask the volunteer to place each token on one pile or the other to direct what you do.
   b. Move the number of cards equal to the number of tokens on each pile, one at a time, from top to bottom of that pile.
   c. Remove the top card from each pile and place them aside with one of the tokens on top.
   d. Give any remaining tokens back to the volunteer.

{ Every pair of cards match.}

How It Works

It works because each round of placing tokens, moving cards and discarding the top two as a pair guarantees that the pair discarded matches. We have said this is so but how can we be sure it always works? We need to do some logical thinking. It will be based on something called a **loop invariant** and a form of reasoning mathematicians call **inductive proof**.

Thinking Computationally

Loop invariants provide a way to reason about the correctness of loops. They are properties that must always be true at the same point in the instructions of a loop, usually the start. The property holds every time the loop's instructions are executed and get back to that point. The situation is changed by the instructions in the loop so that the property temporarily ceases to hold, but is then restored so the property becomes true again. We use this property as a way to prove that at the end a related desired property holds. In our trick, that final property is that all pairs match. This property is the one the loop is being used to guarantee. It needs a slightly more complicated loop invariant property to guarantee it.

The idea behind **inductive reasoning** in this context is that if we can prove three things about a loop invariant, then we can be sure the algorithm works. We must prove three assertions:

A. The loop invariant property is true at the start, and
B. IF it is true at the start of the loop body, THEN it will always be true again after following the loop body instructions once, and
C. IF it is true at the end of the loop, THEN this implies that the final postcondition holds so the algorithm works.

This is a kind of proof called mathematical induction, and it is the kind of logical reasoning needed to prove that an algorithm containing repetition always works.

Inductive reasoning works a bit like a paper chain, each link in the chain is identical, just as the loop invariant is always the same. On its own, it does not get you very far, but as you chain lots together, you end up at the other side of the room, where you were trying to get to, which can be any distance away. The first link in the chain is like the property being initially true (assertion A above). This is a bit like pinning the chain to the wall. Add a link by applying the reasoning that it remains true (assertion B) and you know the property is true after one time around the loop, one link further. Apply assertion B again, adding another link and you know it is true after twice around the loop. Keep applying assertion B, adding more links, as many times as needed, and you know it is always true: you span the room! Assertion C just checks that you have arrived with the last link applied at the place you want to be (pinning the chain to the opposite wall!). It shows that the algorithm works and the magic effect has been created.

The loop invariant for our trick

If we are going to use this idea to prove our magic trick always works, we first need to decide what its loop invariant is. What is always true for our trick when we return to the start of the loop? The actual number of cards changes as does the number of tokens, so they are not part of the invariant. However, we know several facts that do stay the same, so can form our loop invariant:

(I)   Both piles contain the same number of cards.
(II) The number of tokens is one less than the number of cards in each pile.
(III) All (so far) discarded pairs of cards match.
(IV) The cards in each pile are identical except for being in the opposite order.

Proving that the loop invariant is true before the loop

The first part of our logical reasoning (proving assertion A) involves showing that this property is true when we first enter the loop. This can easily be seen just by looking at each fact (I)–(IV) in turn.

We started with 10 cards and split them into two equal piles, so each pile contains five cards. That means (I) is true.

We gave the volunteer four tokens. That is one less than the number of cards which we just saw was five cards, so (II) is also true.

There are no discarded pairs at the start, so that means (III) is true automatically.

Fact (IV) is also guaranteed at the start because of the setup and false shuffle. The cards started with five cards in some order followed by the same five cards in the same order. The false cyclic cutting left that property the same throughout. We then dealt the first five cards onto the table one at a time so that the first one ended up at the bottom, the second on top of it, and so on. That reversed their order. Finally, we put the other five cards down without reversing their order. Consequently, as required, fact (IV) is true just before the loop is entered.

All of the separate facts we have included in our invariants (I)–(IV) are set up to be initially true, so our invariant holds at the start, just before we allow the volunteer to place tokens for the first time. The first link in our chain of reasoning is in place.

Proving that the loop invariant remains true

The next step (proving assertion B) is to make sure the way the tokens are placed and the way we move the cards ensures our loop invariant is ultimately left alone (even if temporarily disturbed) by the steps we repeat, even as cards and tokens are discarded. Again let's look at each fact in turn.

At the end of each round, we have discarded one card from each pile, so while they both have less cards, both piles still contain the same number of cards as each other given they did initially. Our first fact (I) is still true.

Is (II) also still true? We have discarded a card from each pile, but we have also discarded a token with it. That means that (II) the number of tokens is still one less than the number of cards in each pile, as long as it was at the start of the loop.

Fact (III) is a little more tricky and is the crux of the trick. It again relies on there always being one less token than cards in each pile. The volunteer has a free choice of placing the tokens, so there are several cases to consider. Let's think about just one case first and then see if we can work out what is going on more generally.

If all the tokens are placed on one pile, then the other pile is left alone. Its top card will be the one that is discarded. The matching card is at the bottom of the other pile. However, as there is one less token than cards and all the other tokens are on the other pile, we will rotate all but the last to the bottom, leaving that bottom card now on the top to be discarded. The two cards that will be discarded match as required.

Now let us instead suppose that all but one token is placed on one pile and the last token on the other pile. From the pile with one card, we will move one card to the bottom and that pile's second card will be discarded. It matches the card second from the bottom of the other pile. However, we have two less tokens than cards on the other pile, so we will cycle all but two cards to the bottom, leaving the second from the bottom one now at the top to be discarded. Again the discarded pair match.

The same reasoning applies in each other case we consider in turn. We move one more place down the first pile, but also one less place down the other, so always arriving at the same two matching cards, because of the reverse order property.

This reasoning follows how ever many cards, and no matter how the tokens are placed. It works as long as there is one less token than cards and the cards remain in reverse order. Our other facts mean both are true. In fact, what we have just presented is actually an informal version of another inductive proof. Perhaps you can spell it out more formally in terms of the three conditions once you have read the rest of the proof.

For (IV), we need to be sure the cards remain in the opposite order to the other pile. First, we know the moves we do, moving a card from top to bottom, keep the cyclic order. All it does is change the starting point in a given sequence so that a different card is at the top and bottom of each pile. Do we leave the same card at the top of one pile and the bottom of the other by the number of moves done though?

This relies on similar reasoning to the above. Again we will consider the case where all tokens are placed on one pile first. One pile is left alone. In the other, the cards are cycled so that the bottom card comes to the top. This means the new bottom card now matches the second card of the other pile. However, we then remove both top cards, leaving the bottom card of one matching the top card of the other, but with otherwise the orders the same, as required. The same happens in each other way the tokens are placed because of similar reasoning to the above as we always cycle the top cards to match.

Overall, we have just shown that if our loop invariant property was true at the start of a round of placing tokens, it will still be true when we next get to the start of a new round of placing tokens.

Proving that the loop invariant being true at the end implies our magic trick works

Finally, we need to prove that at the end of the trick, if the loop invariant holds, then that means our magical effect holds: that all the pairs match. Part of the invariant that we have shown holds throughout is that the pairs discarded so far do match. At the end, we have discarded all but the final pair so those are the only ones left to check. However, as we started with two sets of the same five cards, if all the others match, these last two must be the same as there is nothing else left that they can be. Our invariant guarantees that all the pairs match at the end.

Our chain of reasoning has taken us to the place, the conclusion, that we wanted. We have proved the trick always works. Indeed, our proof does not rely at all on the actual number of cards involved, so the trick will work technically (and the proof applies) whatever the number of cards we start with.

Oddly, a property that stays the same is the key to understanding how doing repetitive computation changes things in ways that make an algorithm always work. To really be able to code with loops and be sure the code is correct, you need to be instinctively doing this kind of reasoning every time you write a loop.

Interlude: Adelaide Herrmann

The false stereotype of the magician is, like that of the computer scientist, male. In both cases, many women have led the field even in the early days of computing and stage magic. Adelaide Herrmann (1853–1932) started out as a magician working with her husband Alexander, though was far more than just the stereotype pretty assistant. Her input was integral to many of the tricks, and she was given equal billing. When her husband died, she continued doing magic shows on her own for another quarter of a century, billed as "The Queen of Magic". She was an active role model who encouraged other women to take up magic. Her biggest, Noah's ark-linked, illusion involved a vast parade of animals magically appearing out of an ark filled with water to represent the flood. She is also famous for doing a very dangerous trick that had been the preserve of men, where she stood in front of a firing squad, catching their bullets on a plate.

Chapter 38

The Red–Black Mind Meld
Abstraction, Algebra and Proof

Conjuring

You meld your mind with that of a volunteer so that you can predict a fact about the way the red and black cards fall unseen.

Computation

Rigorous argument is one way to convince ourselves that a trick or program works, but we can go a step further and use algebra to do this. We describe the trick or program with maths, do some algebra on the resulting "mathematical model" and prove desirable properties hold. This approach is a vital way to check safety-critical software is correct.

The Trick

Ask for a volunteer to take part in the mind meld. Shuffle a full pack of 52 cards using a normal overhand shuffle (Chapter 15). Deal the cards into two equal piles and hand one pile face down to the volunteer, keeping the other. The volunteer should not look at their cards, but you turn your pile face up. Now say you are beginning the mind meld from you to the volunteer. You will control their actions even as they think they are making their own decisions.

Select, at random, some BLACK cards from your pile and place them in a face-up pile in front of you, saying how many BLACK cards you have chosen. Ask the volunteer to select the same number of cards (without looking!) from the top, middle or bottom of their pile. They should do whichever feels right as it will be the mind-meld working! They should place their chosen cards, face down, in a new pile in front of your BLACK pile. Explain this pile will be influenced by your BLACK pile.

Now repeat the process but take a random number of RED cards from your hand and place them in a new face-up pile next to your black pile. Tell the volunteer how many RED cards you have chosen. Again ask the volunteer to blindly select the same number of cards from anywhere in their pack. They should place them in front of your RED pile. Explain that this new pile will be influenced by your RED pile.

Repeat the process, alternating between choosing BLACK cards and choosing RED cards until you have run out of cards. If done correctly, the volunteer will run out of cards at the same time.

There is now, on the table (see Figure 38.1):

- **Pile 1:** A face-up RED pile.
- **Pile 2:** A face-up BLACK pile.
- **Pile 3:** A face-down pile in front of the RED pile containing the same number of face-down cards the volunteer chose while under the mind meld.
- **Pile 4:** A face-down pile in front of the BLACK pile containing the same number of face-down cards the volunteer chose while under the mind meld.

Remind everyone that your mind meld influenced the volunteer's choice of random cards and you can prove it. Even though the pack was shuffled and the volunteer chose cards at random, you used the mind meld to

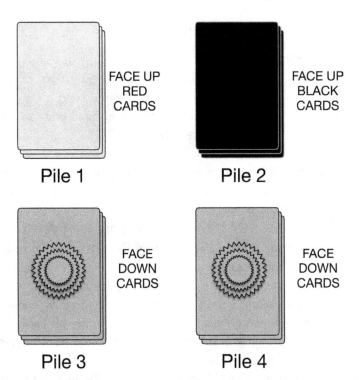

Figure 38.1. The four resulting piles: Piles 1 and 2 face up with each card picked by the magician to be of the right colour; Piles 3 and 4 face-down cards picked by volunteer.

make sure they put exactly the same number of red cards in front of your red pile as they put black cards in front of your black pile.

Ask the volunteer to first take their pile of face-down cards in front of your RED pile and count aloud the number of RED cards in it onto the table. Then ask them to take their face-down cards in front of your BLACK pile, and similarly count aloud the number of BLACK cards.

Through the mind meld, you caused the volunteer to select the same number of RED cards in their RED-influenced pile as BLACK cards in their BLACK-influenced pile. One card out and it wouldn't have worked!

The Magical Algorithm

TO DO the Red–Black Mind Meld:

1. DO an overhand shuffle of a full pack of 52 cards.
2. Ask for a volunteer to take part in a mind meld.
3. Deal the cards into two equal piles and hand one face down to the volunteer, keeping the other.
4. Turn your pile face up.
5. Say you are beginning a mind meld from you to the volunteer. You will control their actions even as they think they are making their own decisions.
6. DO THE FOLLOWING UNTIL there are no cards left.
   a. Select, at random, either some BLACK cards or some RED cards from your pile.
   b. Place them in one of two face-up piles in front of you, based on the colour, saying how many cards you have chosen.
   c. The volunteer selects the same number of cards without looking at the actual cards, taking them from anywhere in their pile.
   d. They place their chosen cards in a pile in front of the pile where you placed yours.
7. Remind everyone that your mind meld influenced the volunteer's choice of random cards and you can prove it. The pack was shuffled, and the volunteer chose cards at random, but your mind meld meant they put the same number of red cards in front of your red pile as they put black cards in front of your black pile.
8. The volunteer counts the number of RED cards in the pile in front of your red pile.
9. The volunteer counts the number of BLACK cards in the pile in front of your black pile.
10. You note that as predicted they are the same number.

How It Works

Of course, it's not mind melding. It's just computation and mathematics. The trick is self-working. As usual, if you follow the steps, it is bound to work because of the mathematics behind the steps the volunteer performed. We can even prove it . . .

Thinking Computationally

So how can we be sure that this trick always works? Rather than doing it lots of times (testing) or just using informal but logical reasoning, we are going to use algebra.

The first step is to create a **mathematical model** of the trick. By that we just mean describe it mathematically. Doing so involves **abstraction**: focussing only on the information about it that matters while ignoring anything that doesn't. A mathematical model is just an abstraction of a part of the world we are interested in. This trick is about the numbers of red and black cards. The actual values and suits of the cards do not matter at all. We can ignore that (abstract away those details) and just focus on the count of each colour that ends up in each pile.

We, of course, have no idea how many reds or blacks ended up in any of the piles as the pack was shuffled. We can't actually put numbers to anything, apart from the fact that there are no black cards in the face-up red pile and no red cards in the face-up black pile at the end. Instead, we just give a name to the unknown numbers of red and black cards in each pile. Then we refer to those numbers by name and do not worry at all about the actual values. Those values, the number of cards in each pile, will be different every time we do the trick. A mathematician calls these names, **variables**, though the word here means something slightly different to the kind of variables programmers talk about, it is a similar idea of giving values names.

First, we give names to the number of red and black cards in each of the four piles. First, consider Pile 1 (your face-up RED pile). We will call the number of red cards there, **RED1**, and the number of blacks there, **BLACK1**. The number of red and black cards in Pile 2 (your face-up BLACK pile) will be called **RED2** and **BLACK2**, respectively. Similarly, we will say that the face-down Pile 3 contains **RED3** reds and **BLACK3** blacks. The face-down Pile 4 contains **RED4** reds and **BLACK4** blacks (see Figure 38.2).

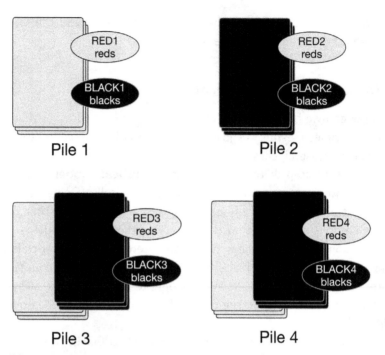

Figure 38.2. The four resulting piles with names given to the number of red cards and number of black cards in each.

Logical thinking: The facts

The next task is to use logical reasoning to work out what facts we actually know and turn them into mathematical equations about the trick.

The first thing we know is that there are no black cards in Pile 1 as you only put red ones there. There are also no red cards in Pile 2 as you only put black cards there. That gives us two facts.

Fact 1:   BLACK1 = 0

Fact 2:   RED2 = 0

Now, we also know that a full pack of 52 cards was used. It contains 26 RED cards and 26 BLACK cards. If you add up the red cards in the four piles, it will come to 26. We can write that as an equation using the names RED1, RED2, RED3 and RED4 for the different sets of red cards in each pile as in Figure 38.2. We can do the same thing for the black cards. We have to use the names here because we don't know the actual numbers.

Fact 3: RED1 + RED2 + RED3 + RED4 = 26

Fact 4: BLACK1 + BLACK2 + BLACK3 + BLACK4 = 26

We can, of course, make use of our first two facts, which do tell us two of the numbers, to simplify Facts 3 and 4. Facts 1 and 2 say we can replace RED2 with 0 and we can replace BLACK1 with 0 as they are the same.

This gives new facts:

Fact 5: RED1 + RED3 + RED4 = 26

Fact 6: BLACK2 + BLACK3 + BLACK4 = 26

We also know something else about the numbers. Whenever we put some number of cards in the red pile, we put exactly the same number of cards in the face-down pile in front of it. That means that the two piles always have exactly the same number of cards, though we have no idea what that number is and it is different each time. We can again turn this into a fact based on the names we have given each number though. The number of cards in the RED Pile 1 (RED1) is the same as the number of face-down cards placed in front of it in Pile 3. Pile 3 is made up of RED3 red cards and BLACK3 black cards. That means that together RED3 and BLACK3 must add up to RED1.

Fact 7: RED1 = RED3 + BLACK3

By a similar argument, we get a fact about the cards in Piles 2 and 4.

Fact 8: BLACK2 = RED4 + BLACK4

Logical thinking: Some rigorous reasoning

The last four facts sum up everything important we know about the cards. They are a mathematical model of the trick.

Just as we did with the first two facts substituting BLACK1 for 0 and RED2 for 0, we can now do a similar bit of logical reasoning substituting for the things we know about RED1 and BLACK2 from Facts 7 and 8.

We replace RED1 in Fact 5 with RED3 + BLACK3 as they are the same value. In the same way, we replace BLACK2 with RED4 + BLACK4 in Fact 6. Our new versions of those facts are:

Fact 9:   (RED3 + BLACK3) + RED3 + RED4 = 26

Fact 10:   (RED4 + BLACK4) + BLACK3 + BLACK4 = 26

Now we have two different things that we know equal 26 so the left-hand sides of both those equal signs equal each other. Combining Facts 9 and 10, we get

Fact 11:   RED3 + BLACK3 + RED3 + RED4

　　　　　= RED4 + BLACK4 + BLACK3 + BLACK4

Things seem to just be getting more and more complicated, but we can now start to simplify things. There is a RED4 on both sides of this equation so they cancel. Put it another way if we subtract RED4 from both sides (so keeping both sides equal still), we get

Fact 12:   RED3 + BLACK3 + RED3

　　　　　= BLACK4 + BLACK3 + BLACK4

Similarly, BLACK3 appears on both sides so can be cancelled.

Fact 13:   RED3 + RED3 = BLACK4 + BLACK4

We have two lots of RED3 on one side and two lots of BLACK4 on the other. That can be written

Fact 14:   2 × RED3 = 2 × BLACK4

Then finally, dividing both sides by two, we get a really simple fact that is guaranteed to be true as it followed mathematically from our original facts.

Fact 15:   RED3 = BLACK4

This tells us that the number RED3 will *always* be the same as the number BLACK4 at the end of the trick.

Back to the real world

Now that is all well and good, but what does it mean? We have to return from our mathematical world of variables to the real world of piles of cards. What do those variables actually represent? RED3 and BLACK4 were actually just names that stood for numbers of cards of particular colours in the face-down piles. RED3 is the number of red cards in the red-influenced pile, Pile 3. BLACK4 is the number of face-down black cards in the black-influenced pile, Pile 4.

The algebra has shown that the number of red cards in Pile 3 is guaranteed to be the same as the number of black cards in Pile 4 at the end of the trick. That is exactly what we predict in the trick ... because it is guaranteed to be true by the algorithm we followed.

Verifying programs

If we can prove that a magic trick always works, then we can prove that a program does too in a similar way. We use abstraction to create a mathematical model of what the program does. We then use algebra to prove properties about the model. Those properties tell us facts about what the program does in the real world. This is called **program verification**. For example, we might prove that if the program controlling a medical device was set to deliver a fixed number of milligrams of a drug over a fixed number of hours, then that is what it always does, whatever the actual numbers involved.

When lives depend on a program always working, it is no good that we tested the program and decided we were 99% sure it won't kill anyone, especially if it is used by millions. Proofs can tell us that a program always works (as well as showing that our tricks do).

PAUSE: Shafi Goldwasser

Shafi Goldwasser's work is about using maths and proof to make computers more secure and private. She studies problems that are so hard that computers would take billions and billions of years to solve them. These are the kinds of problems that the encryption used to secure computer systems is built around. Along with Silvio Micali and Charles Rackoff, she came up with the idea of zero-knowledge proofs. These are a kind of proof that at first sight seems impossible: something that would take actual magic to achieve. The idea is for one person (or computer) to prove that they know some secret information while actually keeping that information a secret. They do not give up the secret even to the person (or computer) they prove they know it too. It is like having a password that lets you into a computer, but without you actually having to type the password. You prove you know it without ever actually revealing it even to the computer doing the checking.

Part 10

More on Computational Thinking

Computational Thinking is a collection of separate skills that we have seen throughout the book including decomposition, abstraction, generalisation, choosing good representations and logical thinking. In this section, we look at some more advanced computational thinking approaches based on them.

Chapter 39

The Doomsday Clock
Generalisation

Conjuring

The Doomsday Clock predicts the most important hour in your future. Even with a free choice to start, its hour hand ends on a predicted hour.

Computation

By abstracting away detail until we get to the very core of a trick, or algorithm, so its most general version, we can then build it back up into new tricks or algorithms.

The Trick

Before you start this trick, you need to create a big clock face with numbers from 1 to 12. Make a single movable hour hand for the clock, drawing a fixed minute hand pointing to 12 (see Figure 39.1). You also need to draw a second smaller version of the clock on a piece of paper with only the number 1 at the 1 o'clock position, and with a fixed hour hand pointing at the 1 (see Figure 39.2). This is your prediction. Place

Figure 39.1. The Doomsday Clock. The minute hand is fixed. The hour hand moves.

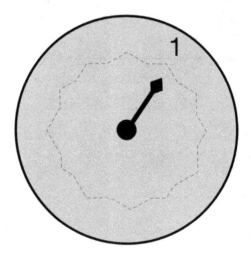

Figure 39.2. Your prediction for the time the Doomsday Clock will stop.

it in an envelope, fastened to the back of the clock. Place the hand of the big clock on 12, and you are ready to start the trick.

Explain that you have made a Doomsday Clock: a clock that can predict the hour that will be most important to someone in the future.

It may be the hour they will get married, their first baby is born, or perhaps the hour they will die. Who knows? What is for sure it will be an hour in the future that will be really important to that person's life.

First, ask for a volunteer. Explain that you will use the clock to find the hour in their future that will be most important to them personally. It will take only a few turns of the hour hand until the hour hand passes 12 once more. Ask them to choose a number from 1 to 12. Write it down as a word (so if they choose 2, write T-W-O). Have them then move the hand of the clock one place round the clock for each letter in their chosen word. If they choose TWO, for example, then they move T-W-O so three places on. Tell them they will be using the words of numbers like this to jump the hand forwards three times. They are now at a new position on the clock and at a new number. This gives a new word to use to count further. They do the same again with that word. They then do it again a final time at the new hour they land on, and then stop the clock at that point.

At whatever place they end up, announce that their personal clock stopped at that time. Point out it was their free choice of the original number. Now, explain that, to show the power of the clock you already used it to do the prediction for them. Turn the clock over revealing the envelope with your prediction. Ask them to open the envelope and read the prediction of their doomsday hour. Amazingly, it is the same as on their clock. That is the power of the Doomsday Clock!

The Magical Algorithm

TO PREPARE The Doomsday Clock:

1. Create a clock face with numbers 1 to 12 for the hours and a single movable hour hand and fixed minute hand pointing to 12.
2. Set the clock's hour hand to 12.
3. Create a clock face with a fixed hour hand pointing to the hour 1 as a prediction.
4. Place the prediction in an envelope fastened to the back of the clock face.

TO DO the Doomsday Clock:

1. A volunteer chooses a number between 1 and 12: one of the hours of the day.
2. Write it down as a word.
3. DO THE FOLLOWING THREE TIMES.
   a. The volunteer moves the hand on one hour, clockwise round the clock, for each letter in the current word.
   b. Write down as a word the hour that the clock hand ends on.
4. Announce the final hour that the clock ends on.
5. The volunteer opens the envelope to reveal your prediction.

How It Works

This trick is based on the same property to do with the randomness of the length of words from the Wizardly Book Magic trick of Chapter 6. It means in this case that in three steps all 12 numbers you can choose take you to the same place. The length of words does not actually vary very much. The words in the clock all have lengths between 3 and 6 letters (see Figure 39.3). As it is the length of the word we use rather than the word itself, that means the original 12 numbers to freely choose from actually only give four possibilities: lengths of 3, 4, 5 or 6.

Since we always start at 12, after counting out the first word, there are only four possible places we could be at after the first step: the hours 3 to 6 (see Figure 39.4). Now the length of THREE is 5, but the length

WORD	ONE	TWO	THREE	FOUR	FIVE	SIX
LENGTH	3	3	5	4	4	3

WORD	SEVEN	EIGHT	NINE	TEN	ELEVEN	TWELVE
LENGTH	5	5	4	3	6	6

Figure 39.3. The lengths of words corresponding to numbers on the clock face.

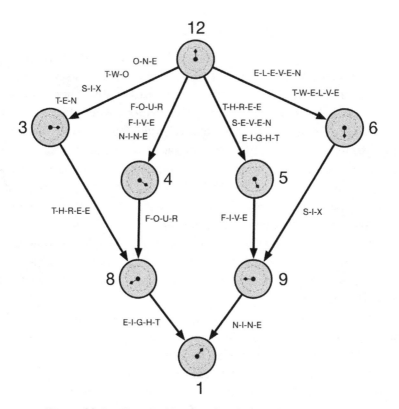

Figure 39.4. The possible ways the clock might change.

of FOUR one place after it is only 4, so they will both count you to the same next place: hour 8. The lengths of FIVE and SIX have the same pattern, and both take you to the position of hour 9. There are now, after 2 steps, only two places you could be. Those positions, 8 and 9, have the same pattern of length, as the previous ones, with the second being one less letter in length than the first. They therefore both jump to the same place: 1. So after only three steps, all options have surprisingly led to the same place. That is your prediction.

Rather than telling the volunteer to stop on the third step, you could alternatively say they will stop when they have passed 12 once more as this is equivalent.

Thinking Computationally

Once you understand the basic principle of a trick, you can reuse that principle as the basis of different tricks. This trick uses exactly the same principle as Wizardly Book Magic (Chapter 6). Rather than using words in a book, here we are just using the words for the numbers on a clock.

If you have invented a trick like Wizardly Book Magic, then strip it down to its core principle (abstracting away the details), and you have a generalised version of the algorithm. You can then build a new trick by providing a new context. Figure 39.5 gives a generalised version of our two variations of this trick. It is just a description of the mathematical principle behind the trick as an algorithm.

Programmers use generalisation like this a lot. Rather than writing code or creating an algorithm just for one specific purpose, once we have solved a problem in a new way, we generalise it so it can be used in lots of situations.

If we have written code to search for names in an alphabetically ordered list of names (e.g., in an online telephone directory), we might generalise it so that it can also be used to search for other text that is ordered alphabetically. We might generalise it further, modifying the code so that it can be used to search for other data ordered in some way (e.g., numbers in numeric order). The increasingly generalised versions have a wider use and are more abstract versions of the original concrete code. They all are based on the same underlying mathematical principle just as in our trick.

1. A volunteer chooses a starting point in some sequence of words.
2. DO THE FOLLOWING UNTIL you get beyond a preset point, after the point that all paths meet:
   a. Count the letters in the word.
   b. Move on that many words.
3. Announce the final word that the volunteer lands on.
4. Reveal a prediction of the word they ended up on.

Figure 39.5. A generalised version of the Doomsday Clock and Wizardly Book Magic.

PAUSE: John von Neumann

To computer scientists, John von Neumann (1903–1957), one of the founders of computer science, is most famous for his paper describing the basic structure of a computer. That structure is now known as the von Neumann architecture, and most modern computers follow the design. It describes a computer as split into a processing unit to do calculation and a control unit that controls which instructions are executed. Data and programs are stored in the same computer memory. It was actually based on the ideas of J. Presper Eckert and John Mauchly for their ENIAC computer. Von Neumann's contributions to the subject were very wide and included, with Herman Goldstine, the suggestion of using assertions to indicate properties that hold at a point in a program. He was a Physicist and Mathematician working on the Manhattan Project to develop the first nuclear bomb. He also came up with the idea of mutually assured destruction, arguing nuclear weapons would never be used in a war if both sides knew everyone would die if they were.

Chapter 40

free My Three
Divide and Conquer

Conjuring

Three cards of a kind chosen by a volunteer are lost in a pack. After repeatedly discarding cards with no sign of the chosen ones, they are eventually revealed as the last cards left.

Computation

Decomposition involves breaking a problem into smaller problems that are easier to solve. Divide and conquer is a powerful version of this where these smaller problems are the same problem as the original (just smaller). Those smaller problems are solved in the same way. This gives a way to create very fast algorithms.

The Trick

For this, you need a full, shuffled deck of 52 cards. Ask a volunteer to find and remove three cards that are three of a kind, such as three of the queens. Have them show the audience, but not you. Everyone must remember those three cards.

Take the pack back, without those cards, give them a shuffle and then casually make three piles. The piles must contain 10, 15 and 15 cards. It's fairly easy to push off blocks of three cards at a time. The first pile, with 10 cards is three blocks of three with one extra. The 15-card piles are simply five blocks of three. You will be left with nine cards in your hand (but your audience won't know that as it looks like you have just built three random piles. Pop these left-over nine cards to the side for the moment.

The three selected cards are put onto the three "random" piles and "lost", but in a special way (see Figure 40.1). The first card goes onto the 10 pile. Next, ask a spectator to cut off a chunk of cards from the adjacent pile, the 15 pile, and pop them on top of the chosen card burying it.

The next chosen card goes on top of the pile they have just cut the cards off. Again, once they place the chosen card on top, they bury it by placing a chunk of cards from the remaining 15-card pile onto it.

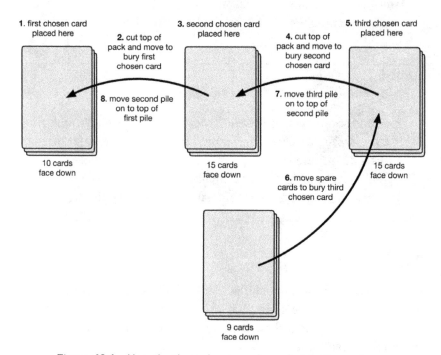

Figure 40.1. How the three chosen cards are lost in the pack.

The final chosen card is placed onto that last pile, and you then drop the nine-card pile on top.

Next, assemble the deck, starting with that last pile you put the nine cards onto. Put this pile on top of the pile next to it and then put this bigger pile on top of the remaining pile. Square the cards.

Now, remind the audience what has happened: you made three random piles, and each of the chosen cards was put into a pile and buried under a random stack of cards from another pile, so no one has any idea where any of the chosen cards are... But you are now going to try to find them and free them from the pack.

You deal the cards into two piles. Start by dealing two piles of two cards each face down, by alternating left, right, left and right. Then stop and say that actually you should make the trick more dangerous by dealing with one of the piles face up. Collect the four face-down cards from the table and put them at the bottom of the pack. What you have just done in this tester deal is shifted four cards from the top to the bottom of the pack, but also built up the tension.

Start again by dealing a card face up. Then, deal the next face down, telling your audience that the trick ends if any of the three selected cards goes in the face-up pile. Deal through the whole deck like this. No chosen cards will be seen.

Put the face-up pile aside, take the face-down pile, and deal it again: first card face up, next face down and so on. Again no chosen card will be seen. Repeat this procedure, dealing the first card face up each time, until the face-down pile contains only three cards. Ask for the names of the three chosen cards. On turning the last three cards over, the three selections are found!

The Magical Algorithm

TO DO Free My Three:
1. DO set up the deck.
2. DO the teaser deal.
3. DO the deal.

TO DO set up the deck:

1. A volunteer finds and removes three matching cards from a shuffled pack.
2. They show them to the audience.
3. DO an overhand shuffle of the remaining cards.
4. Place those remaining cards into piles of 9 cards, 15 cards and 15 cards, face down.
5. Set the remaining cards to one side.
6. The volunteer places one of their three cards onto the first pile of nine cards.
7. The volunteer cuts the top of the next pile and places those cards on top of the chosen card.
8. The volunteer places the second of the three cards on top of the middle pile.
9. The volunteer cuts the top of the last pile and places those cards on top of that second chosen card.
10. The volunteer places their final card on top of the last pile.
11. You place the final pile of cards you placed to one side on top of that card.
12. Place the third pile on top of the second to create a larger second pile.
13. Place this larger second pile on top of the first to create a new full deck of cards.

TO DO the teaser deal:

1. Deal out four cards into two piles face down.
2. Say "Actually let's make this more dangerous. Let's have one pile face up."
3. Collect up the four cards dealt and place them at the bottom of the deck.

TO DO the deal:

1. DO THE FOLLOWING 4 TIMES.
   a. Pick up the remaining cards.
   b. DO THE FOLLOWING UNTIL there are no cards left.
      i. Deal a card face up.
      ii. Deal a card face down.
   c. Discard the face-up cards.

2. Turn over the three remaining face-down cards to reveal the originally chosen cards.

How It Works

You started with four piles of 10, 15, 15 and 9. The first card went into position 11. Then some of the next 15 cards were added on top. This appeared to add some randomness, but actually did nothing important as the remaining cards were later just put back on top of them. That meant there were actually exactly 15 cards separating the first secret card from the next secret card, as it was added to the top of the second pile. This was done again with the next pile meaning another 15 cards separated the second and third secret cards and finally, another nine were placed on top.

At this point, the secret cards, apparently buried randomly, are at known positions from the top: positions 10, 26 and 42. However, in the false start, we actually move the top four cards from top to bottom. This shifts everything up four positions. So when you start the actual deal, the secret cards are at positions 6, 22 and 38 from the top.

That whole palaver was actually a way to take a shuffled pack of cards, but leave the three secret cards at those fixed positions while making the audience think they had been buried randomly.

Why those positions? Well, each deal actually filters out every second card. However, it also reverses the order. It turns out that if you do that repeatedly you will end up with exactly the cards that started in positions 6, 22 and 38. We can see how by working through what happens...

We start with cards as the following where we just note their initial positions:

1, 2, 3, 4, ... , 50, 51, 52.

In the first deal, we start by placing a face-up card, and as we ultimately throw away the face-up cards, we throw away every second card starting with card 1. That means we lose all the odd-positioned cards. We also reverse the order as we do so leaving a new pile:

52, 50, 48, 46, ... , 8, 6, 4, 2.

We do this again, so again take out the current first, third, fifth, etc. cards. This leaves, once reversed, the cards originally in positions:

2, 6, 10, 14, 18, 22, 26, 30, 34, 38, 42, 46, 50.

Another round of the deal takes out every second card and reverses again, leaving:

46, 38, 30, 22, 14, 6.

Finally, taking out every second card one last time leaves us with the cards that were originally in positions:

6, 22 and 38.

Those are exactly the positions we made sure the secret cards were at before the deal started, ensuring the trick was guaranteed to work.

Thinking Computationally

The core of this trick involves the final series of deals, where we repeatedly strip out every second card. This process guarantees we end up with the given three cards. If we went a step further, we would guarantee to have a single card. This magic algorithm is linked to an important decomposition principle called divide and conquer. It is used to create fast algorithms.

You can think about the trick as being an algorithm to find those selected cards. Put that another way, it is about how to discard all the cards aside from the selected ones.

We do that by discarding half the cards on each pass. It only takes four passes to get down to the three secret cards. There is another interesting feature of the way this is done. At the start, you are holding a pack of cards and want to be left with the secret cards. Having done one deal and thrown away half the cards, you are in the same situation: you are holding a pack of cards and want to be left with the secret cards, so you do exactly the same thing again. That leaves you in the same position... so you do the same thing again. Only the number of cards in the pack changes each time: the pack so the problem gets smaller.

This is a special way of decomposing a problem. It has been decomposed into a smaller, simpler version of the *same* problem, not just created a smaller but different problem. Because it is the same problem, we can decompose it again in exactly the same way, and keep doing that until it is a trivially simple version of that original problem. In the trick, that trivial version is we want to find three cards and are holding a pack of three cards (trivial!). This process is called **recursion**. It is actually, computationally, just a version of **repetition**, as it involves repeating the same computation over and over. This is the basis of **recursive problem solving**: finding a way to solve a problem by decomposing it into a smaller version of itself.

Divide and conquer problem solving

Recursive problem solving leads to an even more important decomposition idea called **divide and conquer problem solving**. Rather than finding a slightly smaller version of the problem, this involves finding a way to break a problem into identical problems that are a fraction of the original size. This might involve turning it into one smaller problem that is a fraction of the original size, or two similar problems that are half the size, or three versions that are a third of the size, and so on. As the problem is the same, just massively smaller, we can keep solving the new problems generated in the same way.

Divide and conquer problem solving is a very general way of devising very fast algorithms.

What is happening here is similar. On each pass, we get rid of not just a few cards but half the cards. Each pass leaves us with a single version of the equivalent problem that is half the size by discarding half the cards. We very quickly (in terms of the number of deals of the remaining deck at least) are down to the three cards we are looking for.

This trick doesn't in itself really show off the power of divide and conquer, because we actually spend a lot of time splitting off each card. A variation of the algorithm is in fact the basis of a true divide and conquer algorithm though, where every second card is removed in one go. It was used by early computers to process punch cards: an early way of storing data.

To see the real power of divide and conquer, take a pack of shuffled cards and put them back in order. How? There are lots of different ways (i.e., algorithms) to do it. One way, e.g., is to first scan down the pack looking for the first card (the Ace of Hearts), then scan down it looking for the next (the two of Hearts), and so on. This is very slow. You scan down the remaining pack, on average looking halfway for each card, 51 times. You will likely check individual cards over 1,000 times.

Another way is to start by running through the pack, putting the cards into piles (like in the trick) but one pile for each suit of Hearts, Spades, Clubs and Diamonds. That takes a single scan. We are now left with four versions of the same problem each a quarter of the size. We have the start of a divide and conquer approach! To make it work though, we must be able to do the same again. We must run through each pile in turn and split them into four piles too, each leaving a problem of sorting them. That's easy: a pile for Ace to 3, a pile for 4 to 7, a pile for 8 to 10, and a pile for the court cards. Each has three or four cards. Now taking one of those piles, we do the same again, with three or four piles, smallest to largest again, but this time we end up with piles of a single card. That is trivial to sort! A pile of one card is already sorted. Now we put those four cards on top of each other in the order of the piles and now have those four cards sorted. We move back to the next pile of four and sort it in the same way. It can be placed on top of the first, and so on. Eventually, we have sorted all the Hearts. So we move on to the Spades and do exactly the same, and so on for each suit.

We sorted each pile using the same general divide and conquer method. Split it into four piles and sort them the same way. Once sorted, pile them back up to give a bigger sorted pile. Get a pack of cards and try it.

It probably still sounded slow, but it is actually much faster because rather than working through all the cards lots of times, we have broken them into smaller and smaller piles. The key is that we get down to a single card in only three steps. This essentially means that instead of scanning the whole pack 51 times, we only do so three times: once to split them into suits, once to split them into groups of four, and once to split them into single cards. It is therefore massively faster and involves scanning cards only a few hundred times instead of over a thousand.

Radix sorting

Imagine, now, you have not 52 cards but 5,000 cards (or perhaps, to face a problem I have repeatedly faced in the past, they are exam scripts that need sorting). Each has a four-digit number on it, like 1,234, and you need them to be sorted in order of that number. We can use exactly the same idea but use the different digits to organise each scan. On the first scan, put cards into 10 piles based on the highest (thousands) digit. Next, we take one of those piles and split them based on the hundreds digit. Then do the same on each pile for the tens digit and finally for the units. At that point, we have piles of one script, with the piles in order so we just pile them on top of each other. We then move on to the next pile and so on. This is called **radix sorting**. It is just one of many divide and conquer solutions to the problem of sorting data into order.

Interlude: Alex Elmsley

"Free My Three" is a variation of a famous effect invented by magician Alex Elmsley (1929–2006). He was a graduate of Cambridge University where he studied Mathematics and Physics, before going on to work as a patent agent and then computer programmer. There are very many variations built on the underlying mechanism: see Chapter 49 for another variation of this effect. He also invented a series of other card tricks and wrote about the mathematics underpinning shuffling cards.

Chapter 41

The Double-Destination Deception
Data Representation — Graphs and Cycles

Conjuring

An audience member constructs a trip-of-a-lifetime flight itinerary that crisscrosses the world. They plan it by making a line of tickets. Despite their freedom to choose any itinerary, once completed, you reveal you bought a ticket in advance. Remarkably, it takes them back to their chosen start destination from the place they ended up.

Computation

Graphs are an important data representation used to store and manipulate data when the links between different pieces of data matter. They are also the basis of logical reasoning about whether it is possible to write an algorithm to do certain tasks.

The Trick

Before doing the trick, you need to create a series of tickets. There are two kinds of tickets: flights and hotels. Flight tickets show the start and

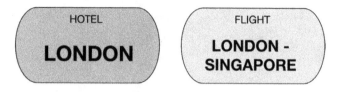

Figure 41.1. Example hotel and flight tickets.

end destinations of flights; hotels just show a city name (see Figure 41.1). The full set of flights and destinations is:

Hotel tickets:
London, Singapore, New York, Delhi, Sydney, St Petersburg, Beijing

Flight tickets:

London–Singapore	New York–London
New York–Singapore	Delhi–London
Delhi–Singapore	Delhi–Singapore
Delhi–New York	Sydney–London
Sydney–London	Sydney–Singapore
Sydney–New York	Sydney–New York
Sydney–Delhi	St Petersburg–London
St Petersburg–London	St Petersburg–Singapore
St Petersburg–New York	St Petersburg–Delhi
St Petersburg–Sydney	St Petersburg–London
Beijing–Singapore	Beijing–New York
Beijing–Delhi	Beijing–Sydney
Beijing–St Petersburg	

As long as you have seven cities with a flight ticket for every pair and a hotel for every city, you can actually use any city. Place one of the flight tickets in an envelope, and you are ready to start the trick.

Give the envelope with the selected ticket to a member of the audience to look after saying that it holds a special prize ticket. Ask another volunteer to use the remaining tickets (flights and hotels) to plan an itinerary crisscrossing the world. They should place them in a line to show their planned route. Explain that it doesn't matter where they start and finish. Flights can be used to fly in either direction. Each ticket must be used exactly once. The volunteer should match up start and end cities of adjacent tickets as they must also always arrive and depart from the same destination: no overland treks from one city to another! Hotel tickets can be used at any time when they are in that city, though they can only stay in a hotel in each city once. At other times, they are just in transit elsewhere.

Once they have created their itinerary, point out they had a completely free choice about the order of the tickets including where they started and ended. Have them write down their start and end destinations so everyone can see. Point out that it is a bit of a shame to do a round-the-world trip but not end up where you started. Luckily, you thought of this for them. Have the person holding the envelope reveal your pre-bought ticket. Amazingly, it is a ticket between the volunteer's start and end locations. It will complete their personal round-the-world trip.

The Magical Algorithm

TO PREPARE the Double-Destination Deception:

1. Create a full set of tickets for seven cities consisting of seven hotel tickets and 25 flight tickets, one between each pair of cities.
2. Place one flight ticket in an envelope marked "Special Prize Ticket".

TO DO the Double-Destination Deception:

1. Give the envelope with the prize ticket to a volunteer.
2. A second volunteer creates a line of the tickets to be their itinerary crisscrossing the world so that the start and end destinations of each pair of adjacent tickets match.
3. The volunteer writes their final start and end destinations for the whole trip where everyone can see.
4. You point out that "You had a free choice of the itinerary, and it would be a shame not to end up back where you started. Luckily, I thought of that."
5. The first volunteer opens the envelope containing the special ticket, to reveal that it is exactly the ticket they need to take them back to their start point.

How It Works

An alternative way to do this trick is using a set of dominos. The trick is based on a little-known mathematical fact about a full set of dominos. You can place all the domino pieces in a circle, matching the numbers on the tiles, and this line will in fact join up making a complete **cycle** with all adjacent dominos matching. The actual order of the pieces may vary, but if you have a full set, you can always find a chain that will join with itself. The tickets in the trick correspond to dominos. A ticket linking each pair of destinations (the flights) is like a normal domino with different numbers. A hotel ticket corresponds to a "double" domino with the same number twice.

Knowing this, it's easy to see how the trick works. You have removed one flight ticket so have removed one link in the cycle. The volunteer won't notice one piece is missing, but when they are challenged to put all the tickets in a single chain, the end of their chain will be missing that link that joins it back to the start. When the ticket is revealed, you are just completing the cycle. The destinations will match your prediction.

Now you know the pattern that makes it work, you can of course generalise it in your own way and so transfer this basic idea for a prediction trick by using your own cycle of data. For example, rather than destinations or the two numbers on a domino, one of the attributes of your piece could be a colour and the other a letter say. Or a piece could have just text on it like a singer's name with one of their songs for a music top 40-type presentation. Just make sure that at the beginning, you write down the full cycle on paper before you transfer the numbers, letters, songs or whatever, to individual pieces.

Thinking Computationally

We've said that this is a property of dominos, but why does that property hold? To a computer scientist, this is a **graph** problem. Graphs are a data representation, used as an abstraction of real-life things. They make that original thing (whether dominos or flights) easier to compute with, model or reason about. Road networks, communication networks and social networks (and dominos) are all things that can be represented by a graph. We have actually used graph data representations to explain tricks in this book already (see, for example, Figure 39.4 in Chapter 39, the Doomsday Clock). A graph consists of points or **nodes** (think of these as places) and lines or **edges** (links between those places). So our cities can be represented by the nodes of a graph, and the tickets or flights linking them can be represented by edges. Nodes don't have to be actual places though. Each number in a domino set (from 0 to 6) can be represented by a node. Each domino in a set is then represented by an edge linking two different numbers or a number to itself.

Now let's start thinking about why our trick works by looking at a simpler version with only three cities: London, Singapore and New York. We then have six tickets as follows:

Hotels:
   London, Singapore, New York

Flights:
   London–Singapore
   London–New York
   Singapore–New York

Drawing these as a graph, we get a clearer picture of what is going on (Figure 41.2). Hotels are just drawn as edges from a place to itself.

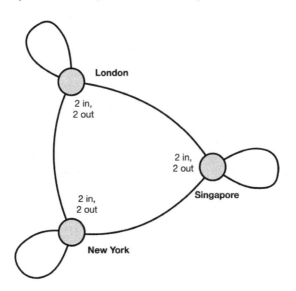

Figure 41.2. The graph representing the tickets when there are three cities.

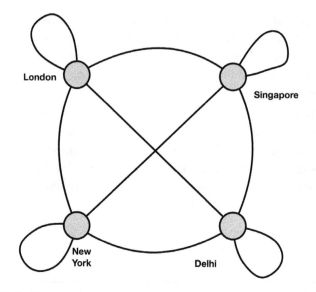

Figure 41.3. The graph representing the tickets when there are four cities.

Each node has two edges leading into it and two leading out. There is an obvious cycle. Removing any flight would break the cycle, and the ends of the chain would correspond to that flight. The trick would work (though not be so magical).

However, if we now add an extra city with a hotel and a flight from it to each other city, things go wrong (see Figure 41.3). The tickets are now as follows:

Hotels:
London, Singapore, New York, Delhi

Flights:
London–Singapore   London–New York   Singapore–New York
Delhi–London   Delhi–Singapore   Delhi–New York

It turns out that it is impossible to create a cycle with four cities (try!). Next, add another city and try again before reading on.

As we keep adding a new city, so its hotel and the flights from it to everywhere else, a pattern seems to emerge. For some, you can create a cycle (3, 5 and 7 cities). For some, you can't (4, 6 and 8 cities).

The Bridges of Königsberg

At this point, we take a detour and go to the very birth of the idea of a graph. It is 1736 and Leonhard Euler has solved a puzzle about the Prussian town of Königsberg. The river Pregel runs through the middle of the town. In the river are islands connected by bridges to either bank (see Figure 41.4). The puzzle is to find a way for a tourist to complete a walking tour of the town crossing each bridge *exactly* once. We will consider a variation where you must also end back where you started.

Euler realised that he could simplify the problem (always a good idea) by drawing the banks and each island as circles and the bridges between them as lines (Figure 41.5). He had invented the abstraction of the graph. In computer science terms, this is a data representation or data structure, but a very general one. Simplifying things down to a graph allowed Euler to see the answer to the problem. Our problem has become a question of whether you can find a **cycle** in the graph that passes along every edge (the bridges) exactly once returning to where you started. He had generalised the problem to one about graphs.

Euler realised that there was an easy, and general, way to work out whether paths like this were possible or not in any graph. Look at any one node. For a cycle to pass through that node, every route (edge) in must have a different route (a different edge) out. The edges of the graph at each node must pair up. If there are an even number of edges

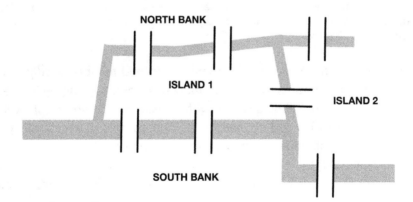

Figure 41.4. The Bridges of Königsberg map.

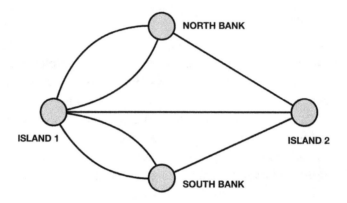

Figure 41.5. The Bridges of Königsberg as a graph.

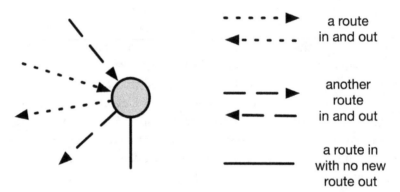

Figure 41.6. A node can only be in the middle of a path (or part of a cycle) if there are an even number of edges to it so that for every way in there is a way out. Here the extra edge makes an odd number, so if followed into the node, there is no way left to leave that node.

in the node, that is possible. If there are an odd number of edges in a node, then it is impossible. In that impossible case, one edge will always be left unused. It will be a way in with no way out to carry on the cycle (see Figure 41.6). For a cycle visiting all nodes, this rule must apply to all the nodes: all nodes must have an even number of edges.

In the Königsberg graph, all the nodes have an odd number of edges (three or five edges) into them. Therefore, by Euler's theorem, a cycle is impossible. There is no algorithm that would take you on a tour that crosses all bridges, visit all islands and back to the start. It is actually impossible to do even without returning to the start as Euler proved with similar reasoning.

Back to the magic

We can apply the same logical reasoning to any graph. That includes the graph of our magic trick. If we look at the graph for a version of the trick with three cities, each city is connected to the two other cities and itself. Ignoring for a moment the hotel edges that come and go from the same node, there is an edge in and an edge out of every node: an even number. There is an obvious cycle. Adding in the hotel links doesn't change that as even though each hotel link is a single edge it counts as a pair: an edge going in and out.

When we add a city to make four cities, we have added a new edge into each node linking it to the new city. Each node now has five edges instead of four (just as in Figure 41.3). That is an odd number, so by applying Euler's theorem, we immediately know there is no cycle. The real trick used seven cities, meaning eight edges at every node (six to link to each other city and a hotel that goes in and out). That is an even number of edges, therefore there is a cycle.

Now, what happens when we remove one flight as in the trick? We are removing one edge. The nodes of those two cities now have one less edge. There are now two nodes with an odd number of edges, so any chain of links will have to start and end at those nodes. We said that the ticket removed by the magician should not be a hotel. We can now see why. If we remove a hotel, we are removing two links from a single node. It remains even and there will still be a full cycle, and the volunteer could start and end it anywhere.

Dominos

We noted that the trick also works with dominos instead of tickets. Follow similar reasoning and draw a graph for the possibilities with dominos. Exactly the same graphs result, so all our above logical reasoning works exactly the same for a domino version too, as long as you use a full set of dominos with tiles with 0 to 6 spots. Try it for yourself.

Interlude: Dynamo

Magician, Dynamo (real name Steven Frayne), baffled the audience on his TV show with a variation of this trick. He grew up in a deprived area of Bradford. His grandfather taught him his first trick, a way to make himself look bigger to deter other children from bullying him. He is one of the first-generation Internet magicians: posting online videos of his street magic helped launch his career. His stage name, after Faraday's invention of a device that produces electricity, came from an audience member who shouted out that Frayne was like a dynamo during a performance he gave when he was still a teenager. It was part of celebrations for the legendary magician, Houdini's centenary.

Part 11

Cyber Security, Privacy and Society

Spies and hackers exploit both legitimate and covert channels in computer systems: ways that information can leak from the system without anyone knowing. Magicians similarly build tricks around such channels: ways that information can leak from the magical system to the magician without the audience realising. Magicians often pretend to know amazing things about us, and some charlatans use tricks to con people. Technology is taking away our privacy for real and often using information gained in bad ways. Skills and technology should be used for good, not harm, which is why professional ethics matter.

Chapter 42

Sniff Out that Card
Steganography

Conjuring

A volunteer chooses a card and holds it to their chest while memorising it. They then place it back in the middle of the pack of cards while you look away. You work through the pack, smelling the backs until you find the one that they picked, detected due to the trace smell left behind.

Computation

Steganography is a way of hiding secret messages in apparently innocuous things. What looks like a normal message or image disguises the real thing being communicated.

The Trick

You shuffle a pack of cards thoroughly using a normal overhand shuffle (Chapter 15) in front of the audience. You then fan the pack and ask a volunteer to pick a card. They pull it out, look at it to be sure what it is, and then hold it against their heart for a few moments while they memorise it. You then hold out the pack for them to reinsert it in a random place. You shuffle the pack again, and then holding the pack with the faces to the audience, work through them a few at a time sniffing the backs, searching for the smell of their card. Triumphantly, you pull out a card, and it is theirs.

How It Works

You need a special pack of cards for this trick that has a picture or pattern on the backs that is not symmetrical. Normal packs of cards have symmetrical patterns, but it is fairly easy to buy a souvenir pack of cards that either has a picture on or some other pattern that is not symmetrical. Magic shops also have cards with patterns that look symmetrical at a casual glance but actually are slightly different at the corners.

Before the trick, you ensure all the cards are the same way around. Then, when the person takes the card and is holding it to their heart, you surreptitiously turn the pack around in your hands. When they reinsert the card, it becomes the only card the other way around. As you go through the cards supposedly smelling them, you are actually looking for the one card that has been turned around (Figure 42.1). When revealing the card, put the rest of the pack face up on the table in a neat pile, the right way around and keep the back of their chosen card facing you so no one can spot what is going on.

The Magical Algorithm

TO PREPARE Sniff Out that Card:
1. Take a pack of cards that contain a non-symmetrical image on the back and turn them all the same way.

TO DO Sniff Out that Card:
1. DO an Overhand Shuffle of the pack of cards.
2. Fan the pack.
3. The volunteer chooses a card.
4. They look at their card, show it to the audience, remember it, and hold it to their heart.
5. You turn the pack around.

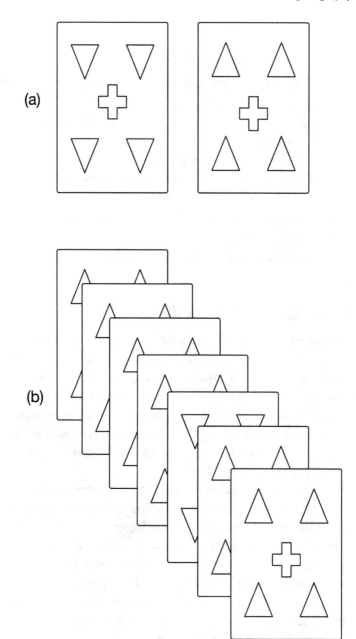

Figure 42.1. (a) Cards with a non-symmetrical pattern look different when turned around. (b) This allows a single card that is turned the other way to the rest to be easily found.

6. They insert the card back somewhere in the middle of the pack.
7. DO an Overhand Shuffle of the pack of cards.
8. Hold the pack with the faces of the cards to the audience.
9. DO THE FOLLOWING UNTIL you come to a card that is turned the wrong way around:
   a. Look at the back of the card to see if it is turned the right way around.
   b. Sniff the back of the top card.
   c. IF the top card is not the wrong way around.
      THEN move it to the bottom.
10. Place the pack face up and neatly squared on the table apart from the top card.
11. Reveal the top card as their chosen card.

Thinking Computationally

Steganography is a way of ensuring a message, and more generally information, is secret by hiding it in some other innocuous thing. The aim is that no one realises there is a secret message there at all. One of the earliest versions from Ancient Greece involved a message being tattooed on the shaved head of a messenger. They had to wait for their hair to grow back before taking the message. Mary Queen of Scots also used steganography. She famously plotted while under house arrest by hiding messages in barrels of ale.

Information can be hidden in apparently innocuous messages in all sorts of ways. Different patterns in an image could stand for different letters, or a subtle difference in the way letters are written could stand for 1s and 0s with a message then stored as binary (see Chapter 28). Different groups of 1s and 0s then represent different letters in the secret message. A Tudor master of spycraft, Sir Francis Bacon, came up with the original version of this kind of steganography. His version used capital and lower case letters for the two binary symbols in writing that was apparently about something completely different.

In the trick, one bit of binary information (a single 1 or 0) was stored in the image on the back of each card, based on which way up it was. The right way up (0) meant "I am not the chosen card". The wrong way up (1) meant "I am the chosen card".

You could store even more information in a pack of cards in this way. For example, take a pack of cards and turn each card the right way up (meaning 0) or the wrong way up (meaning 1) to spell out a message in binary through the whole pack. Every group of five cards would then represent a letter of the alphabet running from 00001 meaning A to 11010 meaning Z. Send the pack of cards to someone supposedly as a present but where the real reason is the message you are sending them. Of course, one pack of cards could only hold a 10-letter message this way.

In the computer age, there are all sorts of ways to hide messages. One way is in a photo. Digital images are ultimately stored as binary, so binary can be hidden there. An image is split into a grid of tiny squares, called pixels (see Chapter 29), and the colour of each is stored as a binary code. The more binary bits used for each pixel, the more colours can be used.

Now imagine an image of a beach with a blue sky with wispy clouds. Perhaps the sky uses two shades of blue, a deeper blue and a lighter blue. Suppose the difference between the binary version of the two colours is one binary bit. If that bit is a 0, then the lighter blue is used there. If it is a 1, then the darker blue is used. A message could be hidden by setting the blue of specific pixels (perhaps every 10th pixel) based on the binary of the message to be stored. If the image is of high resolution and so has thousands of pixels in each row, this will be hard to spot unless you know it is there, and a fairly long message might be hidden. Of course, binary can represent anything so what is hidden could even be a different smaller image spelled out in the changed 1s and 0s.

PAUSE: Sir Francis Bacon

Tudor philosopher, Sir Francis Bacon (1561–1626) is best known for pioneering the scientific method. He was also a Tudor master of spycraft. He invented a form of steganography that was the first use of a binary system for encoding letters. Each letter in a message was represented by a different sequence of five As or Bs. These were then hidden in writing that was apparently about something completely different, using other things in place of A and B. There are various ways this can be done. He used one font for A and a different font for B letters. Another simple version he used was capital letters for A and lower case letters for B. This also demonstrates how any symbols can be used for 0 and 1 in binary.

Chapter 43

Classic Mentalism
Codes and Ciphers

Conjuring

One of two magicians leaves the room while a card is chosen. When they return, they instantly announce the card that was chosen.

Computation

Cryptography, the use of codes and ciphers, to make messages unreadable, is a core part of how computers are made secure. Used by rulers, the military and spies for thousands of years to keep their secrets safe, it is now the way banks can send digital money around the world, how we keep documents, chat and video meetings secure as well as the basis for preventing anyone logging into our computers.

The Trick

In this trick, there are two magicians. One stays with the audience, while the other, "the receiving magician", leaves the room. A brand new pack of cards is opened. A member of the audience chooses a card from the pack. The chosen card is placed back in the pack. The pack is put back in the box and placed back on the table. The receiver is called back. When they return, they immediately tell the audience the chosen card.

How It Works

The secret to this trick is in the table. Once the card has been selected, pack and box are placed on the table in a position that depends on the card selected. The two magicians agree on a secret code of where the box will be placed in advance such as (see Figure 43.1):

If the box is face up and its flap is closed: Clubs.
If the box is face up and its flap is open: Spades.
If the box is face down and its flap is closed: Diamonds.
If the box is face down and its flap is open: Hearts.

That's the suits taken care of. Now for the value. The performers again agree in advance, this time on how to chop up the card table into mental zones. Horizontally, you have the top row, centre row and bottom row of the table and far right, mid right, mid left and far left. That's 3 × 4 unique locations. You have 12 places for 12 of the 13 card values. Ace is top-far-left. Two is top-middle-left, and so on (see Figure 43.2). The magician places the pack of cards in the correct pre-agreed position, box face up or not, flap open or closed as needed (see Figure 43.3).

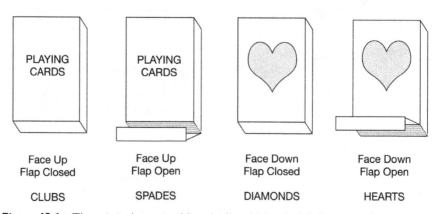

Face Up	Face Up	Face Down	Face Down
Flap Closed	Flap Open	Flap Closed	Flap Open
CLUBS	SPADES	DIAMONDS	HEARTS

Figure 43.1. The suit is determined by whether the box is left face up or face down and with the flap open or closed.

TOP ROW FAR LEFT ACE	TOP ROW MID LEFT 2	TOP ROW MID RIGHT 3	TOP ROW FAR RIGHT 4
CENTRE ROW FAR LEFT 5	CENTRE ROW MID LEFT 6	CENTRE ROW MID RIGHT 7	CENTRE ROW FAR RIGHT 8
BOTTOM ROW FAR LEFT 9	BOTTOM ROW MID LEFT 10	BOTTOM ROW MID RIGHT JACK	BOTTOM ROW FAR RIGHT QUEEN

Figure 43.2. Divide the table into mental areas like this to indicate what the card value is. If the card is a King, put the box in the volunteer's hand.

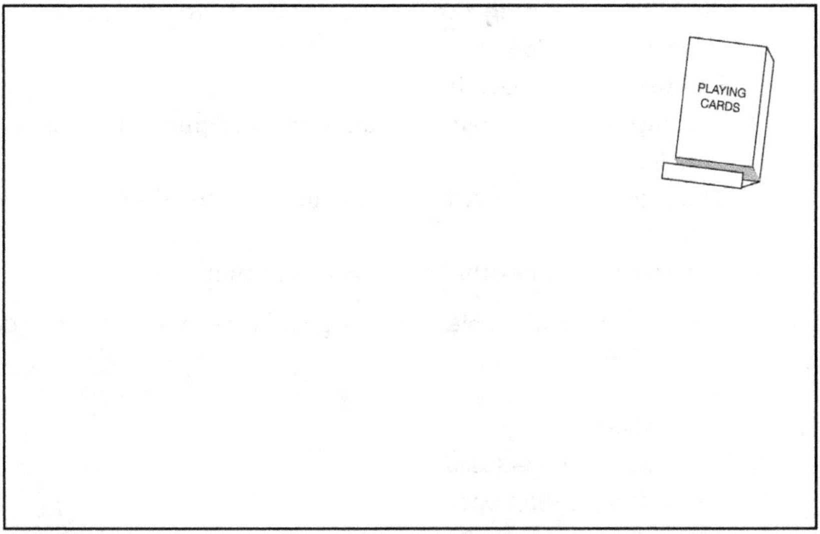

Figure 43.3. The cards are in the top row, far right (4), and the box is face up, with flap open (SPADES), so card indicated is the 4 of spades.

What about the 13th possibility? That is when the card is the King. If the card isn't the King (most often), you leave the pack of cards on the table. If it is the King, have your volunteer place their hand out flat and leave the box of cards on it. Ask them to concentrate on the card they chose while staring at the pack.

The Magical Algorithm

TO DO Classic Mentalism:

1. The receiver leaves the room.
2. A new pack of cards is opened.
3. A volunteer chooses a card and shows it to you and the audience.
4. They place the card back in the pack.
5. You put the pack back in the box.
6. Orient the box using the Suit Code to encode the suit as an orientation.
7. Place the box using the Face Value Code to encode the face value as a position.
8. Call the receiver back in.
9. The receiver works out the suit using the Suit Code Table to decode.
10. The receiver works out the face value using the Face Value Code Table to decode.
11. The receiver names that face value and that suit.

To encode, read the code tables left to right. To decode, read the code tables right to left.

Suit Code Table:

CLUBS: face-up-flap-closed.
SPADES: face-up-flap-open.
DIAMONDS: face-down-flap-closed.
HEARTS: face-down-flap-open.

Face Value Code Table:
  ACE: top-far-left.
  TWO: top-middle-left.
  THREE: top-middle-right.
  FOUR: top-far-right.
  FIVE: middle-far-left.
  SIX: middle-middle-left.
  SEVEN: middle-middle-right.
  EIGHT: middle-far-right.
  NINE: bottom-far-left.
  TEN: bottom-middle-left.
  JACK: bottom-middle-right.
  QUEEN: bottom-far-right.
  KING: hand.

Thinking Computationally

This trick is using steganography again. However, it is also using a secret **code**. In a simple version of steganography, a message is just hidden (like growing hair over it or hiding a letter in a waterproof package inside a barrel of ale). In more complex versions as in both the last trick and this one, information is transformed into a different form that also hides it using a secret code.

A **code** is just an algorithm that transforms information from one form into another. **Encoding** transforms the information and **decoding** transforms it back to the original form (see Chapter 25). The information encoded can be in any form, whether spoken, written, gestures or implicit in the form of objects. The decoded version of the information can also have any form. For example, a semaphore encodes written or spoken letters into the positions of a person's arms holding flags. A secret code is one where the code is being used in a secret way. Only some people know the secret, know the code.

In the last trick, we had a very simple encoding of one piece of information "It is this card" into the orientation of the card. In this trick, we use a code again, but a more complicated one that encodes more information: that of the details of one out of 52 cards. Separate codes are used for the suit and for the value of the card. Codes like this are the basis of a wide variety of mentalism acts. They only appear magical because they are both secret and hidden. For example, in an act where the magician takes an object from an audience member and their partner blindfolded can say what it is, different words the magician says in asking them what they are holding might mean, "It's a watch", "It's a mirror", and so on . . .

Computer scientists also use a wide variety of codes to make information easier to store and transmit. Most codes are not secret so are not a secure way to keep information secret. However, secret codes have also been used throughout history to keep information secure. This is known as **cryptography**. Even if the message is intercepted, if the enemy can not decode it, they cannot read it. They may though be able to infer something useful just from the fact that it is written in code, who it is from and who it is to. Magicians use codes in this way, usually combined with steganography, explicitly to also hide the fact that information is being passed. Many of the tricks in this book have used information secretly both hidden and encoded one way or another.

The word **code**, in general use, means any kind of secret message. In cryptography, it means a specific kind of encryption algorithm where a word or phrase in the message is allocated a code word, symbol or phrase. Mentioning, as part of a conversation, the code word "Phoenix" might mean "Attack at dawn", whereas "Vulture" means "The attack is aborted". That is what our trick did. The word "Clubs" is given a code word "face-up-flap-open" which is then translated into the corresponding physical positioning: the box is placed face up with its flap open. What we do not do is give the separate letters C-L-U-B-S their own code word and try and spell them out in code. Native American languages were used as codes in World War II as very few people spoke them. Navajo words were used as code words for their English equivalent.

A **cipher**, by contrast, works on individual letters (or syllables). A simple cipher encrypts each letter to a new symbol or symbols to encrypt a message. Modern encryption generally uses ciphers rather than codes as it is more flexible. The **Caesar cipher** is a simple example used since Roman times. Each letter of the alphabet is replaced by the letter three places earlier in the alphabet. Today, complex ciphers are used in all sorts of ways, from password-protecting your documents to securing instant messaging conversations and transferring money securely between banks and businesses across the Internet.

Interlude: Reginald Scot

The first English book giving details of conjuring tricks was *The Discoverie of Witchcraft* by a member of parliament, Reginald Scot (c.1538–1599), published in 1584. His aim in the book as a whole was to prove by reason that witches did not exist. This was in the midst of witch hunts that were persecuting thousands of innocent women across the country. His section on conjuring aimed to debunk charlatans. It included a way to communicate secretly by code with a confederate from behind a door. The confederate would indicate whether coins have been arranged in a pile or as a cross, using a simple code: the difference between him saying "What is it?" versus "What ist?" The book also included a trick of how to appear to chop off your head. Shakespeare supposedly used the book for inspiration about the witches in *Macbeth*.

Chapter 44

Call the Clairvoyant
Legitimate Channels

Conjuring

A friend picks a card from a normal pack of cards. You phone the mysterious "Clairvoyant". The "Clairvoyant" is able to name the chosen card.

Computation

Computer systems are kept secure by having separate areas with different security levels. Nothing from a high-security area should be able to leak to a lower-security area. Hiding information (steganography) in a legitimate channel (an allowed way to communicate) is one-way information that might be leaked. Hackers often exploit legitimate channels in computer systems. Magicians build tricks around them too.

The Trick

This is a trick that could be done with an audience or just with a friend. You announce that you know an amazing person who goes by the name

"The Clairvoyant" who can do amazing things and if you like you will ask them to do a demonstration of their powers. Close any doors and curtains of the room you are in so no one outside can see in. Next, ask the friend (or a volunteer) to choose any card from a face-up pack, allowing everyone, you included, to see the card they choose. Next phone the Clairvoyant. When they answer you simply say, "I have a call for the Clairvoyant". After listening for a moment, you say "Thanks". After a further pause during which you say nothing, you finally say, "Let me pass you over." You hand the phone over to the friend/volunteer (and/or put the phone on speaker phone so the audience can hear) telling them to just say "Hello" to the Clairvoyant and then listen. They speak to the Clairvoyant. Despite the Clairvoyant not being in the room, having apparently no way to know what happened, and you saying nothing to indicate what the card was, they dramatically tell your friend the card they chose... and they are right.

How It Works

When you first phone, your accomplice, the Clairvoyant, just names the card suits, saying: "Clubs... Spades... Diamonds... Hearts". You say "Thanks" when they reach the suit of the chosen card (which you, but not they, have seen). Your phoney Clairvoyant accomplice now knows the suit and starts counting out the values, Ace to King. Again you stay silent until they get to the chosen card, at which point you this time say: "Let me pass you over." Figure 44.1 shows an example of how the 5 of spades is communicated. Your accomplice now knows both suit and value. Once they are passed to the person who chose the card, they

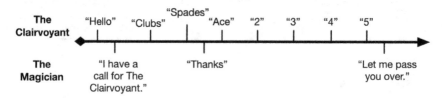

Figure 44.1. Communicating the 5 of spades to the Clairvoyant. The Clairvoyant lists the possibilities until interrupted by the magician speaking.

know the suit and value and so can surprise them by immediately telling them what it was.

The Magical Algorithm

This trick involves two algorithms that work together to allow information to be communicated.

The first, followed by the Clairvoyant, the receiver of the information, is:

TO DO Call the Clairvoyant, the Clairvoyant must:
1. Answer the phone when it rings.
2. IF the person phoning says "I have a call for the Clairvoyant," THEN
   a. Name the suits slowly "Clubs, Spades, Diamonds, Hearts", stopping when the other person says "Thanks", writing the last suit spoken down.
   b. Name the face value of cards slowly "Ace, Two ... Queen, King", stopping when the other person says "Let me pass you over," writing the last value spoken down.
   c. When they hear the second person, say "Hello", they say "Your card was...", and name the value and suit they wrote down.

The second algorithm followed by the magician is:

TO DO Call the Clairvoyant, the magician must:
1. Tell the friend about the Clairvoyant.
2. Close doors and shut curtains so the room is secure.
3. Ask the friend to pick a card, showing you what it was.
4. Phone the Clairvoyant (the person who has agreed to follow the first algorithm).
5. Say "I have a call for the Clairvoyant."
6. Listen to them saying the suits and as soon as the chosen suit is spoken, say "Thanks".
7. Listen to them saying the values and as soon as the chosen value is spoken, say "Let me pass you over."
8. Hand over the phone to the friend, telling them to say "Hello" and then listen to what the Clairvoyant has to say.

9. They say "Hello" and listen to the Clairvoyant naming their card.

Thinking Computationally

This trick requires a shared understanding that the two algorithms will be followed. Such a pair of algorithms used to pass information is called a **communication protocol**. Even though you apparently say nothing to give away what the card was (and in fact say the same thing every time you do the trick), you do pass the information on to your accomplice. You do it not by *what* you say but in the timing of *when* you say it. Your silence passes information!

Computers that are intended to be secure use **secure operating systems**: software that controls the computer but does so in a way that is supposed to not allow information to be passed around. For example, it may be divided into high-security "Top Secret" and low-security "Unclassified" areas. Top-secret information is stored in the high-security areas which only certain people can access. Meanwhile, everyone else has access to the "Unclassified" areas where only non-confidential material resides.

In our trick, think of the room where you, the magician and your friend are, as being the top-secret area. That is where the chosen card resides. You are both there so know the secret information, that is the chosen card. The Clairvoyant, on the other hand, is elsewhere. They are in an unclassified area.

An important part of the setup for the trick is that they should clearly not be able to just see the information (the card) that resides in the top-secret area. This is clear because they are not in the room, just on the end of the phone, and you have closed all doors and curtains. Your accomplice cannot see in! Let us call that BELIEF 1.

Legitimate channels

The only way information can pass out of the top-secret area to the unclassified area is therefore via the phone. This is what a computer scientist would call a **Legitimate Communication Channel**: one built into the system. However, it is monitored; the volunteer and audience hear everything you say, so they apparently hear all information being passed *out* of the area. Think of this as BELIEF 2. You apparently cannot pass information out. (Except you can!).

For the trick to seem magical, the audience have to hold both beliefs. It works because you do have a secret, undetectable way of passing the card details out undetected: the secret pair of algorithms allows the top-secret information to pass out of the top-secret area and be written down in the unclassified area! It is using the legitimate channel of the phone call, but in a hidden way (so using steganography, see Chapter 42).

Secure computer systems are split into areas with different security levels like our top-secret and unclassified areas, and there are two important rules built into secure systems that match the two beliefs behind our trick:

1. Those in lower-security areas (like the unclassified area) should not be able to read any information in higher-security areas (the top-secret area).
2. Someone with access to the top-secret area should not be able to pass information out (accidentally or maliciously) into the unclassified area. The security system should not allow it. Some people, however, may be given the status of being *trusted*: they are able to pass information out but are trusted not to do so with information they should not.

The magician is acting as a **Trusted Person** here. They could actually communicate information out, but everything they say is monitored, so you are led to believe that you would know if they did. The flaw in the security here is that you are not monitoring what the other person is saying.

The typical spy and whistleblower scenarios, where a trusted person inside an organisation passes information out, are working in this way. For example, Edward Snowden, as part of his job, was given, copied and leaked hundreds of thousands of classified US documents to journalists in 2013. These revealed to the public the massive extent to which the US was spying on them, in breach of the US constitution.

Snowden took the information with him which is a bit like our magician leaving the room having seen the card (not very magical). In the trick, we are using steganography to hide the information being leaked in plain sight through the legitimate channel. The message about which card is chosen is passed in an apparently run-of-the-mill conversation. It is not what is said that communicates the information but the timing of when it is said that matters.

In fact, in a more sophisticated variation of the trick, the magician and the Clairvoyant could pass the information without the Clairvoyant saying anything or saying something innocuous, and instead just timing the gap between the magician speaking. This would work as long as the pair had agreed in advance the timings of each suit and face values. So a pause of 5 seconds from saying "I have a call for the Clairvoyant" to saying "Thanks" means Clubs. A pause of 10 seconds means Spades, and so on. Then the whole conversation could be on speakerphone the whole time, and the information still passed.

Timing can similarly be used by a program to communicate covertly out of a secure network. Information might be communicated by the time a message is sent rather than its contents, for example. Alternatively, information might be passed based on whether a particular encrypted file exists or not. They cannot be read, but they can still leak information as a program on the inside could create and delete files to communicate. Making a system really secure is actually quite tricky!

Interlude: Sydney and Lesley Piddington

In the 1950s, Australian couple Sydney and Lesley Piddington took the entertainment world by storm. They had the nation perplexed, puzzled and entertained. They were seemingly able to communicate telepathically over great distances. It all started in World War II when Sydney (1918–1991) was a prisoner of war. To keep up morale, he devised a mentalism act where he "read the minds" of other soldiers. When he later married Lesley (1925–2016), they perfected the act and became an overnight sensation, attracting BBC radio audiences of 20 million listeners.

They communicated random words and objects selected by the audience, even when Lesley was in a circling aeroplane or Sydney was in a diving bell in a swimming pool. To this day, their secret remains unknown, though many have tried to work it out. Perhaps they used a hidden transmitter. After all, that was fairly new technology then. Or perhaps they were using their own version of the old mentalism trick: a code to transmit information hidden in plain sight.

Sydney had a severe stutter, and some suggested it was the pauses he made in words rather than the words themselves that conveyed the information. Using timing and silence to code information may seem rather odd, but it can be used to great effect both in tricks and espionage and has been suggested as a way to hide messages in video calls, for example.

Chapter 45

Call the Clairvoyant a Second Time
Covert Channels
and the Surveillance Society

Conjuring

The Clairvoyant is called once more, this time able to tell exactly which object from a table full of objects a member of the audience chose even though called on a speakerphone, so all could hear everything that was said.

Computation

Another way hackers do damage is to set up covert channels: ways of communicating that are not supposed to be there. Magicians build tricks around covert channels too.

How to Do the Trick

Explain (as in the previous trick) that you know someone with amazing powers who goes by the name "The Clairvoyant" and you will ask them to do a demonstration. Arrange on a table a range of different everyday objects, perhaps borrowed from different members of the audience, together with some magical objects you provide: a pen, a watch, a coin, a silk handkerchief, a wand, a top hat, a pack of cards, and so on. Shut curtains and doors to ensure no one can see in.

Have a member of the audience study the objects and choose one, pick it up, and show it to the audience and then ask the whole audience to think hard about that object only.

You then phone the Clairvoyant using a speakerphone. When they answer, you simply say "I have a call for the Clairvoyant." They say in a mysterious voice (perhaps covering the phone with a handkerchief) "I am she." You then ask them "I have a group of people with me thinking of a single object. Can you say what that object is?" After a silence of several seconds, they correctly announce what the object was.

How It Works

You simply set up a small but hidden webcam somewhere in the room where it has a clear view of the objects on the table, or of where the volunteer will stand holding the chosen object (perhaps poking through curtains at the side of the stage). The webcam livestreams the images so that the person at the other end can see everything. This could just be done by setting up a video call to the computer the webcam is linked to. The Clairvoyant watches the show via the video call (with the sound off!) and so sees the object taken.

When internet-based video calls were new, famous magicians used such technological variations of this. Given such video surveillance is now totally pervasive, making this magical today will depend on your presentation skills distracting the audience from thinking it is a possibility!

The Magical Algorithm

This trick again involves two algorithms that work together to allow information to be communicated.

The first, followed by the Clairvoyant, the receiver of the information, is:

TO DO Call the Clairvoyant a Second Time, the Clairvoyant must:

1. Watch the video stream until the volunteer picks an object.
2. Answer the phone when it rings.
3. Say in a mysterious voice: "I am she" (or he as appropriate).
4. Pause.
5. Name the object that was chosen.

The second algorithm, followed by the magician, is:

TO DO Call the Clairvoyant a Second Time, the magician must:

1. Tell the audience about the Clairvoyant.
2. Close doors and shut curtains so the room is secure.
3. Lay out a mixture of normal and magical objects on the table.
4. Ask a volunteer to pick an object, showing it to the audience.
5. Have the whole audience concentrate on the object, thinking only about it.
6. Phone the Clairvoyant (the person who has agreed to follow the first algorithm) putting the phone on speakerphone.
7. Say "I have a call for the Clairvoyant."
8. Say "I have a group of people with me thinking of a single object. Can you say what that object is?"
9. Listen to their answer and thank them, announcing that they were correct.

Thinking Computationally

Covert channels

The trick is similar to the last though done in a different hi-tech way, using the hidden webcam in the room that was positioned to be able to see the object so the Clairvoyant can watch proceedings via the camera streaming images from the room. For the trick to work, the presence of the hidden camera needs to be unknown to the audience (unlike the phone connection which everyone knows exists). The phone connection to the Clairvoyant is a legitimate channel. In this trick, by contrast, we are using a **covert channel**: a way of communicating that should not exist and is not known to exist by anyone but those using it.

Hackers create covert channels as a way of gaining information too. For example, if you visit a dodgy website, and allow it to execute code on your phone or computer, then the website might insert a program (a **trojan horse program**) that is unknown to you. It records and sends to the hacker details of all your keypresses, say, or allows them to switch on your phone's mike or camera so they can see or hear what you do. This would be a covert channel leaking information from your computer or phone to the hacker's computer, just as the webcam in this alternative version of the trick does.

Surveillance society

The trick depends on camera surveillance. This has now become ubiquitous in many western countries. As you walk through the centre of a city like London, cameras are everywhere mounted on buildings. You are potentially constantly being watched. As you drive around the motorway system, your number plate is constantly being logged. As you move anywhere, your phone logs your position as you connect to different phone masts. This is an example of technology being used for good purposes that could easily be subverted, whether by individuals such as stalkers, companies or states. More recently, companies selling hacking tools to countries have provided them with ways of taking over a person's phone including the microphone and camera, so they can see and hear everything you can. Supposedly only used for legitimate policing, it has been used repeatedly to monitor political opponents of oppressive states, legitimate journalists, lawyers and more, in clearly unethical ways.

Privacy can no longer be taken for granted.

PAUSE: Hedy Lamarr

Hollywood actress, Hedy Lamarr (1914–2000), was a film superstar playing parts such as Helen of Troy, Joan of Arc and Delilah. Most definitely not just a pretty face, she was also an inventor. Working with film music composer, George Antheil at the start of World War II, she came up with a way to guide radio-controlled torpedoes to their targets. The idea was ignored at the time but is now an absolutely central part of wireless communications. We now call it frequency hopping: the idea is that rather than sending out control signals on one frequency, the frequency constantly changes. Only the transmitter and receiver know the frequency it will jump to next (stored on a piano roll in their design). This made it hard both to intercept the radio signals and to jam them: exactly what was needed for torpedoes had it been taken up.

Chapter 46

Reading a Personality with Hot Chocolate
Big Data and Privacy

Conjuring

You make a mug of hot chocolate. The person whose personality you will read stirs it five times and then drinks. You stare into the sludge of chocolate left behind and from it read the personality of the volunteer.

Computation

Tech companies collect data about everyone who uses their services so they can use the information to sell advertising and target services at you. They build up a very detailed picture of each person, their personality and their lives. Their aim is to know you better than you know yourself.

The Trick

You explain that some fortune tellers can read people by looking in a crystal ball, others in tea leaves. You, however, having spent so much time studying chocolate, can tell a person's personality by looking at the dregs left behind when they drink hot chocolate. You make a small mug of hot chocolate. The person stirs it five times and then drinks it. Why five times? Five is a special magical number, the number of pentagons and pentagrams. Once they have finished, you stare into the empty mug at the undrunk chocolate sludge stuck to the bottom.

After a few moments, you tell them something about their personality,

> *At times, you are overly critical of yourself, but you also have a deep desire for others to appreciate you. Sometimes, you are very confident but there are times when you are less sure of yourself. You often worry about whether you have made the right decision and some of the things you try to do do not work out. You like variety and dislike it when prevented from doing things because of rules imposed by others. Sometimes you are sociable, but you can also be much more reserved. You have occasionally found it to be a bad idea to reveal too much of yourself to others too freely. In general, you are an independent thinker who doesn't just believe things you are told without some kind of evidence. Most of the time, you can overcome the flaws in your personality.*

Ask them to rate how accurate your description is, and whether they recognise themselves.

How It Works

You just say the same thing whoever the person and whatever the state of the chocolate mug, occasionally poking at the chocolate as though it is revealing new facts.

The effect used in the trick is called the Barnum–Forer effect after showman Phineas T. Barnum and psychologist Bertram R. Forer. It is relied on by the likes of astrologers and fortune tellers.

The personality prediction is full of the same kind of statements you find in horoscopes, called Barnum statements. Those above are variations on ones used in a classic experiment by psychologist Bertram R. Forer which demonstrated the effect. In 1948, he gave a "psychology test" to his students and then gave each student what he claimed was a personalised summary of their personality based on the test. He asked them to rate the summary, and on average, they rated them at over 4 on a scale of 0–5 suggesting they thought they were very accurate summaries of their personality. In fact, he gave them all an identical summary based on the same statements that he had pulled from an astrology book.

Barnum statements aim to be very general statements that sound specific but that lots of people would agree with. People can apply their own meaning to them, matching them to things they believe about themselves. Some of the statements include phrases like "At times" or "Sometimes" that mean they are likely to apply to anyone. Whilst overall they should be mainly positive traits (as people are more likely to accept positive statements about themselves), they also mix positive and negative statements about the same thing: saying things like "Sometimes you are confident but sometimes you aren't", that are just bound to be true, though saying it in a more long-winded way. It is also important that the person believes the summary is personal to them and that they trust in the authority of the person doing the test.

The Magical Algorithm

TO PREPARE Reading a Personality:

1. Memorise a series of Barnum statements such as those in the given paragraph.

TO DO Reading a Personality:

1. Tell the person you can read their personality in the chocolate dregs of a mug of hot chocolate.
2. Make them a mug of hot chocolate.
3. They stir the drink five times.
4. They drink the hot chocolate.
5. You stare into the chocolate sludge left behind.

6. You "describe their personality" while staring into the mug, poking at the sludge with a teaspoon occasionally and saying a series of Barnum statements.

7. Ask them to rate your accuracy on a scale of 1–5 with 5 meaning fully accurate.

Thinking Computationally

Fortune tellers have long used this kind of fraudulent reading to take people's money. Oppressive regimes have also long collected information dossiers on their citizens so they know who is likely to oppose them. Hackers and fraudsters also use **social engineering** to get people unwittingly to give up personal information, pretending to be people they aren't for example and asking for passwords and credit card details. Magicians have also used a version where they just ask for information for mentalism and spiritualism acts. One version involves collecting information about their audience members before the show to use to make predictions seem more realistic.

Now technology allows it to be done for real on a mass scale. We blithely give away lots of information about ourselves to technology companies in exchange for their services in a way that allows them to both know and predict a lot about us. The way we follow other people on social media combined with our "likes" can be used to fairly accurately tell things like our ethnicity and gender and who we are likely to vote for, for example. Companies also collect your browsing history, what kind of music you listen to and films you watch as well as what you buy or think of buying. Technology companies sell the data to marketing companies who then compile very detailed sets of statements about every one of us based on the mass of information collected and combined. These are no longer Barnum statements but accurate guesses about very intimate aspects of your personality: interests, habits and life.

All this, once private, information can be used for good or bad. It can be used to make life more convenient but also to manipulate us. Advertisers use the information to sell you things you probably don't need or really want, political parties use it to target messages suggesting they support the things that matter to you to change the way you vote, and other companies use it to run promotional campaigns to change your opinion so you think they are good companies, or to change your mind about issues that further their aims. Governments use it to promote their messages and sway opinion of those in other countries in ways that favour them and undermine democracy. Some governments use it to identify people likely to oppose them.

It is done using **big data** processing. Similar data is collected about large numbers of people, and general patterns are gleaned. The more data collected, the more detailed the patterns that can be determined. **Machine learning** algorithms are used to spot the patterns and then apply them. They are artificial intelligence algorithms, partly modelled on the way our brains work, but all they really do is find patterns in their vast store of data. They then look for matches to those patterns in new data, about a new person, say, using the links found to form conclusions about that person.

People who watch particular news stations and follow particular people on social media have been found to be grouped with people who believe abortion is bad, and also those who vote a particular way. If a new person is found to watch that station and follow the same people, then it can be predicted they believe abortion is bad and vote the same way too. If messages are sent to those people claiming an election candidate is pro-abortion (whether they are or not), then that may help swing the vote. Meanwhile, a different group of people identified as being interested in the environment because of programs they have watched are sent messages suggesting that the politician being promoted cares deeply about green issues (whether they do or not).

The predictions are far more powerful when combined with actual data about whatever an organisation wants to predict. Many people make such data freely available: perhaps they both give facts about themselves and state their beliefs about the environment in their social network profile, for example. That hard data can be used as the basis for predicting private information of others. One ruse is to use bogus "surveys" to ask people for specific information. This known information then ties patterns to specific beliefs and personality traits. It can then be used to predict that others that have been grouped with those people will be similar in other aspects of the grouping detected. It therefore gives away similar information about lots of people who refuse to fill in the surveys because they prefer to be private. That freedom of privacy is effectively removed from them by the choices of others.

This kind of manipulation of messaging can be helpful, for example, if it helps people understand the true beliefs of the politicians being promoted. On the other hand, if it is used to propagate lies and half-truths, it undermines democracy.

Computer science is not just about technology but also about its place in society. New technology changes the way we do things, but also can completely change the way the world works, for good or bad. Understanding the effects of changes on society is important, and underlying this is also an understanding of, and commitment to, using technology for good, not just personal gain.

Interlude: Phineas T. Barnum

The kind of statements used in the "Reading a personality with hot chocolate" trick is called Barnum statements because showman Phineas T. Barnum (1810–1891) is credited as having used them. He was happy to use effects and tricks to entertain. However, he went out of his way to debunk fraudsters who used the same tricks to actively con people. This included those who tried to convince others of their "psychic" abilities or that they could "speak to the dead", using the tricks as a way of extracting money from the newly bereaved. He testified at the trial of one fraudster who used photos that had ghostly images of dead relatives in the background. Barnum paid a photographer to create a picture of himself with a ghostly Abraham Lincoln in the background to show how easily spirit photos could be faked. This was long before computer software like Photoshop made it easy for anyone to do this kind of fakery with images.

Chapter 47

Ʈhe Chevreuſ Penðuſum
Professional Ethics

Conjuring

A volunteer holds a pendulum over a circle with YES and NO written on it. They use it to "talk to the spirit world" and ask questions about their future.

Computation

Professional ethics is very important for all computer scientists. A person with computational thinking skills and computing knowledge can use it for good or bad: as a black hat hacker breaking into systems stealing data or as a white hat hacker helping protect people's privacy, for example. Big data can be used to spy on people or to improve their lives. Behaving ethically matters.

The Trick

As part of a magic show, ask for a volunteer who is open to the idea that the spirit world might exist. Tell them they will take part in a seance where they will talk to a supernatural Victorian spirit you have made contact with, called Alice. You know Alice likes to communicate in this way and likes to talk about relationships whether past, present or future. Give the volunteer a simple pendulum made from a large, heavy, old-style key hanging on the end of a string 40 centimetres long. Explain that the key is so old and has been around humans and their lives so long, and it has become a link to the spirit world. Have the volunteer hold it over a large circle split into quarters with YES written in two opposite quarters and NO written in the other two quarters (see Figure 47.1). You may wish also to decorate it with runes or other ghostly images. The volunteer should be standing and keep their arm held out straight and unsupported. They should hold it so it hangs over the middle of the circle. Tell them they must concentrate on the pendulum at all times, but not try to consciously move it themselves. They should allow Alice to work through them.

You then ask a series of questions, starting with:

Alice, are you there? . . . we wish to communicate, are you willing to answer our question?

Follow this by the first question. If after a short wait the pendulum starts to swing to yes or no, then announce the answer given. Then ask the

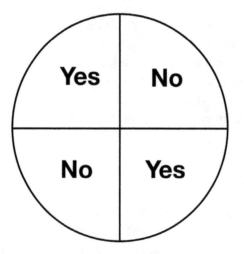

Figure 47.1. The target for the Chevreul Pendulum.

person holding the pendulum (or their friends) to come up with further questions for Alice to answer that they would like to know the answer to, whether about past, present or future relationships. If they are open to the influence of spirits, you say, then the pendulum will swing to give answers to the questions.

The Magical Algorithm

TO PREPARE the Chevreul Pendulum:

1. Make a pendulum by tying an old key on the end of a 40-centimetre long string.
2. Draw a target: a circle split into quarters with YES written on one pair of opposite quarters and NO on the other pair.

TO DO the Chevreul Pendulum:

1. A volunteer holds the pendulum with their arm held out so it is above the centre of the target.
2. Tell them to concentrate on the pendulum but not move it consciously themselves.
3. Ask the volunteer for a YES/NO question they would like Alice to answer about the past, present or future.
4. DO THE FOLLOWING UNTIL the audience do not have any more questions:
   a. Say "Alice, are you there? . . . we wish to communicate, are you willing to answer our question?"
   b. Repeat the question.
   c. Watch to see if the pendulum starts to swing showing Alice is communicating through the volunteer.
   d. IF the pendulum swings,
      THEN announce the answer indicated,
      OTHERWISE announce that you will have to take it as an "Unknown . . . even the spirits cannot tell."
   e. Ask the audience if they would like to know more and if so to give you another YES/NO question they would like Alice to answer about the past, present or future.

How It Works

This illusion is based on an effect called an **ideomotor response** and named after Michel Eugene Chevreul, a French scientist who did experiments about the effect in the 1830s. The same effect leads to the movement of tables and Ouija boards in seances. The movements happen because ideas can lead to subconscious physical changes. An example is the way your mouth waters when you think of something you like such as chocolate (for me at least). In the trick, thinking about questions leads to very small movements of the hand of the person holding the pendulum. The pendulum magnifies the movements particularly if the arm is moving backwards and forwards in a way that matches the natural frequency of the pendulum swinging (which depends on its length). Staring at the pendulum increases the effect as the person thinking strongly about the pendulum swinging one way or the other can trigger the subconscious movements that cause it to happen.

Thinking Computationally

Whilst it is fine to do a trick like this as part of a magic show where it is clearly intended to be just for fun, it would be unethical to use it to really claim to talk to the dead relatives of people as you are not. It would be even more unethical to charge people to do so.

Spiritualism became really popular in Victorian times where seances were held to allow people to supposedly speak to the dead. Whilst a few may have truly believed they were helping people talk to their dead relatives, most were just frauds, unethically preying on people who had lost loved ones. Their aim was to swindle money from them using their false claims. Other people use the same sort of tricks as magicians for a variety of unethical reasons: to cheat when gambling, to claim to do faith healing and to con people out of money.

Behaving ethically is very important to most magicians. They make a clear distinction that what they are doing is a performance for entertainment. Some go out of their way to expose frauds who use the kind of illusions and conjuring tricks we've seen in this book to fleece people by claiming them to be something other than mere tricks that are part of a conjuring show.

Professional ethics is also very important for computer scientists. Those with computing skills can use them for good or bad, and it is important that people do behave ethically. Just as magicians can use their skills to devise tricks to present as other things to fool people, so programmers can devise programs that pretend to be one thing while being something else. Such malware is developed and used by hackers to, for example, steal data for gain, steal someone's identity to defraud them, or lock people out of their computers until they pay a ransom. The computing skills being used are not in themselves bad, it is how they are used that is bad. A magician charging an audience member to see them do tricks that is clearly presented as a night of entertainment is not the same as someone using tricks to convince people they are in contact with gods or ghosts and so take money as a collection "for the work of God" or so they can "speak to dead loved ones". Similarly, those with hacking skills can use them for good or bad. For example, some companies employ **white hat hackers** to search for problems with their security systems so they can make them more secure. They use the same skills as the bad people, also earning money, but in an ethical way.

Interlude: James Randi

James Randi (1928–2020) was a magician famous for investigating fraudulent claims, having shown how a whole series of people claiming to have supernatural powers were actually just using magic tricks. He also demonstrated flaws in research projects supposedly investigating the paranormal. He has shown how claim after claim of paranormal ability was easily done with magic tricks.

Part 12

Advanced Technology

We have mainly focussed on the links between magic and computer science ideas rather than gadgets, but there is a long history of magic tricks being based around novel gadgets based on new science or engineering developments.

Chapter 48

𝕮𝖍𝖊 𝕱𝖆𝖊𝖗𝖎𝖊 𝕮𝖆𝖌𝖊
Augmented Reality

𝕮𝖔𝖓𝖏𝖚𝖗𝖎𝖓𝖌

You show the audience a faerie you have trapped in a magical cage.

Computation

Virtual reality involves creating online worlds that people can move digital versions of themselves around in. Augmented reality involves superimposing virtual elements on the real world so that you can move around both real and virtual worlds together and so that nonexistent things appear to be there in the real world. Applications range from games to the head-up displays in fighter aircraft.

The Trick

Explain that faeries do exist and you have trapped one inside a special box lined with rowan wood, which acts as a barrier to a faerie. You reveal your magic cage. Inside, flying around, for all to see when they peer through the window in the box, is a very angry faerie!

How It Works

This illusion is based on a Victorian stage illusion called **Pepper's Ghost**. In the original trick, a large glass sheet lay at a 45-degree angle between the audience and the stage. Some actors acted just as normal on the stage. Others lay on trolleys on the floor, out of sight, but on the audience side of the glass. When powerful stage lights were shone on them, they appeared (and disappeared) as ghostly figures on the stage. This works because the light reflected on them bounces onto the glass and is reflected out to the audience, making those actors appear as though they are on the stage.

What is happening is the glass acts as a half mirror. Light from behind it can pass through, but also light from below is reflected at 45 degrees out to the viewer too. Because our brains assume light travels in a straight line, the reflected image appears to be in front of the back wall. You can see a weaker version of the same effect at night just by looking out the window. You see a reflection of the room superimposed on the garden next to lit objects actually in the garden.

Trapping a faerie

To create your own (small) version of the illusion, you need to make your own Pepper's Ghost box: the faerie cage. For the faerie itself, you need a smartphone with an animation of a faerie. It doesn't have to be a faerie, of course, you can "trap" any creature that you can find or create an animation of. You could even film your brother or sister lit by a lamp shining on them in a dark room (if you prefer, your story to be about shrinking and trapping your irritating sibling). If you don't have an animation or film, then you can just use a still image on your phone (and explain the faerie is trapped frozen in suspended animation). The phone ensures you have a brightly lit image, equivalent to the bright stage lights of the original effect, which is important if it is to work.

Making the faerie cage

Paint the inside of a small, strong cardboard box matt black. Ideally, it should be just large enough to take a smartphone lying on the base.

Cut a large rectangle out of one side (the lid of the box), leaving a rim all around the box. That is the window through which your audience members can view your trapped faerie. Add bars if you want it to look more like a cage.

Now cut a sheet of stiff Perspex (from a DIY or craft shop) to fit diagonally inside the box at 45 degrees. The top of the Perspex should be towards the audience, above the hole in the box, and the bottom of the Perspex should be at the back of the box. It splits the box into two diagonally. Your viewers can see the back wall of the box through the window and through the transparent Perspex (Figure 48.1).

Now for the secret part. You place your smartphone (ideally, black or covered so only the screen is visible) on the floor of the box, under the Perspex. It should be playing the animation of the faerie on a loop. The phone itself must be out of sight of the viewers who look at the back wall of the box through the window. An overhanging lip at the bottom of the window may help hide it from someone viewing from the front.

If you play an animation of an angry faerie on a black background, then the light from the faerie will bounce off the Perspex and appear to be flying, trapped, inside the cage. The image from the smartphone

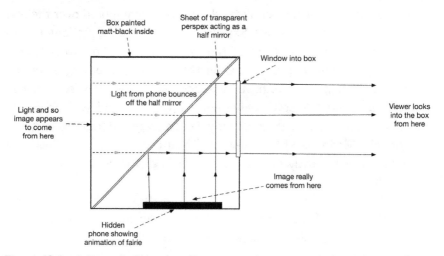

Figure 48.1. A Pepper's Ghost box. Because our brains assume that light travels in a straight line, the image from the hidden camera that bounces off the half mirror appears to come from the back of the box.

appears as if floating in the middle of the box. For a more complex version, you could put props like a miniature bed behind the Perspex to make it appear the faerie is in a prison room. Experiment with what looks best.

TO PREPARE the Faerie Cage:
1. Create or find an animation of whatever you want to trap in your cage such as an angry faerie.
2. Create a Pepper's Ghost box and place a smartphone at the bottom playing the animation on a loop.
3. Cover the box with a cloth.

TO DO the Faerie Cage:
1. Tell the audience you have trapped a faerie in a special magic box.
2. Whip off the cover to show the box.
3. Allow people to look at the faerie through the window, one person at a time.

Thinking Computationally

Essentially the same illusion as Pepper's Ghost is used for **head-up displays**, where a virtual computer display is superimposed over the real world. For example, my car's Sat Nav projects arrow directions in this way so they float out in front of the car as I drive. The arrows appear at the right depth so I can focus on them while still paying attention to the road. Fighter pilots have more complicated versions so they can see information while still looking out the cockpit window. The virtual band, Gorillaz, performed, apparently live on stage, interacting with real singers like Madonna in the same way. You can also see the illusion in museums when ghostly characters appear in dioramas and talk to you about the past.

The same idea of combining the real world with the virtual world forms the basis of **augmented reality**, though modern versions may use different technology to achieve the same effect. Programmers not only can now create whole virtual worlds, but they can also superimpose a virtual world onto the real one using programs that merge live film with the computer-generated imagery. Another way is to have smart glasses that allow you to see the real world but where the programmers superimpose imagery, like Pepper's Ghost, onto the lenses so appearing out in the world.

Interlude: John Henry Pepper and Henry Dircks

When the very first Pepper's Ghost appeared on stage on Christmas Eve, 1862, it stunned the audience. A ghostly figure appeared with the actors out of thin air, interacted with the other, more solid, characters, and then disappeared in an instant. This was more than just magic: it was miraculous. It was so amazing that some spiritualists were convinced John Henry Pepper (1821–1900) had discovered a way to summon spirits. This was no dark seance where ghostly effects happen in a darkened room. Nor did it need the virtual world of a computer (they didn't exist yet!). It was on a brightly lit stage in front of everyone's eyes... Magicians are also often scientists and engineers. They use new innovations, but also invent some themselves. Often they patent their ideas rather than keeping them secret. East Londoner and scientist Pepper co-invented the effect with Henry Dircks (1806–1873), a Liverpudlian engineer. They patented Pepper's Ghost in 1863 as an effect to use in the theatre. It was originally invented far earlier though; Giambattista della Porta (1535–1615) described it in his 16th century Italian book, Magia Naturalis.

Chapter 49

The Down-Under Deal and Robotic Reveal
Robots

Conjuring

A good reveal can make a trick and is also where you can have some creative fun. Here, despite a volunteer having a free choice of where to split the pack, the special Down-Under Deal leads to a final selected card that no one could have predicted. It turns out that the card was forced by the magical influence of your robot assistant down under the table.

Computation

Robots have long been the subject of science fiction but are now reality. Industrial robots work on production lines, building cars, and anyone can buy a robot vacuum cleaner to clean their house while they are out. Robotics researchers are building robots that mimic all kinds of life and, using soft robotics; they are no longer the hard metallic machines of science fiction.

The Trick

You explain that you are going to show a special magical deal called the Down-Under Deal taught to you by an Australian magician (or European one if you are from, for example, Australia or New Zealand). You shuffle a pack of cards and then spread the cards in a line, face up on the table. Point out that it is a normal pack of cards. Saying that the deal will take too long with this many cards, ask a volunteer to point to a card "somewhere in the middle" of the spread deck and then discard half the pack beyond that position. Note that it was their free choice as to the cards discarded as you do so.

Take the remaining cards and, forming them back into a pack, explain you are now going to do the special Down-Under Deal that will leave you with a single chosen card no one could have predicted.

With the pack face down in your hands, deal cards into two piles saying "Down" as you put a card on the first, face-down, pile and "Under" as you place the next on the second face-up pile. When all cards are dealt, discard the face-down pile. Explain that the audience should now be able to see why you wanted fewer cards as it is a very slow deal. Deal out all the remaining cards from the "under" pile, into two piles in the same way, chanting down-under-down-under... as you place the cards, then again discard the down pile. Keep doing this until only one face-up card is left in the un-discarded "under" pile.

Declare this to be the final chosen card that no one could have predicted. Pick up the card and show everyone what it is. Point out again that the volunteer had a free choice of where to split the pack and turn over the pile of discarded cards, showing the top few cards to the audience. Note that if the pack had been split one place further, it would have been a different card chosen.

Finally, you explain that the deal is called the Down-Under Deal, not just because of the way you do the deal, but because the final result is influenced by whatever is down under the table, and throughout the whole trick, your assistant has been down under the table, holding a specific card to try and influence the final choice. You ask your assistant to reveal that card ... and at that moment, a robot pushes itself through the table cloth draped over the table and lifts up a large card to show everyone. It is the same as the final card left on the table. The card chosen was magically determined by the influence of the card your robot helper was holding under the table during the trick.

How It Works

Before the trick, place the card you intend to predict (for example, the 8 of Hearts) in the 16th position from the top of the pack. Place an identical card in the grip of the robot and place it under the table. Have a hidden button that activates the robot somewhere easy to press such as at the back of the table.

The shuffle at the start is just a False Top Overhand Shuffle (Chapter 18). This leaves the top 20 or so cards in the same position, so leaving the 16th card in that position. If you are unsure of doing this successfully, then you can miss out the initial shuffle.

The mathematics behind this trick is a simpler version of that used in the Free My Three trick of Chapter 40. By discarding every second card repeatedly, you will end up with a card that started in a specific position. Starting with 52 cards, so positions 1–52 as below:

$$1, 2, 3, 4, \ldots, 50, 51, 52.$$

we first split the pack somewhere in the middle. It is important that the split happens somewhere between the 16th and 32nd cards, leaving the 16th but discarding the 32nd. If the volunteer points somewhere in the middle, then you will be in this range. We therefore end up, after the discarding part of the pack, with cards such as:

$$1, 2, 3, 4, \ldots, 14, 16, 18, \ldots, 30, 31.$$

The precise last card is unknown, but the above is the worst case that could happen. Note that the critical 16th card is still in the 16th position from the top of the pack.

Deal the odd-position cards into one pile (face down) and the even-position cards into another (face up). Discard the face-down pile containing those in the odd positions. This leaves cards from the original even positions only:

$$2, 4, 6, 8, \ldots, 14, 16, 18, \ldots, 30.$$

Repeat this to leave, after the second deal:

   4, 8, . . . , 12, 16, 20, . . . , 28.

and then again leaving:

   8, 16, 24.

The final deal takes out the odd-position cards of these (so first and last), leaving just the planted 16th card:

   16.

The final reveal can make or break a trick and is a way you can add your own creativity and personal stamp on an existing trick. We have played with different reveals for this trick in different shows and magic workshops. My (Paul's) favourite reveal was kindly filmed (for Peter) by games designer and magician, Richard Garriott. The film shows Richard finding the same card as the one we end up with on the table, buried in the snow at the North Pole during a trip of his there.

   In the 19th century, French clockmaker and magician Robert-Houdin inspired this version of the reveal with his famous trick: the Marvellous Orange Tree. It involves a wonderful reveal using an automaton, an intricate mechanical device. Automata were commonly designed to mimic life in some way. They date back to the Ancient Egyptians and Greeks.

   His Marvellous Orange Tree trick involved destroying a handkerchief, only for it then to reappear unharmed. The reveal involved an automaton of a tree that started bare but grew real oranges, the last one of which when cut open contained the handkerchief (see a version of the trick in the film *The Illusionist*). Robert-Houdin often incorporated automata in his tricks, blurring science, illusion and technology. Was it really done by a machine, or was it part illusion? Perhaps the most famous blurring of this machine–illusion boundary was that of the 18th-century Mechanical Turk of Wolfgang von Kempelen. It was presented as a machine that could beat humans at chess, though in fact was a hoax: it was all illusion. Of course, now computer science has overtaken the magic, and chess computers are easily the best chess players on the planet. What astounded 18th-century audiences, and could then only work by illusion, is now just everyday.

The modern equivalent of using automata in tricks would be to use robots as in this trick. Perhaps you can build a computer-controlled robot with the same artistic flair as Robert-Houdin for an even more amazing reveal, or invent tricks that use robots as an integral part of an illusion.

The Magical Algorithm

TO PREPARE the Down-Under Deal and Robotic Reveal:

1. Place a specific card in the 16th position from the top of a shuffled deck of cards.
2. Place a large version of the same card in the grip of a robot, controlled by a hidden button at the back of the table.
3. Place the robot with the card under the table, hidden from the audience by the table cloth.

TO DO the Down-Under Deal and Robotic Reveal:

1. DO the False Top Overhand Shuffle.
2. Spread the cards face up on the table.
3. Ask a volunteer to point to a card somewhere in the middle.
4. Split the pack at that point.
5. Discard the half from the bottom of the pack, forming the remaining cards back into a deck.
6. DO the Down-Under Deal.
7. Show the final card to the audience.
8. Point out that the volunteer had a free choice, and you could have ended up with any card.
9. Say that this is called the Down-Under Deal, not just because of the down under pattern, but because things down under the table can control what happens on the table. Your assistant who has been under the table holding a controlling card throughout the trick will now prove this.
10. Press the button so that the robot rolls forward from under the table, holding up the matching card.

TO DO the Down-Under Deal:
1. DO THE FOLLOWING 4 TIMES:
   a. Pick up the remaining cards.
   b. DO THE FOLLOWING UNTIL all cards are dealt:
      i. Deal a card face down, saying "Down".
      ii. Deal a card face up, saying "Under".
   c. Discard the face-down cards.

Thinking Computationally

Robert-Houdin's **automata** that mimicked life were sometimes presented as being magical in their own right: how could a machine possibly do what they did? Other automata were mixed with illusion in more complex tricks. Given humanity's long obsession with creating machines that mimic life, it is natural, once computers existed, we would want to give these machine brains bodies too.

The science-fiction versions of **robots** are often either clearly machines or humanoids, sometimes both. Modern robotics is far more varied. Real robots come in all shapes and sizes. While many of the robots now used day to day are very much functional machines with functional forms: working in factories manufacturing cars, in warehouses collecting the items you have bought online, or scuttling around the floor, vacuuming the carpets, many others mimic life, as did the automata. Researchers have created cockroach-like and flea-inspired robots, fish-shaped robots, snake-like ones, and robots modelled on octopuses, to give just a few examples. Animals need to fit many life niches and consequently have evolved elegant solutions to wide-ranging problems that work far better than human-engineered solutions. This has led to the growth of **biologically inspired computing**, including in the area of robotics. Just as automata mimicked many different forms of life, robots do too. If you want a robot that can travel over difficult terrain, then building a variation of a car or a human may not be the best solution. Animals travel across terrain they are adapted to in a multitude of more flexible ways than our vehicles; think of goats on cliffs, for example, or gibbons swinging through the forest. If you wish to move through water, then there are fishes that are far more manoeuvrable than boats and submarines. If you want a machine that can get in and out of tight spaces, then just look at the octopus, which does so in ways that would be a boon for many a magic trick if only a human assistant could do it. Animals provide many wildly different solutions to problems like locomotion, so learning from them can lead to novel engineered solutions.

One area of **biologically inspired robotics** is soft robotics. This is about making robots that are soft, not hard, fixed and rigid, and can also change shape and size. As a result, they can be much more flexible and safer around humans than stereotypical hard robots made of metal. There are many sources of inspiration for soft robotics including the octopus, spiders and plants too. Plants use changing pressures of liquids in cells, induced, for example, by light levels, to change their form to fit needs. It is a mechanism like this that allows them to follow the Sun. Soft robots can use similar systems to move using soft materials.

It is not just the form of animals that researchers copy but also their behaviour. For example, **swarm computing** aims to copy the way birds fly in massive, swirling flocks each following simple rules that maintain the flock. Flocks of drones might follow similar rules to help maintain coverage of an area being monitored. A more futuristic idea is for flocks of tiny, microscopic robots to be injected into the body and work together in swarms to attack cancer cells.

Other researchers explore different uses of robots, creating actor and stand-up comedian robots to explore the art of performance. Even here, Robert-Houdin was there first, having created an automaton to do the cups and balls magic trick. Robots with general-purpose computer brains and fine dexterity as well as programmed showmanship offer the possibility of flexible magician robots able to do a wide range of tricks. A computer brain might even make tricks possible for a robot magician that no human would be capable of. Showmanship and illusion would be needed to make it magical though.

By copying and drawing inspiration from animals, computer scientists have found innovative ways to solve problems. Whilst seeing machines mimic life perhaps does not seem like magic itself anymore, we still find such machines and their abilities intriguing. There is also scope for mixing robots with illusion to make wonderful tricks if you have the creativity to do so. Or perhaps rather than inventing robotic tricks, your interests would lie in making a robot magician do the performances for you.

PAUSE: Ismail al-Jazari

Ismail al-Jazari (c.1136–1206) was a Muslim scholar who lived in Mesopotamia in the 12th century and is famous for his humanoid automata, amongst many other things. They have led to him being called the father of robotics because he was interested in building such machines that had a practical use. The Ancient Greeks by contrast were more interested in automata as illusions and for entertainment. Al-Jazari's inventions included a waitress "robot" that served drinks and one intended to help with ritual handwashing.

Chapter 50

The One True Sovereign
Curtain Call and Creativity

Conjuring

We close with one last trick. Are you the one true Sovereign of the British Isles: can you remove Excalibur from the anvil?

Computation

We overview the main themes of the book, but also explore one last link to computing: how can you be sure someone is who they claim to be?

The Trick

Tell the story of Excalibur, the magical sword set in an anvil, on top of a stone, part of the legend of King Arthur. Merlin predicted that only the true sovereign of Britain, descended from Uther Pendragon, would be able to pull the sword from the anvil. Merlin's magical test showed that the teenage Arthur was the rightful King.

Explain that you have found a new Excalibur, a sword in an anvil. Pull back the curtains to reveal a sword protruding from an anvil, complete with plaque stating that only the heir of Uther Pendragon, and so the one true Sovereign of the British Isles will be able to remove the sword from the anvil.

Allow anyone who wishes to show their strength to try to pull the sword from the anvil. When they fail, apologise that they are clearly not royalty. Once everyone who wants to try has failed, say that perhaps you should try too. Without any effort at all, you pull the sword free. Proclaim yourself heir to the throne. If anyone is sceptical, replace the sword and let them try again.

The Magical Algorithm

1. Explain the story of the sword in the anvil and that you have found Excalibur.
2. Reveal the newly discovered sword in the anvil.
3. Allow volunteers to attempt to pull Excalibur from the anvil (who fail to do so).
4. Explain that this shows they are not royalty, not the true Sovereign of the British Isles.
5. Take hold of Excalibur and pull it out of the anvil.
6. Look surprised and declare you must be the true King/Queen of Britain.
7. Replace the sword and allow anyone who wishes to try to remove it again.

How It Works

We will leave you to work out your own way to make this trick work for now, though building it will take ingenuity, work and lots of both engineering and computing skills.

Thinking Computationally

Algorithms

This book has drawn out the many links between conjuring and computing. Self-working tricks are essentially **algorithms** for doing magic.

Both are sequences of steps that if followed precisely guarantee to achieve a result. In fact, some useful computing algorithms are the mechanism behind actual tricks, like error-checking codes and search algorithms. Showmanship is just added to make the effect of the algorithm seem magical. Both magic and algorithms are ultimately underpinned by mathematics. Inventing tricks and inventing algorithms, so writing programs, involve the same basic skills of **algorithmic thinking**. It is the skill of being able to create those series of steps and to be sure they always work as well as then write them out in a given precise notation. This requires **logical thinking** and **attention to detail**. Both magicians and programmers need to be sure the steps do always work, and that requires **evaluation** skills. In both cases, **testing** (just trying it out some number of times) is complemented by **rigorous argument** and **proof**. These are the basic skills of **computational thinking**.

Decomposition, abstraction and generalisation

Just as programmers use more advanced computational thinking skills, so too do magicians. Programmers **decompose** programs they write into named, reusable and more general parts. They create **generalised** versions of parts that can be used in many situations, and build larger programs from smaller, named parts they already know work.

Similarly, magicians name simple effects that they use in tricks and build tricks by combining together different existing components to make more powerful effects. To create their own versions of a trick, they strip it down to its basic core mechanism and build it back up in new ways to make different tricks. Both programmers and magicians therefore rely on **decomposition**, **abstraction** and **generalisation**.

Data representation

Another important aspect of developing software is the appropriate choice of **data representation**: how is information organised? It needs to be done in a way that facilitates the task. This is also important in many tricks, with different representations used as the basis for organising information in tricks. Whether it is in the organisation of a pack of cards in a certain order needed for a trick to work, in the way information is coded in the props used, or in the way information is passed between magician and assistants, the way information is represented is central to many tricks.

In programming, key things about the choice of representation include how easy the operations are to do, how quickly they can be done, and how efficient their use of storage space is. In a magic trick, the issues are similar. You want a representation that makes the trick easy to perform perhaps or at least possible given constraints on the time and abilities of the magician to do it flawlessly. However, another important consideration is that the representation chosen makes it difficult for the audience to notice vital information about how the trick works.

Computation and cognition

One view of cognition, our ability to think, is that it is just computation. Our brains are **biological computation machines**. Computation is about the manipulation of **symbols** that we then give meaning to. Symbols can be all sorts of things, including physical objects like cards in a deck, that we give meaning to. Symbols can exist in a computer or out in the world. This is the main underlying link between conjuring and computation, they are both manipulating symbols, so conjuring is just computation with the aim of providing surprising and entertaining effects.

This ties in with Edwin Hutchins' ideas of "cognition in the wild". We extend our cognitive abilities by creating a physical system of symbols in the world. We use cultural artefacts as ways to extend our cognitive abilities such as our memories, and to translate information into new representations that make the tasks we do easier. Prayer beads help us count, a shopping list helps us remember, an abacus helps us do arithmetic, and a list of turns helps us navigate to a destination. In this view of cognition and computation, conjuring is using cultural and information artefacts, symbols in the world, to make it harder rather than easier to think: harder to realise what manipulations of the symbols are really going on, whether information in people's heads or in the world as in cards, coins or other objects.

Psychology and human–computer interaction

Tricks are more than the steps. They involve engineering a system where everyone in the audience makes the same mistake at the same time. This relies on a deep understanding of both **cognitive psychology and social psychology**: of the effects of attentional resources, memory limitations, social contexts, and so on. Magicians go out of their way to ensure errors made by the audience are undetected until the final reveal. Creating **usable** and **used** programs involves a similar understanding of psychology, though to use it in a way that ensures no one using the software makes mistakes, or if they do, then they immediately see and correct the error. This is done using similar techniques to the magicians, just with the opposite aim: for example, controlling attention so that everyone looks at the right place at the right time rather than looking at the wrong place.

This leads to the direct link between conjuring and **interaction design** and the study of **human–computer interaction**. Human–computer interaction applies psychology to formulate **design principles** for how to make computer systems **usable**, based on models of how we as users of software get things done. We work from **goals**, creating plans of action that we then try to follow to do tasks based on **signifiers** from an interface. We monitor whether things are going to plan based on **feedback** given by the system. This leads to design principles such as using and communicating clear **conceptual models** of how systems work, ensuring the underlying system state is **visible** so people can track their progress, giving clear **feedback**, being **consistent**, and so on.

Magicians just turn these design principles on their heads. Instead of avoiding confusion, they sow the seeds of it, ensuring the audience lose track of what has happened and is happening: using conceptual models to confuse, not to enlighten, ensuring critical aspects of the system state are hidden so tracking what is happening is impossible, giving misleading feedback, doing things differently to the way expected, and so on.

Engineering of user experience is similar in both conjuring and computing, too. When using computer software, delight occurs when things are surprisingly simple. In a magic trick, delight comes from surprises too, but because the person lost track so that the reveal is surprising! Good system design, whether of computing or conjuring, involves engineering-appropriate experiences.

Computational agents versus practice

There are other differences beyond the opposite ways psychology is used, between writing programs and inventing tricks. Computer scientists have a notion of a **computational agent**: something that follows instructions perfectly and blindly, with no recourse to thinking about what it is doing. Computational agents get things done totally by unthinkingly following the algorithm with no improvisation. Computers are built to be such computational agents.

Magicians, when performing tricks, act as computational agents in that they also just follow the steps. Once well-practised, they should need no improvisation. All possibilities should be covered. A novice can follow the steps of a self-working trick, without thought and without knowing how the magic works, and achieve the effect. However, magicians do need to practise lots and lots to be able to follow the steps of a trick as perfectly as possible. Some tricks, even though just following steps, require a great deal of practice to master the levels of dexterity and timing needed, whether it is palming a coin or doing a perfect riffle shuffle. Computers of course do not need to practise to execute software, they just follow the instructions.

Precise languages

Unlike magicians, computers follow instructions in a **programming language**, a precise mathematical language. A large part of programming is in writing the steps in the constructs that are available in the language being used.

Magicians do not rely on special languages the same way, so the important programming step of writing the instructions in such a mathematically precise language is omitted. Humans work out tricks based on natural language explanations and fill in the gaps themselves if necessary. If a robot were to become a magician, then the tricks would need to be set out precisely in an appropriately precise language. An alternative is a machine would need a similar level of intelligence to humans, but it would still ultimately be following instructions given in a precise language, just ones for intelligence not for tricks.

Scale

There is also a massive difference in **scale** between tricks and programs. Programs can be millions of lines of code, millions of steps long, whereas even the most complex of magic tricks is likely to be only tens or hundreds of steps; after all, you do not want to bore your audience, while they wait for the pay-off of the trick! **Computational thinking** techniques that are used in simple ways with tricks are absolutely vital to manage the complexity of large programs.

Showmanship

Showmanship is all-important in magic, but less so in computing. It is the ability to engage and entertain the audience, to draw them into the world you are creating. It is more than just following the core algorithm of a trick. It is about the presentation around that: the way a trick is weaved into a story, and then the way that story is told, the timing, the flair. Showmanship makes the performance of a trick extra special.

The equivalent to this in computing is **user experience (UX) design**. Something akin to showmanship is just one aspect of this. Similar techniques may draw people into software that aims to entertain like games. Those using the software expect to have an enjoyable, entertaining experience in a similar way as a magic trick. Educational software is often **gamified**, for this reason: trying to make it entertaining so children will want to use it repeatedly, rather than it being a chore. Just as magicians want to engineer delight, often software engineers do too. After all, if a shopping website or app is a delight to use, you are more likely to return and so buy more.

However, user experience design is about more than this kind of showmanship. It depends on the specific task at hand. For some software, a good experience is about being able to do the job quickly and easily with the minimum of fuss; about the software being very easy to use, without frustration. A good experience may even be an experience where you do not notice you have interacted with software at all. For example, to open my car, I just grip the door handle, and it recognises me and unlocks automatically. That is far better than having to dig around in my pockets for keys.

Security and privacy

There are big overlaps between **cyber security** and a variety of magic tricks. One of the aims of cyber security is to prevent **leakage of information**, allowing only certain people access to resources, and often ensuring that no one else even knows they exist. Many mentalism tricks rely on **secret codes** to pass information between magician and assistant, whether by known **legitimate channels** or hidden **covert channels**. **Steganography** techniques hide the fact that any information is passed between magicians.

Some tricks actively involve a magician gathering information about members of the audience. In others, they just pretend to know things. Information about people can now be gleaned from a variety of sources, and big data techniques mean your **privacy** is lost if enough people, even ones you have never met give up information about themselves. Undoubtedly, such technology can form the basis of new tricks too.

Science and technology

Magicians have always been at the forefront of science and technology: having a better understanding of physics, mechanical engineering or electronics than their audience can be a basis of a trick if the effect is combined with illusion. This was part of what drove the golden age of magic and illusion, from Victorian times into the early 20th century. Pepper's Ghost, for example, uses some simple physics of light; automata-based tricks involved intricate mechanical engineering, and there are many opportunities to base tricks around electronic gadgetry. Computing gadgetry offers yet more new opportunities.

Sometimes magicians are ahead of the game, rather than just following science and engineering. For example, a hot research topic at the moment is **wearable computing**, where electronic gadgetry is built into clothes, but magicians have been doing this for years. What tricks can you imagine doing with electronics, whether hidden controls, sensors or displays built into your stage clothes? What might you do with **body-centric networks** that use a person's body as a network to pass signals between different gadgets detecting things you touch? How about buttons for controlling things built into your skin, or **brain–computer interfaces** that can pick up a person's simple thoughts and pass them to a computer. A magician who is ahead of the game with mathematics, science and technology can always invent new tricks and new ways of doing old ones that baffle and entertain.

Creativity

Being a magician, inventing new tricks and adding new twists to old ones, is not just about being on top of technology but all about **creativity** too. Computer science is a similarly creative subject. In fact, some computer scientists have gone a step further and see creativity as something to investigate algorithmically. **Machine creativity**, computer programs creating poems, jokes, songs, stories, films, and so on, is a major area of research.

Machines have long ago been created to perform tricks but in future they could create new ones too. Researchers have started to explore this with **artificial intelligence** programs that develop the most magical version of a trick. PhD student Howard Williams developed a program modelled on evolution that created its own version of a jigsaw trick: the teleporting robot trick (Chapter 11). It used a kind of algorithm called a **genetic algorithm** to "breed" better and better versions of the trick, selecting for ones that would appear most magical, exploring many more possibilities than any human magician trying to develop a trick could. True computer magicians are still in the future, but one day they may be inventing their own completely novel tricks.

An authentication problem to finish

If you want to become a magician, inventing new effects and mechanisms, then you would do worse than to follow science, computer science, electronic engineering and technology closely. Hone your skills at making gadgets, as many magicians over the years have. This approach was exemplified by Robert-Houdin, but to make a trick magical, you will also need to be able to combine creativity with the basic effects: an ability he had in spades.

One way to do Excalibur magic, for example, is based on that of the original version: Robert-Houdin's "The Light and Heavy Chest". He created a magic box that he explained was a perfect way to prevent theft as it sapped the energy of even the strongest people who attempted to open it. An innocent child, however, would not be affected and could open it at will. The strongest volunteers from the audience would try, but no one could lift the box. Once all had given up, a child volunteer would then lift it with ease. How could this be done? Electromagnetism had recently been discovered. If you pass an electric current through a coil of wire, it creates a magnetic field. Wrap the coil of wire around an iron bar and the bar becomes a strong magnet. The more times the wire is wound around it, the stronger the magnet you make. However, switch off the electricity and the magnet switches off too. All it took was a flick of a switch to turn on and off powerful electromagnets that held the iron box to the table.

A modern version could add to the trick, and undoubtedly Robert-Houdin would have done so, had he been alive in the 21st century. In computer science terms, Excalibur's role in the myth was to determine the identity of the person holding it: were they the true Sovereign of Britain or not? If they were, then and only then were they allowed to remove it from the anvil. Excalibur was just an **authentication** device.

Today, it could be done without the need for a secret on–off switch and work actually using modern authentication techniques. A wide range of authentication devices have been invented to do this, so take your pick! Keys and passwords do not really work in this situation, but **keyless locks**, for example, as found now on many cars allow you to open a door just by gripping the door handle, as long as you have an electronic key in you pocket. Sensors in the handle trigger the car's computer to check if the key is close enough to unlock. The hidden key broadcasts a code (the equivalent of a password) by radio. If the right code is detected, then the door is unlocked.

An alternative approach is **biometrics**. Biometric authentication uses unique features of people like their fingerprints to check who they are and what rights they have. My laptop has such a finger pad which I can just touch to unlock the laptop avoiding typing a password.

My tablet on the other hand uses **facial recognition**. It allows me in because it recognises unique features of my face, just as some fast-track passport systems at airports do to get people through immigration quickly. Yet another alternative might be to use **voice authentication**, where unique features of your voice identify you. (That would also be useful to make magic words actually work!)

Any of these (and more) could be used as a way to allow a trick to work for you and only you, as with Excalibur. However, once technology is widespread, it is not as simple as just building it into a trick. Showmanship is needed to distract from what is actually happening so that it still seems magical. Part of this is to embed the trick in a story (such as searching for the rightful King or Queen of Britain). Part is by combining it with other illusions so that an apparent obvious way appears to be impossible. That is where creativity comes in. Over to you.

Interlude: Richard Garriott

Richard Garriott made his fortune as a programmer and games designer, creating massively multiplayer online role-playing games (a term he invented). He is also a keen magician and astronaut, travelling to the International Space Station in 2008, and while there, he performed the first-ever low-gravity magic show in space, broadcast back to earth. There are always new frontiers for science and engineering, and with them, new frontiers for magic.

Invent your own ways to present tricks, invent new versions from old and invent completely new tricks based on your knowledge of and skills in maths, science, technology, and especially computing.

Further Reading

Find resources to accompany the tricks in this book at

https://conjuringwithcomputation.wordpress.com

There is lots more of our magic and computer science at

http://www.cs4fn.org/magic/

Magical computing resources for teachers can be found at

https://teachinglondoncomputing.org/magic/

The History of Magic and Magicians

Hiding the Elephant, Jim Steinmeyer, Arrow Books, 2005.

And that's renaissance magic..., Lucy McDonald, *The Guardian*, https://www.theguardian.com/world/2007/apr/10/italy.books, 10 Apr 2007.

Magic: 1400s–1950s, Noel Daniel (Ed.), Taschen.

Famous Female Magicians Through the Ages, Katherine Mills, https://www.katherinemills.co.uk/blog/most-famous-female-magicians-of-all-time

David Copperfield's History of Magic, David Copperfield, Richard Wiseman and David Britland, Simon and Shuster, 2021.

The Discoverie of Witchcraft, Reginald Scott, 1886. Available from https://archive.org/details/discoverieofwitc00scot/

Dot-dash-diss: The gentleman hacker's 1903 lulz, Paul Marks, *New Scientist* issue 2844, 2011.
https://www.newscientist.com/article/mg21228440-700-dot-dash-diss-the-gentleman-hackers-1903-lulz/

Wikipedia. www.wikipedia.com

Self-working Magic Tricks

Self-working Card Tricks, Karl Fulves, Dover, 1976.

Self-working Mental Magic, Karl Fulves, Dover, 1979.

Self-working Table Magic, Karl Fulves, Dover, 1981.

Self-working Number Magic, Karl Fulves, Dover, 1983.

Magic Tricks in General

Magic and Showmanship, a Handbook for Conjurers, Henning Nelms, Dover, 1969.

Martin Gardner's Table Magic, Martin Gardner, Dover, 1998.

Encyclopedia of Impromptu Card Forces, 2nd Edition, Lewis Jones, 2004.

Optical Illusions and Op Art

Japanese Optical and Geometrical Art, Hajime Ōuchi, Dover Pictorial Archive, 2000 (original edition 1977).

Bridget Riley, accompaniment to exhibitions of Riley's work, National Galleries of Scotland, Hayward Gallery, 2019.

Magic and Mathematics

Mathematics, Magic and Mystery, Martin Gardner, Dover, 1956.

Mathematical Magic, William Simon, Dover, 1964.

Magical Mathematics, Persi Diaconis and Ron Graham, Princeton University Press, 2012.

Magic and Computer Science

The Magic of Computer Science, Paul Curzon and Peter W. McOwan, Queen Mary University of London, 2008.

The Magic of Computer Science II, Now We Have Your Attention, Paul Curzon, Peter W. McOwan and Jonathan Black, Queen Mary University of London, 2009.

The Magic of Computer Science III, Magic Meets Mistakes, Machines and Medicine, Paul Curzon and Peter W. McOwan, Queen Mary University of London, 2015.

Unplugged Computer Science

CS Unplugged. Tim Bell, Ian Witten and Michael Fellows (founders). https://www.csunplugged.org/

Teaching London Computing, Paul Curzon, Peter W. McOwan and William Marsh (founders). https://teachinglondoncomputing.org/

Computer Science

The Power of Computational Thinking: Games, Magic and Puzzles to Help You Become a Computational Thinker, Paul Curzon and Peter W. McOwan, World Scientific, 2017.

Human–Computer Interaction, Cognition and Computation

Cognition in the Wild, Edwin Hutchins, MIT Press, 1995.

The Design of Everyday Things, Donald Norman, MIT Press, 1998.

Movies about Magic

The Prestige, directed by Christopher Nolan, 2006.

The Illusionist, directed by Neil Burger, 2006.

Now You See Me, directed by Louis Leterrier, 2013.

Novels about Magic

The Prestige, Christopher Priest, Simon and Schuster, 1995.

Carter Beats the Devil, Glen David Gold, Sceptre, 2001.

Acknowledgements

Thanks to my family, for putting up with me constantly disappearing to write and especially Daniel for his enthusiasm for my magic. Sam Stein gave advice on the early chapters. Thanks also to all at World Scientific, especially Rochelle Kronzek for seeking us out. Jonathan Black, Jane Waite and Jo Brodie have worked on the cs4fn project as we originally developed the magic ideas. I would also like to thank all those who have supported the cs4fn project at Queen Mary University of London and elsewhere, since its inception, and especially the Engineering and Physical Sciences Research Council (EPSRC) who provided major funding for cs4fn. We also developed many of the ideas of linking magic and interaction design as part of the EPSRC-funded CHI+MED research project on safer medical device design. Other major funders of our public engagement work have included Google and the Mayor of London. The Cyclops Eye was created by Kelly Burrows based on a design by Peter, and the original illusion was made freely available for designers to use by Hajime Ōuchi. Kelly was also the person behind the design of our cs4fn magazine. Paul drew the teleporting robot. Wikipedia has been invaluable in researching the book and particularly for learning more about, and fact-checking, the background of the scientists and magicians. Tim Bell pointed out some of my mistakes. Peter provided the majority of the tricks from his lifetime studying magic. I am also indebted to Jane McOwan and the rest of Peter's family for their enthusiasm and support for me to finish this book and for passing on his collection of magic books; some of my favourites and those I have found most useful learning about magic and its history are included below along with ones I am aware of as being favourites of Peter's. Peter would undoubtedly have included others that I have missed, so my apologies for any such omissions.

Index of Computing Terms

Index of Tricks, Illusions and Conjuring Techniques

(*) means a trick that is described in the book in detail.

Index of People

CPSIA information can be obtained
at www.ICGtesting.com
Printed in the USA
JSHW010453150623
42972JS00002B/150

9 789811 264337